The foe claims in error that a philosopher I am.
God knows I am not what he says I am.
But, having endured this sorrow's nest, I ask:
Why should I not know at least what I am?

—Omar Khayyam

HUMAN ARCHITECTURE
Journal of the Sociology of Self-Knowledge

Editor:
Mohammad H. (Behrooz) Tamdgidi
Associate Professor of Sociology
UMass Boston

Human Architecture: Journal of the Sociology of Self-Knowledge (ISSN # 1540-5699) is published by OKCIR: the Omar Khayyam Center for Integrative Research in Utopia, Mysticism, and Science (www.okcir.com, info@okcir.com) and printed by the Okcir Press, an imprint of Ahead Publishing House (APH), P. O. Box 393, Belmont, MA, 02478, U.S.A., tel/fax: 617.932.1170. Copyright © by Ahead Publishing House, 2002-2010. All rights reserved. *Human Architecture* is indexed in CSA Illumina's *Sociological Abstracts*® and complied in EBSCO's SocINDEX with Full-Text®, ProQuest's *Social Science Journals* full-text database, and Gale's *Academic OneFile* and *Expanded Academic ASAP*.

Submissions: *Human Architecture* publishes both submitted and invited manuscripts as well as the working papers of OKCIR: the Omar Khayyam Center for Integrative Research in Utopia, Mysticism, and Science—an independent research and educational project. Contributors extend permission to *Human Architecture* for the publication of their work in the journal. They retain copyrights to their work and may publish them elsewhere. If the submitted manuscript has been published elsewhere before, written permission from both the author(s) and publication(s) where it earlier appeared should accompany submission to *Human Architecture*.

Editorial decisions: *Human Architecture* adheres to the peer reviewing principle for advancing scholarship—seeking innovative ways to meet the need in favor of liberatory scholarly practices most conducive to the aim and purpose of the journal. Selection of papers from submitted or invited manuscripts are based on their substantive relevance and the coherence and innovativeness of their argument in consideration of the mission of the journal. Views expressed in the journal by contributors are those of their authors and may not necessarily coincide with one another, or with the views of the editor, members of the Editorial Advisory Board, or the institutions with which any of the above are affiliated. Authors are solely responsible for the accuracy and integrity of factual, bibliographic, and referential materials used in their own articles, and for obtaining permissions for using copyrighted material in their manuscripts. Methodological, theoretical, historical, empirical, practical, as well as literary and artistic contributions relevant to the mission of the journal are all encouraged. The primary language used is English, but material in other languages may be included if relevant to the purpose of the journal.

What to submit: All manuscripts should be submitted in electronic format. They should preferably be double-spaced in Times 12 typeface., with 1 inch margins all around. Footnotes, endnotes, or reference lists may be single-spaced. In general, authors should follow a consistent bibliographic and citation style of their choice throughout the manuscript. Using the ASA (American Sociological Association) style is preferred by the editor.

Where to submit: The Editor, *Human Architecture*, Okcir Press, P. O. Box 393, Belmont, MA, 02478, U.S.A., tel/fax: 617.932.1170, e-mail: mohammad.tamdgidi@umb.edu

Subscriptions: *Human Architecture* is a quarterly publication, published in either single-issue or double-issue formats, all issues for each volume becoming usually available concurrently at the end of every summer. Individual and institutional rates are $15 and $30 for single-issues and $30 and $60 for double-issues respectively. *Individual and institutional subscription rates* per year beginning from the most recently published issue (when subscription order is received) are $60 and $120 respectively. Back issues or additional copies of the journal are available upon request at the same rates as indicated above. Rates include domestic shipping and sales tax, where applicable. For international or bulk orders please inquire for special rates & shipping charges. Make checks payable in U.S. dollars to Ahead Publishing House, and send payments to Ahead Publishing House, P. O. Box 393, Belmont, MA, 02478, U.S.A. Contributors each receive one free copy of the issue in which their articles appear. Rates are subjected to change without notice.

Advertisements: Current rates and specifications may be obtained by contacting the Okcir Press, P. O. Box 393, Belmont, MA, 02478, U.S.A., tel/fax: 617.932.1170, e-mail: mohammad.tamdgidi@umb.edu

Inquiries: Address all correspondence and requests to *Human Architecture*, Okcir Press, P. O. Box 393, Belmont, MA, 02478, U.S.A., tel/fax: 617.932.1170, e-mail: mohammad.tamdgidi@umb.edu

Changes of address: Six weeks' advance notice must be given when notifying change of address. Please include both the old and the new addresses in your request. **Postmaster:** Send address changes to Ahead Publishing House, P. O. Box 393, Belmont, MA, 02478, U.S.A.

Human Architecture:
Journal of the Sociology of Self-Knowledge
Volume XI, Issue 1, Fall 2013
ISSN: 1540-5699
ISBN: 978-1-888024-74-6

Editorial Advisory Board

In Honor of

Jesse Reichek (1916-2005)
Professor Emeritus of Design
U. C. Berkeley

Terence K. Hopkins (1918-1997)
Professor Emeritus of Sociology and
Founding Director of the Graduate
Program in Sociology
Binghamton University

Bart Bonikowski
Assistant Professor of Sociology
Harvard University

David Baronov
Associate Professor of Sociology
St. John Fisher College

Anna Beckwith
Lecturer of Sociology
UMass Boston

Jay Dee
Associate Professor of Higher Education
UMass Boston

Estelle Disch
Professor of Sociology
UMass Boston

Alicia Dowd
Associate Professor
Rossier School of Education
University of Southern California

Leila Farsakh
Assistant Professor of Political Science
UMass Boston

Benjamin Frymer
Assistant Professor of Sociology
Hutchins School of Liberal Studies
Sonoma State University

Michal Ginach
Psychoanalyst
The Institute for the Study of Violence
Boston Graduate School of Psychoanalysis

Lewis R. Gordon
Laura H. Carnell Professor of
Philosophy, Religion, and Jewish Studies
Temple University

Panayota Gounari
Assistant Professor of Applied Linguistics
UMass Boston

Ramón Grosfoguel
Associate Professor of Ethnic Studies
U.C. Berkeley

Terry-Ann Jones
Assistant Professor of Sociology
Fairfield University

Philip Kretsedemas
Assistant Professor of Sociology
UMass Boston

Winston Langley
Provost and Vice Chancellor for
Academic Affairs
UMass Boston

Neil G. McLaughlin
Associate Professor of Sociology
McMaster University, Canada

Jonathan Martin
Assistant Professor of Sociology
Framingham State College

Bruce Mazlish
Professor Emeritus of History
Massachusetts Institute of Technology

Askold Melnyczuk
Associate Professor of English
UMass Boston

Aundra Saa Meroe
Senior Researcher of Sociology
University of Chicago

Eric Mielants
Associate Professor of Sociology
Fairfield University

Martha Montero-Sieburth
Professor Emeritus of
Higher Education Administration
and Leadership
Graduate College of Education
UMass Boston

Dorothy Shubow Nelson
Senior Lecturer of English
UMass Boston

Dylan Rodriguez
Associate Professor
Department of Ethnic Studies
U.C. Riverside

Khaldoun Samman
Associate Professor of Sociology
Macalester College

Emmett Schaefer
Senior Lecturer of Sociology
UMass Boston

Ingrid Semaan
Director of Women's Studies
Univ. of Connecticut, Stamford

Tim Sieber
Professor of Anthropology
UMass Boston

Santiago E. Slabodsky
Assistant Professor of Judaic Studies
University of Saskatchewan, Canada

Rajini Srikanth
Associate Professor of English
UMass Boston

Shirley Tang
Associate Professor of
Asian American Studies
and American Studies
UMass Boston

Aleksandra Wagner
BA Program Core Faculty, Sociology
The New School for Social Research

Reef Youngreen
Assistant Professor of Sociology
UMass Boston

Samuel Zalanga
Associate Professor of Sociology
Bethel University

Vivian Zamel
Professor of English
UMass Boston

STUDENT ADVISORY BOARD

Ayan Ahmed
B.A., Sociology
UMass Boston

Keilah Billings
B.A., Sociology
UMass Boston

Bryan Gangemi
Alumni and Activist
UMass Boston

Chris Gauthier
Doctoral Student of Sociology
University of Michigan

Jenna Howard
Doctoral Student of Sociology
The State University of New Jersey at
Rutgers

Tu Huynh
Doctoral Student of Sociology
SUNY-Binghamton

Jennifer McFarlane-Harris
Doctoral Candidate
English and Women's Studies
University of Michigan, Ann Arbor

Emily Margulies
Graduate Student of Sociology
SUNY-Albany

Anthony Nadler
Service-Learning and
Outreach Coordinator
Massachusetts Institute of Technology

Donna M. Rafferty
B.A., Sociology
UMass Boston

Annie Roper
B.A., Sociology
UMass Boston

Frank Scherer
Doctoral Candidate
Social/Political Thought Program
York University, Toronto, Canada

Peter Van Do
M.A., American Studies
UMass-Boston

Rika Yonemura
Doctoral Student of Sociology
äU.C. San Diego

A Peer-Review*ing* Journal

Contributions to *Human Architecture: Journal of the Sociology of Self-Knowledge* pass through a rigorous selective process with respect to their fit, relevance, coherence of argument, and innovativeness in consideration of the scope, nature, and intended purpose of the journal. The journal adheres to the peer-reviewing principle for advancing scholarship, but aims to design and build new scholarly avenues to meet this requirement—seeking mechanisms that foster openness of inquiry and evaluation; mechanisms that invite constructive judgments subject to free, open, and mutually interactive, not blinded and one-sided, peer reviewing practices; mechanisms that can be employed as widely and dynamically as possible among specialist and interested scholars in the field who value the need for the proliferation of new, critical, and innovative personal and global insights and transformations.

To meet the highest standards of scholarship, liberatory editorial practices need to transition from static peer review*ed* to dynamic peer review*ing* models that de-couple publication from defective pre-publication peer review requirements, and engage in alternative peer review practices that remain open to all those wishing to review a manuscript at any time in the post-publication phase—encouraging expanded and deepening exchanges among scholars, authors and readers alike. They need to invite critical thinking about prevailing and dominant paradigms and inflame creative spirits to forge new scholarly horizons and intellectual landscapes. And they need to embrace the subaltern voices in the academia and beyond, voices of those who have been deprived of cultivating their sociological imaginations through formal scholarly publishing avenues.

Human Architecture warmly invites contributors and readers to peer review the articles herein and to openly share their critical and constructive insights with one another in the future chronicles of this journal.

Contents

HUMAN ARCHITECTURE
Journal of the Sociology of Self-Knowledge

Volume XI　　　　　　　　Issue 1　　　　　　　　Fall 2013

---

vii　Editor's Note: I Think; Therefore, I Don't—Tackling the Enormity of Intellectual Inadvertency
　　Mohammad H. Tamdgidi, University of Massachusetts Boston

1　Introduction: Enrique Dussel´s Multiple Decolonial Contributions
　Issue Co-Editors: George Ciccariello-Maher, Drexel University, and Ramón Grosfoguel, U.C. Berkeley

3　Agenda for a South-South Philosophical Dialogue
　Enrique Dussel, Universidad Autónoma Metropolitano, México

19　Justice after the Law: Paul of Tarsus and the People of Come
　　Eduardo Mendieta, State University of New York, Stony Brook

33　Law, Globalisation, and Second Coming
　　Oscar Guardiola-Rivera, Birkbeck School of Law, University of London, UK

57　Philosophy, the Conquest, and the Meaning of Modernity: A Commentary on "Anti-Cartesian Meditations: On the Origin of the Philosophical Anti-Discourse of Modernity" by Enrique Dussel
　　Linda Martín Alcoff, Hunter College and the Graduate School, C.U.N.Y.

67　Thoughts on Dussel's "Anti-Cartesian Meditations"
　　Lewis R. Gordon, University of Connecticut at Storrs

73　The Structure of Knowledge in Westernized Universities: Epistemic Racism/Sexism and the Four Genocides/Epistemicides of the Long 16th Century
　　Ramón Grosfoguel, U.C. Berkeley

91　Exploring Pluriversal Paths Toward Transmodernity: From the Mind-Centered Egolatry of Colonial Modernity to Islam's Epistemic Decolonization through the Heart
　　Dustin Craun

115　The Voice of a Country of Called 'Forgetfulness': Mahmoud Darwish as Edward Said's "Amateur"
　　 Rehnuma Sazzad, Nottingham Trent University, UK

127　Lisa Suhair Majaj's *Geographies of Light: the Lighted Landscape of Hope* (Book Review)
　　 Rehnuma Sazzad, Nottingham Trent University, UK

135　Deep Learning in the Sociological Classroom: Understanding Craving and Understanding Self
　　 Linda R. Weber, SUNY, Institute of Technology, Utica, NY

HUMAN ARCHITECTURE: JOURNAL OF THE SOCIOLOGY OF SELF-KNOWLEDGE
A Publication of OKCIR: The Omar Khayyam Center for Integrative Research in Utopia, Mysticism, and Science (Utopystics)
ISSN: 1540-5699. © COPYRIGHT BY AHEAD PUBLISHING HOUSE (IMPRINT: OKCIR PRESS) AND AUTHORS. ALL RIGHTS RESERVED.

Editor's Note: I Think; Therefore, I Don't— Tackling the Enormity of Intellectual Inadvertency

Mohammad H. Tamdgidi

University of Massachusetts Boston

mohammad.tamdgidi@umb.edu

Abstract: This is the journal editor's note to the Fall 2013 issue of *Human Architecture: Journal of the Sociology of Self-Knowledge*, entitled "Conversations with Enrique Dussel on Anti-Cartesian Decoloniality and Pluriversal Transmodernity." In his invitation for a South-South philosophical dialogue as a prelude to a broader global philosophical conversation to advance anti-Cartesian decoloniality and pluriversal transmodernity, Dussel aptly forewarns those from the South embarking on such a conversation to become aware of and avoid what he calls "inadvertent Eurocentricity." This cautious, self-critical reflexivity not only is indicative of the depth of the project being advanced by Dussel and how he himself biographically arrived at his own world-view, but also points to the enormity of a broader challenge that exists in any liberatory conversation and effort, namely that of intellectual inadvertency. In other words, what can make problems such as ethnocentricity (including Eurocentricity, both as variants of egocentricity), among others, even more of an obstacle in advancing any conversation and practice (be they South-South and/or Global) is the fact that they can also (and often do) take place *inadvertently and subconsciously*, that is, beyond conscious self-awareness of the actors who otherwise explicitly seek with the best of intentions to advance their liberatory cause devoid of such biases. This editorial aims to highlight and further emphasize the significance of the subconscious processes that often accompany all political and cultural, including philosophical, dialogues, and reflects on the ways in which Dussel's conceptual frames and the conversations in the present volume provide opportunities for reflections that may further contribute to understanding the challenge intellectual inadvertency poses in advancing decoloniality and pluriversality. It can be argued that a lack of adequate appreciation of this challenge may also be traceable to the prevailing interpretations of the Cartesian dictum: "I think; therefore, I am"—one that fails to acknowledge the multiplicity and plurality, simultaneously both personal and global, of the selves that constitute the reality of human voice uttering that dictum, leading to a subjective fragmention in discourse that precipitates intellectual inadvertency.

The present, Fall 2013, issue of *Human Architecture: Journal of the Sociology of Self-Knowledge* was originally proposed by the issue co-editors Ramón Grosfoguel and George Ciccariello-Maher in late 2011. In their view, despite the long established recognition and reputation of Enrique Dussel as being "without a doubt the most prolific,

---

Mohammad H. Tamdgidi is associate professor of sociology, teaching social theory at UMass Boston. Most recently he has been the author of *Gurdjieff and Hypnosis: A Hermeneutic Study* (Palgrave/Macmillan 2009), *Advancing Utopistics: The Three Component Parts and Errors of Marxism* (Paradigm Publishers 2007/2009), and "Decolonizing Selves: The Subtler Violences of Colonialism and Racism in Fanon, Said, and Anzaldúa" (in *Fanon and the Decolonization of Philosophy*, edited by Elizabeth A. Hoppe and Tracey Nicolls). Tamdgidi's writings have appeared in *Review* (Journal of the Fernand Braudel Center), *Sociological Spectrum*, *Humanity & Society*, *Contemporary Sociology*, and several edited collections.

creative, and influential Latin American philosopher alive," an astonishingly limited portion of his writings had appeared in English by the time they wrote their proposal. Exiled to Mexico from his native Argentina more than 35 years ago, the co-editors noted, Dussel has written more than 70 books and hundreds of articles ranging from theology to history, from philosophy to politics. Following the publication of Dussel's *Twenty Theses on Politics* (Duke, 2008), the co-editors added, increasing interest in his work has been emerging among students and educators interested in developing liberating social theories and philosophies from the Global South.

The co-editors' own introduction to the present issue following this editorial note provides a brief, helpful overview of the purpose of this volume, one that was aimed, in their words in the original proposal, at contributing to fill "the gap in available secondary material about Dussel's work while also stimulating further interest in the burgeoning field of Latin American philosophy." As the journal editor, I would like to take this opportunity to thank both issue co-editors, George Ciccariello-Maher and Ramón Grosfoguel, for their original proposal and subsequent collaboration in realizing this endeavor.

I also thank all the authors contributing, directly or indirectly, to the conversation on Dussel's work published in this issue of *Human Architecture*. Other than the essay by Dussel entitled "Agenda for a South-South Philosophical Dialogue"—reprinted here by kind permission from the editors of *Budhi: A Journal of Ideas and Culture*—authors Eduardo Mendieta, Oscar Guardiola-Rivera, Linda Martín Alcoff, Lewis R. Gordon, Ramón Grosfoguel, and Dustin Craun contribute to the issue while directly engaging with the works and ideas of Enrique Dussel. As for the contributions of the two other authors, Rehnuma Sazzad (regarding both her article on Said and Darwish and her review of the book of poetry by the Palestinian-American poet Lisa Suhair Majaj) and Linda Weber, even though they do not directly engage with Dussel's work, they can be appreciated in terms of their own contributions and—as I will try to briefly elaborate—in terms of how they, in meaningful ways, shed important light on and provide illustrations for the conversations other authors pursue on the issue's main theme, which is "Conversations with Enrique Dussel on Anti-Cartesian Decoloniality and Pluriversal Transmodernity."

• • •

What I most appreciate in Dussel's work, one that makes his work highly relevant to the focus of *Human Architecture* as a journal of the sociology of self-knowledge, is that his philosophical-political career has been seriously inspired by a self-critical spirit, one that subjects his prior views and inclinations to continual scrutiniy. In his "Transmodernity and Interculturality: An Interpretation from the Perspective of Philosophy of Liberation,"[1] for instance, Dussel chronicles in a detailed way how he became, early on in his career, aware of the Eurocentric biases in his own training and education as a philosopher. He writes,

> It is difficult to evoke in the present the firm hold that the European model of philosophy had on us… With my trip to Europe—in my case, crossing the Atlantic by boat in 1957—we discovered ourselves to be "Latin Americans," or at least no longer "Europeans," from the moment that we disembarked in Lisbon or Barcelona. The differences were obvious and could not be concealed. Consequently, the problem of culture—humanisticly, philosophically, and existentially—was an obsession for me: "Who are we

---

1. http://www.escholarship.org/uc/item/6591j76r

culturally? What is our historical identity?" This was not a question of the possibility of describing this "identity" objectively; it was something prior. It was the existential anguish of knowing oneself. (Dussel, ibid., pp. 28-29)

Dussel's work demonstrates his continuing efforts to, in a self-conscious way, critically learn from and avoid inherited pre-deterministic and reductionist frameworks of the past that in an a priori manner favor one-sided explanations in understanding social change. However, he is also aware of the significance of the philosophical, ontological, and epistemological foundations of the world-views that enable coloniality and, in contrast, those that can alternatively equip liberatory efforts toward ending it. His emphasis on the need for adopting a *creative* approach in pursuing long-delayed conversations among philosophers and intellectuals of the South as part of a critical global conversation in favor of decoloniality is refreshing. His intellectual work demonstrates a genuine effort in reaching out to help others unearth their cultural and philosophical heritage in order to build alternative foundations for contributing to the global conversations on the meaning of human existence, the horrors brought on human life and culture by legacies of colonialism, and in seeking ways out of the present crisis in favor of decolonized and pluriversal human realities.

Judging from the intellectual practices of those scholars attracted to Dussel's work, with whom I have collaborated, I can see the extent to which they have been open to alternative liberatory perspectives, theories, and practices from other cultural traditions. What has impressed me most in Dussel's work, in other words and as noted earlier, however, is the extent to which he invites all joining his conversations to be mindful of their own biases, and to recognize that, simply, a scholar's coming from the South does not mean that he or she is free from Eurocentric and ethnocentric biases.

In his invitation for a South-South philosophical dialogue (as reprinted in this issue) as a prelude to a broader global philosophical conversation to advance anti-Cartesian decoloniality and pluriversal transmodernity, Dussel aptly forewarns those from the South embarking on such a conversation to become aware of and avoid what he calls "inadvertent Eurocentricity." He writes, for instance, about how a philosopher from the South, not having been adequately informed of and trained in his or her own philosophical tradition, may regard the positions of his colleagues from the center as more universal than they are and thereby be unable to establish a symmetry in balancing the conversation with a strong argument in favor of the authenticity of his or her own philosophical heritage. He writes,

When I refer to "symmetry" in this context, what I am suggesting is the need to develop a psychological attitude and approach representative of a certain normality that would make it possible for those of us in the South to consider and treat academic colleagues in Europe and the U.S as "equals." We should free ourselves of false respect for a knowledge with universalist pretensions. This false respect could be overcome by philosophers in the South once they possess the historical, cultural, and philosophical tools of the same quality as their colleagues in the metropolitan centers, which at minimum would enable our peers in the South to uncover the signs within us of an *inadvertent Eurocentrism* which has been ignored. (Dussel, p. 14, this issue; italics added)

This cautious, self-critical reflexivity not only is indicative of the depth of the project being advanced by Dussel and how he himself biographically arrived at his own world-view, but also points in my view to the enormity of a broader challenge that exists in any dialogue and liberatory effort in global social transformation, namely that of intellectual inadvertency. In other words, what can make problems such as ethnocentricity (including Eurocentricity, both as variants of egocentricity), among others, even more of an obstacle in advancing any conversation and practice (be they South-South and/or Global) is the fact that they can also (and often do) take place *inadvertently and subconsciously*, that is, beyond conscious self-awareness of the actors who otherwise explicitly seek with the best of intentions to be advancing their liberatory cause devoid of such biases.

From what I have highlighted above about Dussel's work, and based on what I have read from him so far, and also considering the thoughtful contributions made by various authors in this issue, therefore, I have a sense that Dussel would appreciate a frank dialogue that may make the conversation he is inviting others to join more fruitful, beyond simply highlighting the (deserved) significance of the liberatory intellectual and philosophical-political project he has been building over the decades.

In this editorial note, I wish to briefly highlight and further emphasize the significance of the subconscious processes that often accompany all political and cultural, including philosophical, dialogues, and reflect on the ways in which Dussel's conceptual frames and the conversations in the present volume provide opportunities for reflections that may further contribute to understanding the challenge intellectual inadvertency poses in advancing decoloniality and pluriversality. I will further argue that a lack of adequate appreciation of this challenge may also be traceable to the prevailing interpretations of the Cartesian dictum: "I think, therefore I am"—one that fails to acknowledge the multiplicity and plurality, simultaneously both personal and global, of the selves that constitute the reality of human voice uttering that dictum, leading to a subjective fragmentation in discourse that precipitates intellectual inadvertency.

•••

Let me provide some examples of how the issue of inadvertency may manifest itself amid conversations that journal issues such as the present seek to foster.

In his essay published in this volume entitled "Agenda for a South-South Philosophical Dialogue," in footnote 17, Dussel appreciatively critiques Randall Collins for not referring even once to the Latin American philosophical tradition in his major work. He writes,

> There is not a single sentence dedicated to Latin America in the brilliant book by Randall Collins, *The Sociology of Philosophies* (Cambridge, MA: Belknap/Harvard University Press, 1998), although it does include a good description of the philosophies of China, India, the Islamic world, and Bantu Africa. (Dussel, p. 15)

I recall reading a similar observation on Collins's book in another of Dussel's articles, titled, "A New Age in the History of Philosophy: The World Dialogue Between Philosophical Traditions"[2] where he states,

> *We also need a complete reformulation of the history of philosophy* in order to be prepared for such a dialogue. A 'world philosophy', the pioneering work by the sociologist Randall Collins (2000), points to key aspects that must taken into account. His comparative analysis crosses the geography (space) and history

2. http://psc.sagepub.com/content/35/5/499.abstract

(time) of the great Chinese, Indian, Arab, European, North American and African philosophers, which he categorizes in generations and in terms of their relative importance, although glaring omissions include his failures to devote a single line to 500 years of Latin American philosophy, and to the nascent philosophies of the urban cultures prior to the conquest. ... (Dussel, p. 512; italics in the original)

Now, while reading the latter article, I recall thinking, why does Dussel not refer, even once, to Zoroastrianism alongside other religious or philosophical traditions he lists throughout the latter article in order to argue for his otherwise important project of rethinking the history of philosophy in a more inclusive way? So, at the very same time he is consciously aware (and rightly so) of what another scholar has totally ignored about a particular philosophical tradition he himself is more closely familiar with, Dussel totally omits in the same writing another spiritual/philosophical tradition from his map of world philosophy.

I don't think the omission of Zoroastrianism is warranted, even as an example or simply in passing, in such an article aimed at the project of building an inclusive history of world philosophy. In making the above point, of course, it is obvious that the reason I thought of this point has something to do with my own Iranian heritage as a scholar, even though I am not a Zoroastrian. As I read the article, I also noticed that even when Dussel acknowledges the contribution of "Persian Gnostic thinking" to the Islamic philosophy, his commentary is offered via conversations he has had with non-Iranian Arab scholars[3] of Islam studying, among others, the Iranian contribution to Islamic philosophy. In other words, knowledge of Iranian (including Persian) contributions to Islamic, and world, philosophy was mediated through the work of Arab scholars.

This reminded me of another example. In my reading as editor of the manuscript of Dussel's article that was eventually included in this journal issue as a reprint of a previously published essay by him, I recall noticing how in several references to Iran, there was an ambiguity of representation of the Iranian heritage in distinction from that of Arabs—interestingly amid a passage devoted by Dussel to pointing out the reality that often all regional philosophies are ethnocentric. For instance, where Dussel had written,

My point of departure is that all philosophies (Chinese, Indian, Egyptian, Greek, Roman, Arab, Amerindian, etc.) have inevitably been ethnocentric in character, since their origin lies in a certain ontological ... (p. 5, this volume)

I recall that I commented on the passage as follows:

I wonder if just mentioning Arabs without specifying Islam (which covers a broader field to which the Iranian culture contributed key achievements) is itself limiting. It is impossible to consider Arab contribution to philosophy without considering Islam, and it is impossible to consider Islamic philosophy without considering the contribution of Iranian philosophers (Ibn Sina, Suhrawardi, Ghazzali, Farabi, Khayyam, Rumi, ...). ...

Or, consider elsewhere in his manuscript, where Dussel had written,

... modernity denied any validity to the philosophical narratives (which

---

3. It is important to note that Iran is a multi-ethnic population, comprised, among others, of also an ethnic Arab population. Others include Persian, Azeri, Baluchi, Turkmen, Kurd, Gilaki, Mazandarani, Armenian, Assyrian, and Jewish ethnic groups.

contained myths) of the cultures of the South, including those of China and India which go back for millennia, as well as those of the Iranian-Aristotelian tradition of scientific and empirical inquiry in the Arab world. … (ibid., p. 12)

Obviously, as I noted in a commentary on the above, there was no doubt in my mind that Dussel is generally aware of the distinction (as well as intersections) of Iranian and Arab cultural heritages. However, when reading Dussel for whom respect for and inclusion of all cultural and philosophical traditions in his effort in building a decolonized world philosophy is a vital and central consideration, I, as a scholar from an Iranian heritage that happens also not to be of Arab ethnic background, cannot help but feel somewhat left out. Read his passage below, for instance, in his "A New Age in the History of Philosophy: The World Dialogue Between Philosophical Traditions":

> We must lay the pedagogical foundations by educating future generations in multiple philosophical traditions. For example, in the first semester in the history of philosophy in our universities at the undergraduate level, we should begin with the study of the 'First Great Philosophers of Humanity'—the thinkers who developed the original categories of philosophical thinking in Egypt (Africa), Mesopotamia (including the prophets of Israel), Greece, India, China, Meso-America or the Incas. In the second semester we should continue with study of the 'Great Ontologies', including Taoism, Confucianism, Hinduism, Buddhism, the Greeks (such as Plato, Aristotle and up to Plotinus), the Romans, etc. A third course should explore later stages of philosophical development in China (beginning with the founding of the Han Empire), later examples of Buddhist and Indian philosophy, Byzantine Christian philosophy, Arab philosophy, the medieval European philosophy and so on. This is how a new generation can begin to think philosophically from within a global mindset. The same approach should be reflected in the courses specializing in ethics, politics, ontology, anthropology and even logic (should not we have some notion of Buddhist logic as well?). (p. 511)

Again, let me reiterate, that there is no doubt in my mind that Dussel is aware of and attributes high significance to any contribution the Iranian culture has made to the world's philosophical and spiritual traditions. In his *Politics of Liberation: A Critical World History* (SCM Press, 2011), he does devote pages to delineating the share of Iran in human history, by dwelling, for instance, on the contributions of Farabi. However, the point I am trying to convey here is that the omission of any references in the specific writings considered earlier to Iranian culture (including the Zoroastrian tradition, for instance, but for the same reason one can cite Manichaeism or Mithraism, etc.) and the significant part they played in the development of world spirituality and philosophy is noteworthy as an example of "inadvertent" omission, or, where the heritage is acknowledged, it is "inadvertently" considered as part of the Arab world.

•••

Is this "inadvertency" just a matter of error and omission, or does it arise from a conceptual frame that informs Dussel? For instance, consider what in my previous writings (Tamdgidi 2006[4]), I have argued for

---

4. "Toward a Dialectical Conception of Imperiality: The Transitory (Heuristic) Nature of

regarding the value of considering a typology of imperiality in a world-history context, identifying the modern (economic) form as only one form among a trilogy of political, cultural, and economic modes of imperiality appearing in world-history. Without going into its details here, I wish to suggest, for instance, that one can regard Islamic practice of imperiality (which should always be distinguished from Islam's genuine, original source of spirituality—a distinction that can be made in regard to all genuine spiritual traditions that were later put to imperial practice by some or other of their adherents) as a type of cultural imperiality aimed at subjugating others via cultural conversion. It is in such light that one can understand, for instance, the complaints of scholars such as Omar Khayyam, himself an Islamic scholar, who vehemently resisted, openly or not, the oppressive colonialism of Islamic orthodoxy being imposed on him and his time via the rise of Turkish imperial expansionism spreading under the banner of Islamic Caliphate in Baghdad. So, in a world-historical context, subsuming an Iranian cultural heritage wholly under an "Arab" culture would be equivalent of all that Dussel rightly abhors in the Western imperial practice, so far as ignoring the distinct identity and contributions of a people subjected to imperiality is concerned.

Should not a liberating philosophy be able to help us become aware of not only actual, but also potential modes of imperiality that may still lurk behind seemingly "antisystemic movements" challenging the Western status quo at the present? If we use world-history as a whole (and not mainly focus on the modern times) as our unit of analysis, we may discover that it is as necessary for us to be mindful of Western colonialism and imperiality, as it is to be aware of other non-Western forms of imperiality preceding it, ones that may have become marginalized today along with the genuinely humanistic elements in their local cultures, but may raise their head again amid the antisystemic movements challenging Western imperiality (for instance, consider Wahhabism and Al-Qaeda using Islam to revive their imperial dystopia). But not all imperial contents of "traditional" cultures are so easily discernible. The binary logic that may lead us to consider what opposes the 'bad' Western imperiality is necessarily offering a 'good' alternative, I am sure, is not what Dussel advocates. But, inadvertently, the conceptual architecture and historical foci of the unit of analysis thus used may inadvertently precipitate a one-sided attention to getting rid of the presently dominant modes of imperiality while remaining somewhat less cautious regarding the threats posed by imperial elements that have in time become entangled with the genuinely progressive, decolonial traditions sidelined by the Western imperial conquest.

So, as I read across various of Dussel's writings, I felt as if there is one Dussel that is highly sensitive, and rightly so, when he notices the lack of even a single reference to Latin American philosophies in Collins's book, yet, another Dussel that does the same, as what he critiques Collins to be doing, to another tradition in world philosophy in that very same text. One Dussel that is genuinely and explicitly aware of how Western imperiality has subjugated, sidelined, and ignored other cultural and philosophical traditions, and another Dussel that subsumes, say, Iranian contributions to Islamic philosophy under a general "Arab philosophy" rubric.

•••

the Primacy of Analyses of Economies in World-Historical Social Science" *Review* (Fernand Braudel Center), Vol. 29, No. 4 (2006), pp. 291-328 (http://www.jstor.org/discover/10.2307/40241670?uid=3739696&uid=2129&uid=2&uid=70&uid=4&uid=3739256&sid=21102774501037)

Another conversation that took place among the editors may illustrate intellectual inadvertency in a different way.

I recall a while ago when starting working on this issue with the co-editors, I read for the first time Dussel's *Twenty Theses on Politics*, following which I wrote to them:

> I read Dussel's *Twenty Theses* during my trip to Iran. I must say that I found it rather dense and somewhat not convincing at times, somewhat left with questions regarding what is so distinctive or new about what Dussel is contributing that has not been in other forms brought up by others. I can see where he is heading with matters such as "obediential power," etc., but in real social contexts, things get a bit more complicated when constituents [to be "obeyed"] are [themselves] conflicted. …

In response to my comments, co-editor Grosfoguel wrote:

> … The *Twenty Theses on Politics* of Dussel is based on an experience that is quite unknown outside Latin America. The concept and practices of "obeying power" or "commanding while obeying" are coming from indigenous thought in the Americas and is a living practice in many indigenous communities in the region. The concept of pluri-national societies that is now in the constitutions of Ecuador and Bolivia is a radical critique to the nation-state and is a consequence of the indigenous proposals in the region. What Dussel is doing here is taking these experiences as the basis of doing political philosophy. If the French Revolution has been the basis of Eurocentric political philosophy, for Dussel Latina American Revolutions such as the Cuban, Nicaraguan, Zapatista, Bolivarian revolutions are his raw material for doing a different political philosophy. Moreover, the *Twenty Theses* is just a very brief and sometimes simplified summary of a three volume work entitled *Politica de Liberacion* of which only one volume is out in English and only two volumes are out in Spanish. The only volume in English is this one: *Politics of Liberation: A Critical World History* … Let me just say about this volume, that this is the first world-history of political philosophy that is non-Helenocentric and non-Eurocentric. This is a masterpiece in my humble opinion.
>
> Why did he write this volume? Because in order to begin his political philosophy with the "commanding while obeying" or the "obeying power" of indigenous peoples in the Americas and not with Plato, Aristotle, Rousseau, Kant, Marx or Hegel, he needed to justify it with a different world history of political philosophy. For philosophers—remember Dussel is a philosopher—it would have been awkward to begin his political philosophy this way without a radical questioning of Helenocentric and Eurocentric narratives of political philosophy. His original intention was to write one chapter on world-history of political philosophy, but it turned out into a volume of more than 700 pages. I highly recommend it! He begins in Mesopotamia 5000 years ago, he discusses Chinese philosophy and other philosophies before the Greeks. Then the Greeks political philosophy arrive about 2500 years later and the Europeans about 4500 years later as a crossroad of concepts of political philosophy

coming from Egyptian, Persian, Phoenician and other civilizations in the case of the Greeks or Byzantine, Roman and Muslim civilizations in the case of Europe.

Grosfoguel continued:

> I am saying this to say that there is more to Dussel's political philosophy than what is portrayed in the *Twenty Theses*. Why did he then write the *Twenty Theses*? He wrote it fundamentally for activists in Latin America. He organized seminars with political activists all over Latin America using his *Twenty Theses* as a starting point to discuss his political philosophy. So, what you are reading in the *Twenty Theses* is a material he uses to provoke debate in order to explain orally and more in-depth his political philosophy. It is not his definitive work on the topic.
>
> I wanted to clarify this because in English his first publication on his political philosophy is the *Twenty Theses*. This led to many misunderstandings because people did not know about his trilogy in *Politics of Liberation*. While in Spanish he published his *Twenty Theses* once the first two volumes of his *Politica de Liberacion* were already published. In the Spanish-speaking world, when people read the *Twenty Theses*, many already knew that this was just a condensed summary of his volumes on *Politica de Liberacion*. For those who did not know and wanted to know more, Dussel could always refer them to the volumes. In English this was not possible because the volumes where not out in English language when his *Twenty Theses* were published. The only volume that has been published so far is the first volume on world-history of political philosophy. By the way, George [Ciccariello-Maher] is the translator of the *Twenty Theses* into English.

In response to Grosfoguel's thoughtful clarifications, I shared the following:

> Thanks for taking the time to comment on Dussel. I appreciate George's translation work, and I don't think my sense of any critique I may have reading the book had to do with its translation—which I think is well done. It is just that even in a synopsis some outline of the overall work must be apparent, and it is worthwhile and useful in that capacity as well to consider the book for what it is, while not forgetting all the good points you have brought up regarding the broader context of Dussel's writings and historical context of them in turn. I will try to keep all that in mind as I am reading him and in providing feedback. I have a copy of the first volume in English and make sure to consult it as well. …
>
> I hope that in my reading and feedback via editorial note I can also contribute somewhat as an outsider to all the contributors' conversations, hoping for the spirit of what may be regarded, borrowing from Dussel, as obediential scholarship (I am not particularly fond of the notion of anyone obeying anything or anyone, though I see the point Dussel is making in critiquing top-to-bottom leadership models). As I was reading him, I did not help but notice that at times, what he rightly critiques as the Euroncentric may be coming around unconsciously from another entry in the form of

disciplinary boundaries and conceptions that, at least, from other indigenous context he wishes to converse with, may be regarded as divided knowledge.

The very notion and identity one may have as a "philosopher" or even the very focus on "politics" as such, may be problematized sub-textually as a practice in disciplinarity and particular ways of knowing and relating to the object. One thing I appreciate in him is his openness to learn from other traditions, even though, at times I feel some opportunities are missed in taking other traditions seriously. Even though *Twenty Theses* is a synopsis, still, some trace of the detailed work elsewhere should be present to indicate some sensitivity to other traditions. For instance, I have marked in *Twenty Theses* all the times the issue of reflexivity and self has come up, and I can clearly demonstrate that except in one or two places, it is referred to in a derogatory way, in its capitalistic selfish (rightly so, in this case when referring to capitalist notions of selfhood) interpretations/application, but then the value of that gets lost in the analysis. When a whole synopsis is constructed, even then one should be able to know to what extent consciously and intentionally someone has taken a particular issue seriously. His notion of the 'social' purposely, and I can show consciously, defines sociality in interpersonal terms [only, and not also intrapersonally] (he is clear in that, and frankly, I find that to be very much an inheritance from Marx[5] that, despite other critiques

of him, has not left him—and as such, the question raises whether in fact the traces of Marx's Eurocentricity are continued, intentionally or not, in Dussel). This brings up other issues regarding historical unit of analysis used, and attention to alternative modes of thinking, and other matters, that perhaps I can expand on further when I draft my editor's note.

My point here is, if we regard how Dussel has himself read world-history, and done so via a particular regional experience of it, we may lose his other and more important point that his synthesis and/or detailed reading may be coming from a particular standpoint when this is supposed to be a broader dialogue intended to show both the contributions and limits of present thinking in favor of more inclusive ones. Given his stature intellectually among those interested in him, it would then be important to borrow from his notion and advance an obediential type of scholarship where the leadership pays attention to the differences people may have with them or others, for otherwise we will miss the forest for the tree.

I think the journal issue is serving its purpose well by generating a dialogue, and hopefully it will be done in a constructive way taking us in new directions in favor of what Dussel appreciates in opening new conversations creatively, and not habitually, which is a good point that emerges from his *Twenty*

---

5. For a detailed discussion of my critique of Marx in this regard, see *Advancing Utopistics: The Three Component Parts and Errors of Marxism* (Boulder, CO: Paradigm Publishers, 2007/9; http://www.paradigmpublishers.com/Books/BookDetail.aspx?productID=151470.

Theses continually in terms of the whole problematization of fetishism. Ultimately, I think Dussel himself would prefer not to be fetishized. Sorry, I don't mean to say anyone is doing so, but overall we wish not to give the impression that the journal issue devoted to him inclines in that direction. (all email exchanges in July 2013)

Now that I have a chance to further elaborate on the conversation I had with Grosfoguel on Dussel, and having read more of the latter's texts since then, I can see the issues I was raising then from another vantage point. Now, on one hand, I do recognize how seriously Dussel has taken the issue of self-critical reflexivity in moving beyond his own and his intellectual roots in order to embrace a decolonized vision of world philosophy, one in which he is always mindful of the diverse forms in which philosophy itself has been defined and practiced across cultures, and one in which he is highly critical of the Eurocentric efforts to belittle other philosophical traditions simply because the West's own ways of defining and practicing philosophy does not conform to the mythical, religious, artistic, and other forms human questions about the nature of existence and the place of humanity in it have been reflected upon.

While recognizing this, I also see, on the other hand, that textual practice is not always intentional and entirely wakeful. I may think one thing, but at the very same time say or do something that contradicts it in a practical way. I simply don't see Dussel's attention to reflexivity, and the role it played in his own autobiographical making, present in *Twenty Theses*. Somehow in the process of "synopsis" writing, the most essential elements of what made Dussel who he is are lost, to the point where self-reflexivity is not only not made a central attribute to be cultivated by the people or leaders alike, but the notion of "self" is only touched upon mostly (except for a few instances where there is a reference to to self-management) in its negative and derogatory sense prevalent in capitalist society. When speaking of reflexivity, I am not only speaking of it in collective terms, but also of individual, and highly personal terms. When reading Dussel in his autobiographical writings, one can appreciate the very personal nature of the revelations he arrived at with regard to the Eurocentric foundations of his early educational training. Why should not such a highly personal self-inquiry be an attribute to be cultivated by others, especially political leaders, who are his audience in *Twenty Theses*? Somehow, it appears to me that it is as if *Twenty Theses* is written by another self in Dussel, whose thoughts are less accessible, more "philosophically" abstracted in the conventional and academic sense of the term, and one that disciplinary foci on "theoretical" work and seeking of a "philosophy of politics" has led to a distanciation of the voices of the two Dussels across the texts. And the very central focus of that synopsis on "politics" sounds to me like a fetishization of it, as if the most effective way of exerting power is through the traditional, organizational or movement forms of it, rather than via knowledge, culture, and philosophy itself, or even poetry, for instance. And the disciplinary fragmentations that inadvertently manifest themselves amid our busy-bodied professional activities and self-identities as "philosophers" of "politics" play a part in shaping our epistemic orientations.

•••

Having felt the depth of sincerity with which Dussel has written and practiced his scholarship, I wish to use these examples of my editorial experience to highlight an important matter that I think should also be a part of the conversation Dussel is inspiring us to engage in when writing his "Agenda for a South-South Philosophical Dialogue."

Dussel himself has critically demonstrated the problematic meaning in a world-history context of the Cartesian dictum, "I think, therefore I am"—one that in the context of Western imperiality and colonialism served well to philosophically justify an egocentric elevation of the West's own philosophical insight onto an allegedly universal world-view.

One interpretation of such a dictum from a critical point of view, and as one that may be relevant to this editorial commentary, is the observation that when I think, the "I" that thinks is not a singular entity, as the Western "universalist" philosophy amid an individualistic culture proclaims, but is multiple. There is still a reluctance on our part to recognize that this presumption of human selfhood as a singular entity is also a significant, culturally perpetuated artifact of the West enabling its imperial practices. At the same time that one imperial 'I' thinks, another forgets; one 'I' fights Islamic fundamentalism in Afghanistan, while another "I" continues to promote a policy toward its "friendly" Islamic states in the regions that has been one of the primary causes of the modern rise and spread of Islamic fundamentalism.[6]

An important reason why this happens may be that "thinking" itself is isolated from feelings of empathy toward others, and from sensing of others' suffering resulting from one's own actions. This multiplicity of not only the thinking 'I's but also across the thinking-feeling-sensing faculties of our being, may itself also be a product of a Eurocentricity in which the splitting of the "rational" from the feeling and sensing makes it possible to engage in the kinds of scientific, political, and philosophical practices that justify relating with others without feeling or sensing empathy toward them.

It is in the context of such an awareness of the limits of philosophy and politics itself as universally defined and practiced that one can arrive at an appreciation of what other authors in the present issue of *Human Architecture* contribute, directly or indirectly, to the conversation. The co-editors have commented on the contributions of those directly engaging with Dussel in this issue. What I wish to further highlight in what remains of this editor's note are the contributions of Dustin Craun, Rehnuma Sazzad (and through her book review, of Lisa Suhair Majaj), and Linda Weber, who make equally relevant contributions as those by Mendieta, Guardiola-Rivera, Alcoff, Gordon, and Grosfoguel.

What I wish to highlight in Dustin Craun's contribution is how his emphasis on the Sufi way of the heart, in contrast to the way of the mind alone, may provide a way out of the one-sided "rational" way Western epistemology is constructed in the first place. In other words, as we engage in a "conversation," we should be mindful of the limits of the "mental" apparatuses we use to conduct that conversation, since "thinking" is not, and should not be, the only way we converse. The very notion of why we would care, or not, to engage in a conversation, is pre-verbal and engages faculties of sensation of and empathy toward others who have decided to join a conversation. Dussel himself is highly aware of the diverse ways "philosophy" have been defined and practiced across cultures, and is rightfully critical of the extent to which Western philosophy has marginalized and ignored other cultural, philosophical, and spiritual traditions, simply because they are not offered in the "rational" form in which Western philosophy and scholarship is con-

---

6. For further commentaries on this theme see my article entitled, "Beyond Islamophobia and Islamophilia as Western Epistemic Racisms: Revisiting Runnymede Trust's Definition in a World-History Contest," *Islamic Studies Journal*, vol. 1, issue 1, 2012. (http://islamicommentary.org/2012/11/new-islamophobia-studies-journal-debuts/#sthash.B2UJsciZ.dpuf). Also see my "Abu Ghraib as a Microcosm: The Strange Face of Empire as a Lived Prison," *Sociological Spectrum*, Vol. 27, Issue 1, 2007, 29-55 (http://www.tandfonline.com/doi/abs/10.1080/02732170601001185?journalCode=usls20#preview).

ducted. This also brings up important question that had been raised thoughtfully by Anders Burman in a recent issue of this journal (Winter 2012[7]) regarding contrasting epistemologies prevalent in what Grosfoguel calls Westernized universities and those advanced by Anders's shaman guide and teacher in Bolivia. The notion that "we think with places" is important, and I think any conversations on Dussel's or even of our own contributions cannot avoid asking the extent to which conversations via academic settings can help or limit the kind of pluriversal and anti-Cartesian conversations we wish to pusue in favor of what Dussel calls trans-modernity.

If we are truly appreciative of Dussel's advocacy of pluriversality—which I think should encourage us to explore *both* the ways of the mind and the heart, *as well as* of sensibility—we should be appreciative of other, including poetic and literary, forms of conversation that have also set their aim at combatting colonialism in favor of just social outcomes. I think Rehnuma Sazzad's work may best be characterized as most poignantly representing that trend in cross/inter/transdisciplinary scholarship focusing on literary studies that puts poetry at the center of what may be an alternative way for bringing about social transformation from within in favor of global social justice, in contrast to the failed efforts of one or another kind in the past. This is perhaps one important reason why I was impressed with her work when she originally submitted her manuscript—leading me to also suggest to her to review the book of poetry by the Palestinian-American poet Lisa Suhair Majaj.

In her essay, Sazzad is highly self-conscious of this agenda, and uses all her creative skills while studying her subjects to press forth the notion that the best way to bring about the good society is to practice what Mahmoud Darwish characterizes as a mode of understanding that 'touches one's heart.' The multidimensional mode of understanding, or what Jürgen Habermas calls "communicative action," is translated in Sazzad's cross-culturally enriched intellectual agenda to an highly focused attention to the integral nature of mental, emotional, and sensual ways of knowing that alone can touch the heart and soul of all those involved in the struggle for a better world. When she studies a poet, say Mahmoud Darwish, or a literary figure such as Edward Said, or reviews the poetry of a scholar such as Majaj, her reflections on the text reflects in turn the lucidity and power of her own intellectual attention to the complexity of the multidimensional nature of what needs to be touched in the human reality to bring about a transformative experience.

When reviewing Majaj, for instance, and regarding the significance of self-transformation as a path to global social change (as one, for instance, also centrally advanced in Gloria Anzaldúa's poetic and literary praxes centering on her thesis of the simultaneity of self and world change as expressed in her expression, "I change myself, I change the world"), Sazzad writes,

> In my view, maintaining a complex existence of being both from 'the Iowa farm' and a troubled Arab land by following a beacon of light for the continuous self-transformation towards a better pattern of socio-political existence is the root out of which this beautiful collection of verses branch out. ...

> Therefore, beauty, not the horror of the attacks, is the truth that inspires him [Darwish] to knit a strong hope in an otherwise bleak war diary. That is why we are told not to expect the poem to be a journalistic report or a detailed record of the invasion. Rather, the beauty emanates

---

7. See his "Places To Think With, Books To Think About: Words, Experience and the Decolonization of Knowledge in the Bolivian Andes" (http://www.okcir.com/26HAX1W2012.html).

from the pieces of feelings, fragments of thoughts, and strings of emotions with which Darwish represents the collective suffering of his people. As with most Darwish poems, the personal is political …

Sazzad is deeply attracted to poets and poetry in the Saidian sense of "amateurism," i.e., a poet that, while being substantively sophisticated, is not detached from people as a professional, but is deeply loving of and dedicated to what he or she does without becoming a professional (ibid.). Sazzad's is also a unique approach to literary studies that strongly favors not severing the poet and the poetry from its social and political context, but embedding it as an integral part of it in terms of the dialectics of simultaneity, of the identity of self and social transformations, and a mode of knowing and changing reality (within and global) in which poetry does not simply reflect reality, but *is it*, and thus the transformation induced by poetry is at the same time a poetic transformation and revolution in the true senses of the words.

Linda Weber's study may seem at first to have little to do with what Dussel has devoted his life to accomplish. However, a closer reading of Weber's article in the context of the theme of this issue may illustrate well that what one may think at first to be not relevant to a subject matter, may prove to be at its heart. As a teacher, Weber is interested in understanding how she can help her students "deeply learn" about why they have habits they may struggle with. She conducts an exercise in class where students abstain from a habit for a couple of weeks so that they can observe their thoughts and feelings (and sensations) in the process to arrive at a better understanding of themselves and the society in which they live. Her study demonstrates the extent to which even the spacetime of a senior seminar classroom can be transformed into a learning experience through which students realize knowledge is not merely a matter of thinking, but also feeling (and sensing their bodies).

It takes more than thinking to engage in a conversation, since the modes of conversing are also multi-form, and habits can play enormous role in shaping, and limiting, our philosophies and politics in favor of decolonized outcomes in self and broader society. As the saying goes, "the devil is in the detail," and our conceptual and practices all count, even when they take inadvertent turns. I sincerely believe that no significant effort can be made toward anti-Cartesian decoloniality and pluriversal transmodernity, unless we find ways of becoming, first and foremost in our own personal lives and scholarship (to the various extents engaged in), but also as part of the communities to which we belong, aware of our thinking habits that are often accompanied by intellectual inadvertency, since the causes of perpetuation of such habits of thinking cannot be readily found in our thoughts only. They arise from the multiplicities and fragmentations of our being across our thinking-feeling-sensing faculties.

Only a pluriversal epistemology that involves all the pluriversal aspects of our learning faculties can enable us to fully realize what coloniality has done to our nature in a world-history (and not just in the modern) context, and how we can creatively absorb all the liberating aspects of the world's traditions, Eastern and Western, in a pluriversal spirit while discarding the imperial habits of political domination, cultural conversion, and economic exploitation that have been the defining features of imperial practice in world-history.

•••

In his article published in this issue, Dussel advises,

But together with this dissemination of histories and reflection by philosophers of the South—researchers, students, professors, and intellectuals in general—upon the most valuable aspects of their own philosophical traditions, it is also necessary to develop a creative discourse which is *properly philosophical* in character, and which thus goes beyond mere commentaries on either one's ancestral tradition or that of Europe. This implies contributions that take the reality and history of the treatment of key specific themes in the corresponding regional or local philosophy of the South. Philosophical reflection should enrich these realities critically with one's own tools, and in dialogue with the best expressions of modern European philosophy (which the philosophers of the South must know *how to select and incorporate into their own projects of distinct, autonomous thought*). All of this should be deployed with an emphasis on producing *clear thinking* which is well-founded, coherent, and understandable by those responsible for the concrete political, economic, aesthetic, technological, and scientific realities of the countries of the South. In sum, what is aimed at is a *proper philosophy*, which is both an expression of the South and a useful contribution to its community of reference. (Dussel, p. 15; italics added)

Dussel writes that in order to engage in South-South philosophical conversation, we need to find ways to interpret the rich philosophical traditions that we come from—all in their multifaceted and pluriversal forms—through a hermeneutic method that brings them to a philosophy "proper." While what he proposes is an important part of the project to be undertaken, I think a word of caution about the limits of this strategy is also warranted.

I wonder if by doing so we deprive the very nature of alternative philosophical insights of their epistemic multi-dimensionality, reducing them to mere thought forms, and dislodge them from their contextual settings, when they are (as is, for instance, the genuine forms of meditation often practiced in non-"university" settings) holistic practices that engage all of our beings' sensing, feeling, and thinking faculties at the same time. So, in the very process of our translating these rich cultural traditions into "proper philosophy" we may ourselves commit—unconsciously and habitually following Westernized university prevalent practices, what Grosfoguel calls (in his important paper in this issue) while drawing on Boaventura de Sousa Santos—"epistemicide," and as such engage in an "inadvertent," subtler form of Cartesian, modern coloniality in the very process of our scholarly conversations about how to transcend them.

I recall a while ago, when working on my editorial note for an issue of *Human Architecture* on Islamophobia, I was asked to delete a quatrain from Khayyam from my draft, simply because someone feared institutional backlash from her (perhaps more orthodox Islamic) peers for using "wine" as a Sufi metaphor while commenting on Islam. It was an odd experience to me, being asked to censor myself in an editorial note to a journal of my own founding. And the substance of the request amid a journal issue dedicated to Islamophobia seemed itself to be surreally interesting. I respected the request at the time, but I can use the experience now and here to illustrate how it is possible to inadvertently and unconsciously commit Islamophobia in our every day intellectual projects at the very lines we devote to conversing about what (unconscious) Islamphobia is and how to rid the world of it.

In fact, the very process of reducing a quatrain into "proper philosophical" language can deprive it of the very nature of its creative force in transforming not only our minds, feelings, and senses, but even—if we are persistent enough—of the very contextual "places" with which we think and thereby perpetuate our inner and broader slaveries.

This may explain why Khayyam chose to convey his philosophy via poetry. Perhaps, it may take practicing obediential scholarship to learn from Linda Weber and her students—in our case, of "abstaining" and 'de-tiring' from our busy institutionalized academic (and editorial) habits—to come to a better understanding of ourselves and of our world, in favor of happier outcomes. And it may be worth, following Sazzad's findings, to become an amateur again so as to detach ourselves consciously from the institutional slaveries and preoccupations that have divided and ruled our colonized inner lives for a while.

ما خرقه زهد بر سر خم کردیم
وز خاک خرابات تیمّم کردیم
باشد که ز خاک میکده دریابیم
آن عمر که در مدرسه ها گم کردیم

We Hung Piety's Cloak on the Barrel of Wine.
And Abluted with Dust in the Ruin's Shrine.
So we may Recover from the Tavern's Dust
The Life that we Lost in the Schools' Confine.

—Omar Khayyam

HUMAN ARCHITECTURE: JOURNAL OF THE SOCIOLOGY OF SELF-KNOWLEDGE
A Publication of OKCIR: The Omar Khayyam Center for Integrative Research in Utopia, Mysticism, and Science (Utopystics)
ISSN: 1540-5699. © COPYRIGHT BY AHEAD PUBLISHING HOUSE (IMPRINT: OKCIR PRESS) AND AUTHORS. ALL RIGHTS RESERVED.

Introduction:
Enrique Dussel's Multiple Decolonial Contributions

Issue Co-Editors: George Ciccariello-Maher and Ramón Grosfoguel

Drexel University and U.C. Berkeley

gjcm@drexel.edu • grosfogu@berkeley.edu

Abstract: This is a brief introduction by the co-editors of the vol. XI, no. 1 (Fall 2013) issue of *Human Architecture: Journal of the Sociology of Self-Knowledge*, titled "Towards a Decolonial Transmodern World: A Conversation with Enrique Dussel."

Recent years have witnessed a growing interest in Enrique Dussel's work, to which this volume seeks to contribute. With the appearance in English of his accessible handbook *Twenty Theses on Politics* in 2008 and the monumental *Ethics of Liberation* earlier this year, both from Duke University Press, it is safe to say that this long-prolific and influential Latin American philosopher of liberation is breaking new ground and gaining adherents in the English-speaking world. And yet his production in Spanish continues to dramatically outpace available translations: at the height of the global upsurge of 2011, Dussel published *Carta a los indignados*, and he has recently finished a companion piece to the *Twenty Theses*, which dedicates sixteen theses to the subject of political economy. He continues to work on the expected third volume of his massive *Política de la Liberación*, the first of which recently appeared in English, and the second of which garnered Dussel the prestigious Liberator Prize for Critical Thought in 2010.

Central to Dussel's massive and continually expanding body of work is a profound political decolonial engagement which nevertheless refuses to shun thought: his is a *philosophy* in the fullest sense of the word, but *liberation* is its express objective. Or, as he put it in his 1971 *Philosophy of Liberation*: "Politics introduces ethics, which in turn introduces philosophy" (173). That these aspects should not be considered in isolation from one another, that philosophy should not be locked in the ivory tower as political practice and not be isolated from theory, is also attested to in Dussel's recent decision to accept—at the demand of organized student movements—the interim rectorship of

---

George Ciccariello-Maher is assistant professor in the Department of History and Politics at Drexel University, Philadelphia, PA. **Ramón Grosfoguel** is associate professor in the Department of Ethnic Studies at U.C. Berkeley.

the Autonomous University of Mexico City (UACM). Stepping into the contentious political fray in such a way was not something any philosopher could take lightly, but nor was it something that a philosopher *of liberation* could easily refuse.

It is in this spirit of engagement that we offer the essays collected here, which range from theoretical reflections on aspects of Dusselian thought to attempts to concretely apply his concepts to different aspects of reality. While reflecting the importance, coherence, and power of Dussel's work, these essays also reflect the range of this philosopher-historian-theologian-political theorist.

Eduardo Mendieta and Oscar Guardiola engage Dussel's recent intervention into rekindled debates on the importance of Saint Paul of Tarsus for radical thought, on which Dussel published yet another book in 2012. Linda Martín Alcoff and Lewis Gordon reflect on Dussel's polemical engagement in his "Anti-Cartesian Meditations" with the ostensible founder of European philosophy. Ramón Grosfoguel engages a broad range of Dussel's work, drawing epistemology and geopolitics into conversation to press forward the task of a decolonial epistem-ology by linking the four genocides/epistemicides of the long 16th century with modern/colonial racist/sexist structures of knowledge. Finally, Dustin Craun turns Dussel's work toward pressing contemporary efforts to rethink Islam's contribution toward pluriversal transition to transmodernity. In the spirit of the conversations begun here, we also reprint Dussel's own "Agenda for a South-South Philosophical Dialogue" that seeks to transcend the false universalism of European philosophy in the hopes of ushering in a truly universal "pluriversal, trans-modern age." For decolonial thinkers around the world, there is a before and after Enrique Dussel's Liberation Philosophy.

REFERENCES

Enrique Dussel, *Philosophy of Liberation*, trans. A. Martinez and C. Morkovsky. Eugene, OR: Wipf and Stock: 1985.

HUMAN ARCHITECTURE: JOURNAL OF THE SOCIOLOGY OF SELF-KNOWLEDGE
A Publication of OKCIR: The Omar Khayyam Center for Integrative Research in Utopia, Mysticism, and Science (Utopystics)
ISSN: 1540-5699. © COPYRIGHT BY AHEAD PUBLISHING HOUSE (IMPRINT: OKCIR PRESS) AND AUTHORS. ALL RIGHTS RESERVED.

Agenda for a South-South Philosophical Dialogue

Enrique Dussel

Universidad Autónoma Metropolitano, México

dussamb@servidor.unam.mx

Abstract: The intercultural dialogue that has been developing since the beginning of the 21st century as a cultural and political priority should have an inter-philosophical global dialogue as its epistemological and ontological foundation. However, given the asymmetric relation between the Global North and the Global South, it is necessary that this global dialogue begin with an inter-philosophical dialogue among the world's post-colonial communities. This essay argues that it is imperative for philosophers of the South to come together to define and claim for themselves a philosophical practice—generating its topics and methods from its own historical, socio-economic-political realities and traditions—that is critical of and goes beyond the European "I" which, by virtue of its colonial history, has asserted itself as the universal standard of humanity and philosophy. In asserting the particularity of their own traditions and the creative possibilities of their own situations, dialogues among the philosophers of the South work towards the realization of a pluriverse, where each culture will be in dialogue with all others from the perspective of a common "similarity," enabling each to continuously recreate its own analogical "distinction," and to diffuse itself within a dialogical, reciprocally creative space.

The intercultural dialogue that has been developing since the beginning of the 21st century as a cultural and political priority should have an inter-philosophical global dialogue as its epistemological and ontological foundation. Nonetheless, given the disproportionate concentration of cultural, political, economic, and military power in the Global North and given the exercise of power characterized by inequalities of race and gender, among other factors, against the Global South—i.e., the former colonial world whose configurations emerged in the 16th century and have intensified since the

Enrique Dussel was born December 24, 1934, in the town of La Paz, in the region of Mendoza, Argentina. He first came to Mexico in 1975 as a political exile and is currently a Mexican citizen, Professor in the Department of Philosophy at the Iztapalapa campus of the Universidad Autónoma Metropolitana (Autonomous Metropolitan University, UAM) and also teaches courses at the Universidad Nacional Autónoma de México (National Autonomous University of Mexico, UNAM). He has an undergraduate degree in Philosophy (from the Universidad Nacional de Cuyo/National University of Cuyo in Mendoza, Argentina), a Doctorate from the Complutense University of Madrid, a Doctorate in History from the Sorbonne in Paris, and an undergraduate degree in Theology obtained through studies in Paris and Münster. He has been awarded Doctorates Honoris Causa from the University of Friburg in Switzerland, the University of San Andrés in Bolivia and the University of Buenos Aires in Argentina. He is the founder with others of the movement referred to as the Philosophy of Liberation, and his work is concentrated in the field of Ethics and Political Philosophy. **This paper was presented at the first South-South Philosophical Dialogue organized by UNESCO in Marrakech, Morocco, June 2012. It was originally published in** *Budhi: A Journal of Ideas and Culture* **17.1 (2013): 1–27. We are grateful for permission by the editors of** *Budhi* **to republish it here.**

Industrial Revolution in Latin America, Bantu Africa, the Arab and Islamic world, Southeast Asia and India, including China which, although it was not directly colonized, has borne the effects of Western power since the 19th century—it is necessary that this process begin with an inter-philosophical dialogue among the world's postcolonial communities.

This is also necessary because modern Western philosophy decreed the inexistence as philosophy, strictly speaking, of all of the philosophical exercises undertaken in those countries which have borne the effects of the colonialism imposed by the European metropolitan powers. It is thus imperative that the philosophers of the South meet in recognition of their existence as such—grounded in the traditions that they have cultivated in the regional philosophies from which they have emerged—in order to clarify our positions, develop working hypotheses, and then, upon this basis, initiate a fertile North-South inter-philosophical dialogue with a well-defined agenda that has been previously developed by the philosophies based in the so-called "underdeveloped" countries or nations of the global periphery who have the material basis to affirm that they have been exploited by a colonialist capitalism that today has become globalized and is in crisis.

My approach to these issues is set forth here in the form of simple theses that might contribute towards this dialogue, with the intention that they be tested in forthcoming debates as bases for possible consensus regarding central themes which must be ranked in the order of their importance with a view towards more focused, specific dialogues at later stages of this process. Those themes could then be explored in greater detail as part of agreed frameworks that could be taught in high schools, universities, and other institutes of learning, and help spark new working hypotheses and innovative research projects, derived from the new philosophical paradigm presented here.

1. The Significance of an Agenda of Philosophical Themes to be Discussed Within the Framework of a South-South Dialogue

In the first instance, I believe that a necessary precondition for a fertile overall dialogue in the future is the meeting of a group of critical philosophers from the Global South (not those who simply teach or comment on the philosophers of the North) in order to undertake deep discussions, with sufficient time, to determine which are the problems, themes, and hypotheses for reflection that they should focus on in the future. These meetings would provide the participants the opportunity to explore each of the most fundamental themes or hypotheses in order to assess their deeper significance within a community of dialogue, and arrive at the levels of consensus necessary in order to define minimum ranges of agreement, that in turn could lay the basis for a truly planetary philosophy (not just for the South, but for the Global North as well).

Such a consensus (and its respective priorities) could only be arrived at upon the basis of a determination of the most relevant themes. This in turn presupposes a degree of critical philosophical reflection necessary in order to initiate such a dialogue from a new point of departure. It would not be necessary to discuss a specific theme in this first encounter, but instead to undertake a reflection regarding the significance and implications of the current situation of contemporary postcolonial philosophy, the causes of its prostration, as well as of its supposed inexistence, lack of fertility, and invisibility in the eyes of our fellow philosophers in the so- called "periphery." How did this situation come about? How can this apparent inexistence of the regional philosophies be overcome? Which are the themes that should be explored, and in what order? In some regions of the South or postcolonial world, the histories of our regional philosophies, some of which have ancient roots dating back for centuries and even thousands of years, have begun to be written for the first time and to be renovated with new criteria. It has been a long time since the history of our philosophies ceased to be a central aspect of the formation of our university students of philosophy. The prevailing tendency has long been to simply transplant the curriculums developed in European or U.S. universities (the latter, particularly, since the end of the so-called "Second World War"). All of this reflects a dismal state of affairs, which is one of the manifest fruits of a cultural colonialism that must be confronted.

The discussion regarding the *factors that impeded the development of our regional philosophies in the South*, and the order in which they arose, ought to be the first item on the agenda that must be explored upon the basis of a full awareness of its importance.

2. Metropolitan Modernity and the Colonial Worlds

My point of departure is that all philosophies (Chinese, Indian, Egyptian, Greek, Roman, Arab, Amerindian, etc.) have inevitably been ethnocentric in character, since their origin lies in a certain ontological ingenuousness which considers their own world (their cultural totality assumed as a complete grasp of the meaning of human existence) as the center around which the rest of humanity revolved. This ethnocentrism, however, was empirically local and regional in character. Even the immense Chinese empire, which always assumed itself to be the "center" of the universe, never ceased to be centered around its particularity, with only the most incipient consciousness of its near and distant surroundings. It considered other peoples if not inferior then as causes of disquiet within its apparent imperturbability, because it suspected that its knowledge was inherently limited, and that an immense unknown exteriority lingered in the shadows of the unexplored and might erupt into visibility at any moment. The accounts of sporadic travelers, which told of adventures in unknown regions, were not given much credit but could in any case illuminate that consciousness which was never clear about the phantoms, monstrous beings, and bottomless depths that surrounded it, like those strewn throughout the Atlantic in the equivalent representations imagined by the Europeans under siege by the Arab and Islamic world in what they referred to as the so-called "Middle Ages."[1]

But it was only in the European context that for the first time in the history of humanity such traditional expressions of ethnocentrism reached the most distant confines of the planet itself, and began to be diffused around the Earth beginning in the 15th-century of the Common Era. As a result of rapid technological development, Chinese, Portuguese, and Spanish navigators for the first time achieved the circumnavigation of the globe, which made it possible for the European version of what was merely yet another *particularist*, localized ethnocentrism to be transformed into an ethnocentrism on a *global* scale. This included first the *modern* expansion of Mediterranean Europe, and later that of Northern Europe, which together marked the inception of what we describe today as globalization.

European modernity emerged simultaneously with this process, thanks to the mercantile centrality of the North Atlantic (which displaced that of the Mediterranean), leading to the emergence of capitalism as a historical phenomenon, and to Eurocentrism and the scientific and technological revolution which would result from the combination of all of these factors. All of these were also the origin of a *modern* philosophy, which would lay claim to the privilege of supposedly being the sole

---
1. The name of a historical epoch that is only valid in the European context. The Islamic world experienced a stage of urbanized and mercantile splendor during the same period.

vehicle for the deployment of human reason capable of transcending the narratives of mythology, thus discrediting all of the religions of the South. This philosophy did not only have the pretension of being universal, planetary, and the expression of human reason as such, but also categorized all other regional philosophies of the South as "backward," naïve, and particular. Once the process of the Spanish conquest of the Americas began at the end of the 15th century in the Caribbean (with all of the cultural conflicts that were inherent in this process), all of its argumentation was focused on the demonstration of the superiority of European civilization, and thus gradually that of its philosophy. Europe's military conquests and the destruction of pre-existent commercial routes would help impede the possibility that other cultures might subsequently match European levels of development, and would seek to prevent them from progressing upon the basis of a new perspective on world history distinct from that which had been inaugurated by the original *world-system*. The cultures which were colonized sought to defend themselves by reiterating the value of their past glories, but this was not a sufficient basis for them either to resist the new developments which ensued or to formulate arguments that were effective against the superiority assumed by their European adversaries. In the end, they were largely swept away by events and were not able to confront the new European philosophy for centuries.

This overall landscape should not be exaggerated, because in reality there were significant moments of specific creativity in all the regions of the South. But such moments were soon excluded from the regional histories of these philosophies in favor of the prevalence of the advances achieved by modern European philosophy beginning with Descartes, which would attain a hegemony that is still unsurpassed among the colonial élites.

A specific kind of historical judgment soon became diffused throughout the periphery. It was true that a certain kind of philosophical discourse was conducted with locally important figures, but how could this be compared with the thought of Kant, Hegel, Nietzsche, Heidegger, Sartre, or Carnap? This question was poorly formulated and, as a result, the responses it inspired were incomplete and complicit, serving only to blur and bury the historical truths at issue. In Latin America, until recently, it was said, "There is no Latin American philosophy!"—if by philosophy one understands the practice of the same kind of theoretical discourse which had been developed in the context of modern European philosophy. But certainly in the Latin American context, there have been numerous philosophers and philosophical currents which have helped lay the basis for cultural, political, economic, or technological processes, and which interpreted the meaning of life within the cultural contexts of our region. But these efforts obtained regional, not global, recognition, as might be expected within the framework of a peripheral culture.

One must therefore meditate in detail on the causes which produced the eclipse of the philosophies of the South in order to be able to clearly comprehend the negative factors which must be overcome to undertake the process of developing the philosophies of the postcolonial, peripheral, or dominated regions of the world, subjected to the colonialism of the European metropolises, whose domination has not only been military, economic, or political, but also ideological, cultural, and at its roots *philosophical*.

3. THE COLONIAL DIMENSIONS OF ECONOMIC AND TECHNOLOGICAL EXPANSION

At the end of the 15th century, Europe was completely limited, surrounded by the walls of the Ottoman Empire. The Muslims laid siege to Vienna well into the 17th century, and did not cease to occupy Granada (the last region representative of the splendor of the ancient Califate of Cordoba) until January 1492. The Latino-Germanic region of Europe (not that of the Byzantine or oriental Empire) was peripheral, under-developed, and cornered by the Islamic world, and thus unable to connect itself with the "Old World" envisioned by Adam Smith. Its only path in that direction was through the ports of the Italian cities, which dominated the traffic of the Eastern Mediterranean, and from there to Fatimid Egypt or Syrian Antioch, which led eventually to Baghdad, or to the caravans which reached China through the deserts of the north, or India via Kabul. The other way was north of the Black Sea all the way to Constantinople, or across the Red Sea or Persian Gulf towards Hindustan and the China Sea. This Europe, which was dark (during the so-called "Middle Ages"), could only break through its isolation from the Northeast through the Principality of Moscow (which would reach into Siberia and arrive at the Pacific at the beginning of the 17th century), or via the West, through Portugal and Spain. The discovery of the caravel in 1441, and the slow dominion of the Oceans—thanks to the Chinese maps of the Atlantic and Pacific, the compass, and other instruments of navigation equally of Chinese origin (China had an advantage of more than 400 years with respect to the technology, science, and astronomy characteristic of Medieval Europe)—enabled it to discover and manage the Atlantic Ocean, which would become the geopolitical center of European modernity. The development of naval and military technology would enable Portugal to take control of the maritime commercial routes of Africa, the Indian Ocean, India, the Moluccas, and the coasts of China and Japan. And it would be Spain which established the *first European continental colonialism* in Latin America and imposed it upon the continent's original inhabitants (Meso-Americans, Incas, Tupi-Guaraní, etc.) for three hundred years (from the end of the 15th century until the beginning of the 19th century, approximately).

This expansion, due to the greater levels of development of military strategy and technology in comparison with the cultures of native Latin America, would establish, in the first phase of Early Modernity,[2] an economic system of mercantile and monetary capitalism based upon the extraction of silver, gold, and colonial goods, founded upon the inhuman domination of the continent's indigenous peoples and the Atlantic slave trade, which would incorporate West Africa into a triangle of death structured around the relationship between Africa, Latin America, and Europe: Europe would transport arms to Africa; from there slaves would be transported to the Americas (and later to the English colonies in North America); the sale of these slaves would permit silver and gold (money) and tropical products (sugar, cacao, tobacco, etc.) to be sold in Europe or accumulated in its banks. This was the period of capitalist "primitive accumulation." Later, the Dutch, English, French, and Danes would land in India and the rest of Asia, and capitalist commerce with its center in Europe would achieve global dimensions.

The tragic component inherent in the process which produced the configuration of a capitalist economic *world-system* is that the colonial world would be interpreted as one which is inhabited by human beings who are exploitable and are treated as if they belonged to a secondary class of human beings in anthropological, ontological, and ethical-political terms, as we shall see. The original inhabitants of the colonized regions of the Global South were thus assumed to be sub-humans whose domination by Europeans supposedly endows them at the same

---

2. The second phase of *Early Modernity* would be characterized by the hegemony of Holland (from 1630), and its third phase by that of England (from 1688), which in turn laid the basis for *Mature Modernity*, thanks to the Industrial Revolution, which began in China's Yellow River Valley and flowered definitively in the United Kingdom at the end of the 18th century.

time with a limited dosage of enhanced humanity. Coloniality was interpreted from the European perspective as a kind of gift, the endowment of humanity. This ideological core which underlies all the other modern ideologies has prevailed up until the present.

4. The Political and Military Dimensions of Colonial Expansion

Political and military forms of aggression always precede economic expansion, as expressed within the context of the capitalist mercantile system in Latin America in the form of big landed estates (*haciendas*) and systems of forced miner community labor (the *mita*), the African slave trade and slavery, and through unequal forms of commerce such as the Opium Wars in the Far East. It was a Eurocentric "will to power" which organized armies of occupation, whose strategic and technological advantages were able to overcome the resistance of the political structures of power (sometimes regional and sometimes local or ethnic in character) they encountered in their path, first in Latin America (beginning at the end of the 15th century) and then in Africa or Asia (on a continental stage from the end of the 18th century). The emerging modern states (in Spain, Portugal, the United Provinces of Holland, England, France, Denmark, etc.) from their origins combined the following characteristics, which developed together in an intertwined manner: a) royal domination of state churches (*Christendoms*[3]), b) *coloniality*, c) mercantilist versions of *capitalism*, and d) *Eurocentrism*.

The *coloniality of power* (a concept clarified by the sociologist of Peru, Aníbal Quijano) of the European colonial metropolises was expressed in diverse forms of domination imposed upon their dependent colonies. The European king at the head of each of the metropolitan powers exercised an unquestioned monopoly of power over their colonial subjects. The coloniality of the members of the colonial communities impeded their participation as proper citizens; they were the subject neither of political rights nor human rights equivalent to those of the European metropolitan subjects. None of this was contradictory from the European colonialist perspective, given the premises of the European conception of law (which Carl Schmitt describes accurately, although he is incapable of perceiving its Eurocentrism). This explains how it was possible, within the constraints of this framework, for the French Revolution to issue the Declaration of the Rights of Man and the Citizen in August 1789 (the first list of its kind of ostensibly universal human rights),[4] and at the same time to apply its *Code Noir* (*Black Code*), which was the governing law in the French colony, to define the duties and restrict the rights of the slaves it possessed in the Caribbean (in Haiti, whose slave rebellion in 1791 finally led to the independence in 1804). These slaves evidently were not considered to be human or to be the subject of the new *universal human* rights proclaimed by a bourgeois, colonialist revolution in metropolitan France (which considered the citizens of the metropolis to be *equal, fraternal,* and *free,* but considered the *non-humans* of the South to be slaves who were inherently unequal and thus the legitimate objects of *domination*).[5]

---

3. See the concept of *Christendom* (*Christlichkeit* in German), that is not Christianity, in the fifth chapter of the second part of Karl Loewith, *Von Hegel zu Nietzsche* (Stuttgart: Kohlhammer, 1964); and also in the fourth chapter of my *Politics of Liberation* (London: SCM Press, 2011).

4. Which means that the "universality" of these rights excluded colonial subjects; it was in fact a particularity imposed with universalist pretensions, or an ideological universality which was actually particular and exclusionary regarding the colonial sectors of humanity, which is a theme within the political philosophy of the South that was not addressed by Hobbes, Locke, or Hume, etc.

5. The *non-humanity* of the human beings of the South or post-colonial regions of the world continues today. The deaths of the civilian populations which have been the victims of aggression in Iraq and Afghanistan count much less

The European metropolitan countries had political institutions in charge of administering matters related with their overseas territories, beginning with the Spanish *Council of the Indies* established at the beginning of the 16th century. These institutions combined political and military dimensions in charge of *vigilance* and *punishment*, when necessary (as suggested by Foucault's book *Discipline and Punish*), related to the extraction of wealth from the colonial regions, without any concern whatever for their reciprocal duties to colonial workers (including indigenous peoples who worked for them for free, African slaves, and exploited *mestizos*). The idea was never that of a symmetrical commercial exchange (involving the payment of the value equivalent to that of the commodity transported from the periphery to the center); instead, the essence of the matter was a theft of the exchange value which had been expropriated thanks to the presence of a military power that impeded the colonial world from demanding a just payment for the extraction of wealth from the South. Violent military coercion guaranteed economic theft, which was not considered to obligate the metropolitan center in terms of a debt owed to the colonies (and which would involve a just payment of interest). Rather, what was at issue was the direct appropriation of goods belonging to someone else pursuant to a purported right of conquest, which always in fact implied an imposition grounded in superior military force. Jürgen Habermas has correctly emphasized that any consensus must be achieved as the result of the symmetrical rational participation of all those affected; but the political dimension of colonialism implied instead the asymmetrical imposition by force, not of a rational consensus but of an irrational *will to power* exercised by the center against the periphery. Nonetheless, the philosophers of the center speak today of rights, symmetry, and democracy (and do

than those of the soldiers (*boys*) who lose their life waging these wars.

not criticize the wars conducted today to "establish democracy" in the "backward" countries of the South), without ever having acknowledged the last 500 years of irrational, colonialist, and anti-democratic political and military violence, in which they are implicated, and its negative effects.

The political philosophy of the South today must rethink all of the philosophical tradition from Hobbes or Locke up until the Frankfurt School, C. Schmitt, A. Badiou or G. Agamben, to name just a few, who have not yet succeeded in overcoming the Eurocentrism which has always accompanied the political expansion of Europe, and now that of the United States as well.

5. The Ontological-Philosophical Justification of Colonialism

Colonial praxis has from the beginning relied upon a philosophical justification as its foundation, and this is the point of departure for modern European philosophy with its universality claim, which unfortunately is accepted by most of the members of the philosophical academies of the South. This justification also had an anthropological character (expressed in the assumption of the superiority of European human beings over those of the South, as reflected in the interpretation of that superiority by Gines de Sepúlveda in his re-reading of Aristotle in the 16th century, or by Kant in the 18th century, based upon his conception of the origins of such inequalities in the climates of the Earth and its regions)—one aspect of which was historical (where Europe was, for example, the "center and end of universal history" for Hegel) and another which was ethical (in terms of the inclusion within European culture of the peoples of the Americas, Africa, or Asia, upon whom was imposed its vision of an ethics which is non-conventional, individualist, founded upon rational argumentation, universal, and not merely particular such as those characteristic of the cultures of the South, etc.)—which served to demonstrate the legitimacy of colonialism.

But the ultimate foundation of colonial praxis was ontological in character. The European "I" which had enunciated to the South for over a century and a half, beginning in 1492, its formulation, "I conquer the New World," now assumed itself as a universal ontological foundation as "I." This central *Ego* (*Ichheit* in German), around which everything revolved, was inadvertently European: a European "I" with the pretension of discovering itself to be universal and ultimate, which knows itself, and which can reconstruct *all of the world* (including all of the worlds contained within the South). It is within this context that René Descartes, during the second phase of Early Modernity, in Amsterdam (a Spanish province until shortly before his emergence), a student of the Jesuits (a Spanish religious order) enunciates his *ego cogito*. This *ego*, this metropolitan *European* "I"[6] is the ontological-philosophical foundation of what Martin Heidegger will denominate as the "world" (*Welt*) in *Being and Time* (1927).[7] In 1637, Descartes's *Discourse on Method* serves as the manifesto of modern European philosophy, which assumes its role as the supposed universal philosophy throughout the next 400 years.[8] The need to overcome this Eurocentric vision must precisely be the primary objective of a dialogue among the philosophers of the South, among those of us from the post-colonial regions, who continue to be treated as if we were still colonial subjects in epistemological and philosophical terms, in the vast majority of our spaces for philosophical and academic reflection within the universities of the South. In large part, the function we fulfill and have assumed is as mere commentators at the periphery of modern European philosophy, and not as thinkers with reflections regarding our reality, which has been negated and which has not been the object of thinking by that philosophy which claims universality for itself.

Philosophical coloniality has dual aspects: a) in the center, Spain of the 16th century, due to the universality claim of its European metropolitan regional philosophy since the 16th century which at the same time has negated and marginalized the contributions of the pre-Cartesian ethical and political philosophy that flourished during the period of the First Early Modernity and has disappeared from the histories of modern philosophy; and b) in the periphery, the South, because of the prevailing, unquestioning acceptance of the supposed evidence that the said European philosophy is in fact the universal philosophy, which has imposed itself throughout the last few centuries. This latter aspect presupposes for its part: i) an ignorance of the regional philosophies of the periphery from their origins (prior to and together with that of European modernity); ii) the negative evaluation of the significance of its own philosophies throughout the last 500 years; and iii) the definition of philosophy (in the colonial philosophy of the South) as commentary regarding the European modern philosophy (that has a universal claim) that denies even the very existence of the South's own philosophies. In addition, there is a marked tendency in these colonial philosophies of the South towards argumentation in favor of their impossibility and as to their uselessness or superfluity.

The colonial philosophy of the South then, in a negative sense, is that which is practiced in the periphery by those who act based on the premises of Eurocentrism and deny their own regional and local philosophy. From the perspective of the center, it is modern philosophy which negates all other

---

6. I repeat: *inadvertently*. "European," and also male, white, adult, metropolitan, etc.

7. Of course Heidegger seeks to demonstrate that this "I" is founded upon a "being-in-the-world" which is always presupposed.

8. See my article: "The Anti-Cartesian Meditations," *Polígrafi* 41–42 (2006): 5–60, http://www.enriquedussel.com, (under "work" and "philosophical articles").

philosophies (from the South), and which categorizes them as being equivalent to mythological, folkloric, conventional, backward, particularist, and/or pseudo-philosophical thinking.

6. The Economic and Political Liberation of the South

The concrete historical processes of national or regional liberation in the face of European colonialism—which began in the South with Tupac Amaru and Tupac Katari between 1780–1781, and then in Haiti between 1791 and 1804 against France, in 1810 with Latin America against Spain and Portugal, and in Africa and Asia following the Second World War—laid the foundation for the emergence of a philosophy of liberation from colonialism. These events determine a creative moment which should be taken into account.

These political, economic, and cultural moments of liberation must also be considered to be culminations of a philosophical process, as well as the birth of a philosophy which is intertwined with praxis and which lays the foundation for a justification of this age of emancipation from colonialism. It will be necessary, therefore, to be especially *attentive* to the historical reconstruction of the philosophy of the South (in singular or plural, for it is also necessary to highlight the "philosophies" of the South). It is simply impossible to conceive of an autonomous, creative, truly free philosophy in the South within the tortuous, suffocating limits of the political, economic, and cultural horizons of a community which has been colonized, subjugated, exploited, and oppressed. As Augusto Salazar Bondy wrote in 1969 in neocolonial Perú, it is very difficult to construct an authentic philosophy in a colonial and dependent context.[9]

The post-colonial situation (which is not exempt from neoliberal or other new economic, political, geopolitical, or epistemological variants of colonialism) is the contemporary framework of conditions which make liberation from colonial philosophy possible within the context of a new stage of creativity. In my view, this is the current responsibility of philosophers who have the pretension of being thinkers regarding the reality that surrounds them, as European philosophers did in the context of their reality, in their metropolitan and colonial context. This goes much beyond merely being the *commentators* of philosophical works, from which a great deal can be learned, but which must be understood as the expression of thinking grounded in *another reality*. To confuse European or U.S. reality with our own simply constitutes a *fallacy of dislocation* (the fallacy of taking the space or world of another culture as one's own, and thereby rendering invisible the distinct originality inherent in the other reality and its very differences with one's own).[10]

7. The Affirmation of the Ancestral Cultures of the South

Philosophy does not imply an isolated process of theoretical production, but instead one that involves a commitment to the world surrounding us. The pretension of such absolute autonomy is what character-

---

9. Augusto Salazar Bondy, ¿*Existeuna Filosofía en Nuestra América*? (México: Siglo XXI Editores, 1969).

10. This *fallacy* encompasses many additional errors: not to recognize that the other's reality is different from one's own; therefore, not to know that it is impossible to assume reality as a given as it is lived in Europe or the U.S., because one is not existentially, originally part of that other-world (which one might fictitiously live as if it were one's own, as a colonial person with a metropolitan soul, a ghost or phantom); to negate the knowledge of the evolving historical identity of one's own reality and not differentiate it from that of others; to thus think of that which is alien falsely as one's own, and therefore to define as philosophy what is in essence commentary, and not to aspire to create something different; and in, ethical terms, to be responsible for rendering invisible, for hiding, for making disappear, or for failing to perceive what is one's own, etc.

izes the efforts of a certain school of Anglo-Saxon analytical philosophy, which nonetheless supposes all of the history of philosophy from the Vienna Circle to the philosophy of language in the British Isles, to be itself the history of philosophy as such, when in fact all of this must be situated in specific cultural worlds, located in the universities of certain countries in certain specific historical moments with concrete characteristics that explain their emergence, development, and current crisis. The Frankfurt School, French existentialism, phenomenology, etc., all argued that a philosophy without historical commitment (that is, one that is isolated from specific philosophical, cultural, economic, and political moments within their historical contexts) is impossible. Thomas Kuhn demonstrated that scientific revolutions (and thus those of a philosophical character as well) depend not only on intra-scientific events, but also on extra-scientific factors which help determine their emergence.

For their part, Eurocentric philosophies in the South, in post-colonial countries, equally seek to practice a universal philosophy of the modern European type within their own cultural horizon, that of the South in Latin America, Africa, or Asia.[11] This compels them to accept certain apparent forms of evidence that constitute unquestionable dogmas within modern European philosophy, such as the idea that philosophy itself is of Greek origin marked by the transition from *mythos* to *logos*. Both of these formulations—that is, philosophy's Greek origin and the overcoming of *mythos* by *logos*—are unacceptable. Today it is widely recognized that long before Greece, there was philosophy in the Mesopotamian kingdoms dating back to the 4th century BCE, and in Egypt. Thales of Miletus, the first recognized Greek philosopher, came from a family of Phoenician origin.[12] And as to the relationship between mythology and philosophy, Aristotle considered the latter to be a form of *mythopoiesis*, and Greek philosophy as a whole (beginning with the post-Socratics such as Plato or Plotinus) were completely immersed in a world permeated by myth: What, for example, is the *psyche* (soul) in Plato but a myth of Hindustani origin, which cannot be demonstrated by means of empirical evidence (a myth which is handed down all the way to Kant)? What are the *Enneads* of Plotinus but an expression of the metaphysical cosmic mathematics characteristic of Egyptian culture?

It is upon the basis of the allegedly irrational and anti-philosophical character (according to the modern European definition of philosophy) of myths and religious narratives (which, according to Paul Ricoeur, one of my professors at the Sorbonne in Paris, are *rational* philosophical narratives based on symbols), that modernity denied any validity to the philosophical narratives (which contained myths) of the cultures of the South, including those of China and India which go back for millennia, as well as those of the Iranian-Aristotelian tradition of scientific and empirical inquiry in the Arab world.

In order to reconstruct the philosophies of the South, it is necessary, as part of a pendulum swing in the inverse direction from that imposed by the pretensions of modern European secularism (which necessarily implied the negation of the ancestral cultures of the South), to restore the validity and significance of the traditions of these regions of the world, including those of a mythical character, and to subject them to an adequate hermeneutical interpretation. It is the methodology of interpretation (hermeneutics) which is philosophical; although

---

11. I should be more specific here: the *South* which I have been referring to includes at minimum: a) Latin America (and its indigenous peoples); b) the Islamic world (from Morocco to Mindanao in the Philippines); c) Sub-Saharan Bantu Africa and its diaspora; d) India; e) Southeast Asia (in part Hindustani, such as Burma, Nepal, etc., and also countries linked to China, such as Korea, Vietnam, etc.); and (f) China.

12. See the third section of the first chapter of my book, *Politics of Liberation*.

the text or narrative subjected to this process can be mythical, poetic, or non-philosophical, the result of this interpretation would thus be hermeneutically a work of philosophy.

It is thus necessary to recover the symbolic narratives of our ancestral cultures in the South, regardless of whether they are philosophical, mythical, or religious in character or not (even those texts categorized as theophanic or revelatory), in order to subject them to a *philosophical labor* within the overall framework of reconstructing our traditions. The local *reality* of the South which I have alluded to is enveloped in myth, as is that of modern philosophy,[13] and must be considered a humanist, rational, and symbolic point of departure for a history and philosophy of the South.

8. The Philosophy of the South as a Critique of Coloniality

The *philosophy of the South*, as a *front* or philosophical consensus consisting of many philosophies of the post-colonial, underdeveloped, or exploited world (in some cases, only recently free of direct colonial domination)[14]—with some sectors in the process of achieving greater autonomy than others[15]—should in the first place take into consideration the themes described above. The point of departure must be an understanding of the epistemologically colonial character of its methods, themes, use of sources, and manners of discourse; the reality in which it is immersed and the community to which it is directed—whether it be the philosophical community of the South, the intellectual community, or peoples of the post-colonial world which is in process of liberation—are unavoidable themes integral to the philosophy of the South.

I also believe that there is a specific aspect which should be prioritized; it is a question which we have analyzed in certain dialogues between Arab and Latin American intellectuals, namely: *What were the causes which led to the virtual "disappearance" or loss of overall creativity of the philosophies of the South since the emergence of modern European philosophy?* Here I am alluding, for example, to the disconnection of the Islamic world (as I have suggested, from Morocco to the Philippines, passing through Tunisia and Egypt, through Iraq and its center in Baghdad, Afghanistan, the Mogul empire in India, the commercial sultanates of Indochina, and the Moluccas or Spice Islands) due in part to its disruption by Portuguese colonialism and to the indifference of mercantilism and of Arab culture with regard to the use of oceanic navigation (initiated in the context of modernity by China, which discovered the Americas, Africa, and Australia beginning in the early 14th century). All of these factors

---

13. See Franz Hinkelammert, *Crítica de la Razón Mítica* (San José, Costa Rica: DEI, 2009). The "myth of progress," for example, is at the foundation of all of modern science, and cannot be proven empirically; it is in fact a transcendental postulate and supposition (which is also dangerously false, as Walter Benjamin argued).

14. And I say "only recently" advisedly, because since the beginning of the 21st century, the failure of the U.S. to impose its military domination throughout the world (as the result of its defeats in the wars in Iraq and Afghanistan) and the emergence as new global powers—namely, China (with 1.3 billion inhabitants and an average growth rate in its production of 9% over the last few years), India, Russia (in an intensified process of reorganization), and Brazil (gauging from a distance its implications as a nation of 200 million inhabitants)—the geopolitics of the world has moved away from a unipolarity of the North (centered around the U.S., Europe, and Japan, today in crisis). The philosophy of the South, therefore, includes these new powers in the South (China and Russia were never colonies, but were definitely underdeveloped and exploited for a long time), which in turn define the need for a new nomenclature, since there are new powers emerging that no longer fit into the category of the North as it was developed in the 20th century, and the South itself is no longer what it was in that same century.

15. The situation of South America (as differentiated from that of "Latin" America as a whole) in particular, and that of the "Arab Spring" or "Jasmine Revolution" are key indicators of deep processes of political renewal, that also demand correspondingly new levels of philosophical production.

together produced the absence of a joint reaction and effort to resist European expansion. The Ottoman Empire itself, defeated at Lepanto in 1571 (due in part to the flow of Latin American silver towards Spain), lost the capacity to control its territory because of economic crises (which included the devaluation of that same silver in the Islamic system due to the influx of cheap silver from Latin America). The Arab world was impoverished without losing money because of the devaluation of its currency. This is how it ceased to be the necessary "center" capable of connecting all of the cultures of Asia, Africa, and the Mediterranean; thus began its long slide into peripheral coloniality.

Although global commerce was centered around relations between China and Hindustan up until around 1800, the impact of the crisis in its own first industrial revolution would lead China to retreat into itself and thus lose the possibility of developing the potential of its own technological inventions which it had achieved between the 7th and 18th centuries,[16] which in turn helped spark the Italian Renaissance and the English Industrial Revolution.

Once this question has been fully explored (here I have only begun to sketch an initial approach), a philosophical critique focused on the destructive tendency of philosophical colonialism with regard to the impact of European modern philosophy must be developed. In the absence of the kind of critique of the coloniality of each of the national and regional or continental philosophies of the cultural entities of the South, it will not be possible to undertake the subsequent stage of unleashing a moment of philosophical creativity and symmetry throughout the South. When I refer to "symmetry" in this context, what I am suggesting is the need to develop a psychological attitude and approach representative of a certain normality that would make it possible for those of us in the South to consider and treat academic colleagues in Europe and the U.S as "equals." We should free ourselves of false respect for a knowledge with universalist pretensions. This false respect could be overcome by philosophers in the South once they possess the historical, cultural, and philosophical tools of the same quality as their colleagues in the metropolitan centers, which at minimum would enable our peers in the South to uncover the signs within us of an inadvertent Eurocentrism which has been ignored. A well-founded accusation of Eurocentrism (expressed either as an ignorance of the South or as an ignorance of one's own Eurocentrism) places the colleague from the center or North in an uncomfortable and unaccustomed situation (which destabilizes their previously assured centrality and universality and ultimate superiority) before the philosophers of the South. When a philosopher of the South falls into the trap of formulating a Eurocentric judgment (for example, due to their ignorance regarding the history of philosophy in the South), they could exclaim: "What you are reflecting is the expression of a Eurocentric philosophy that judges what is in fact unknown to you." It is likely that the confident, secure professor or academic from the center will lose their serenity or get angry, which would only make things worse (intensifying the arguments deployed against his or her positioning), or might begin to reflect and accept the criticisms proffered. It is only at this stage that a slow dialogue between the philosophy of the North and that of the South can truly begin, which is both so necessary and virtually inexistent, within an ethical framework of symmetry, respect, and openness to the truth.

9. The Unfolding of a Philosophy of the South

A key priority which should be included in the initial stages of development of a

---

16. Regarding science and technology in China, see Joseph Needham, *Science and Civilisation in China*, 7 vols. (Cambridge: Cambridge University Press, 1956–2012).

network of philosophies of the South is to begin with the study, debate, exposition, and publication of *histories of philosophy* in each of our countries, continents, and regions. It is notable that the first histories of the national philosophies of the South are beginning to appear.[17] At the same time we must also prioritize the publication (electronic and by other means) of the classical works of the philosophies of the South, at least since the end of the 15th century. It would be even better if all of the classic works since the origins of these regional histories were included.

These publications should be the result of debates regarding the corresponding periods of philosophical history in each context, their significance and contents, and the works which should be taken into account. It should be evident that this process of critical reconstruction must be open to varying contents with wide-ranging interpretations, including those which are philosophical in content but not simply imitative of foreign philosophies, and which engage themes emerging from the historical process of the peoples themselves. These historical processes are the points of reference for the most important philosophers who accompanied these processes, and sometimes, these philosophers influenced such processes to a greater or lesser extent. Undoubtedly Confucius or Lao Tse were key constituent factors in the configuration of Chinese culture, Budhha or Sankara in Hindustan, Al-Farabi or Ibn Sina (often referred to by his Latinized name as Avicenna) in the Arab and Iranian contexts, or Bartolomé de Las Casas in the Latin American context of the 16th century.

But together with this dissemination of histories and reflection by philosophers of the South—researchers, students, professors, and intellectuals in general—upon the most valuable aspects of their own philosophical traditions, it is also necessary to develop a creative discourse which is properly philosophical in character, and which thus goes beyond mere commentaries on either one's ancestral tradition or that of Europe. This implies contributions that take the reality and history of the treatment of key specific themes in the corresponding regional or local philosophy of the South. Philosophical reflection should enrich these realities critically with one's own tools, and in dialogue with the best expressions of modern European philosophy (which the philosophers of the South must know how to select and incorporate into their own projects of distinct, autonomous thought). All of this should be deployed with an emphasis on producing clear thinking which is well-founded, coherent, and understandable by those responsible for the concrete political, economic, aesthetic, technological, and scientific realities of the countries of the South. In sum, what is aimed at is a proper philosophy, which is both an expression of the South and a useful contribution to its community of reference.

In order to achieve these objectives it is also crucial to avoid a kind of fundamentalism that would lead to the exclusion of other philosophical currents (beyond those of the South, including those rooted in European modernity), and mere commentaries on European contributions. The exclusionary approach is disdainful of dialogue and fails to have due regard for the best of European modernity. It has to be noted, however, that the latter conceives of itself as modern but

---

17. The most recent World Congress of Philosophy in Seoul, Korea, organized by FISP included the presentation of the first history of the philosophy of Korea. In Latin America we have published, as I noted above, a large-format initial overview of Latin American, Caribbean, and Latino philosophy from an integral perspective; see Enrique Dussel, Eduardo Mendieta, and Carmen Bohórquez, eds., *El Pensamiento Filosófico Latinoamericano, del Caribe y "Latino" (1300–2000): Historia, Corrientes, Temas y Filósofos* (México: CREFAL/Siglo XXI Editores, 2009). There is not a single sentence dedicated to Latin America in the brilliant book by Randall Collins, *The Sociology of Philosophies* (Cambridge, MA: Belknap/Harvard University Press, 1998), although it does include a good description of the philosophies of China, India, the Islamic world, and Bantu Africa.

does not serve the interests of the South as a community of reference; at the same time, it is disdained by the philosophical community of the European center for its lack of originality, and at best is perceived as simply "registering" the latest intellectual productions from Europe or the U.S., with commentaries which come too late and lack any real importance either in the South (because of their culturally distant character) or in the center (because they lack creativity and a vanguard quality).

Those of us who are able to effectively combine proficiency in our own regional tradition within the South (which is usually less well known than that of our local traditions) with the necessary familiarity with the latest achievements of European or U.S. philosophy, together with a commitment to shed light on contemporary aspects of the regional or local reality in the South, will be best positioned to contribute creatively to the new philosophical reflections which are so necessary. Contributions along these lines which address and describe relevant, previously unknown themes, have the potential to spearhead philosophical thinking that is both innovative and well-founded. The philosophers of the South are uniquely situated to reflect critically regarding the ethical, political, anthropological, ontological, and epistemological dimensions of our realities in the context of examples such as China (amid its hyper-industrial revolution), India (with its developments in electronics), Latin America (given the contributions of its political experiences of transformation in Bolivia, Venezuela, or Brazil), and the Islamic world (in the wake of the "Arab Spring" or "Jasmine Revolution"). All of these reflect relevant themes which the philosophers of the South are ideally positioned to engage as actors in such settings.

Precision, seriousness, well-founded argumentation, relevance to one's own reality, beauty in the process of exposition, pedagogical and explanatory quality, and a sense of conviction as to the positioning one has elected, are all characteristics which should be reflected in the contemporary philosophies of the South. In this manner the community of philosophers of the center will learn about new themes, with new methods, within the framework of a dialogue enriched by new participants. Meanwhile, the philosophy of the South will revive the creativity annihilated at the end of the 15th century, with the inception of the coloniality of knowledge that extinguished the philosophies of the South.

10. Premonitions as to the Dawning of a Pluriversal Trans-Modern Age[18]

The *decentering* of the world-system (which is taking place before our eyes towards countries with increased political, economic, and military autonomy, including the emergence of BRICS,[19] among others), the intensification of economic crises in Europe and Japan, and the limits confronting U.S. militarism, have laid the foundation for the following questions: a) What is modernity? b) Was there, is there, and will there be one or several different modernities? c) Is it possible for a *new age* to arise in the future, within the framework of a different kind of culture that lies beyond modernity and thus might be described as trans-modern in character?[20] d) And if this

---

18. Both the concept of "trans-modernity" and that of "pluriversality" are explained in this last section of the essay.

19. Brasil, India, Rusia, China, and South Africa.

20. In my essay "Transmodernity and Interculturality" (unpublished paper, 2004, http://www.enriquedussel.com), I explain the difference between this position and that of those who embrace the notion of "post-modernity." The prefix "post" refers to the final critical stage of European modernity, and thus implies a Eurocentric hypothesis rooted in the Global North. It is a particularism with an unfounded pretense of universality; the South is not and will never be "post-modern." "Trans" by contrast has as its referent a point lying beyond modernity, a different

new world age emerges, as Schelling might have imagined, will it be organized according to the framework of a *univocal universality*—which assumes the viability of one culture for humanity as a whole, reflected in one language and one tradition, with the disappearance of cultures which have been vanquished, including the negation of the diversity of other cultures which have existed for millennia—or will it instead be an *analogical pluriverse* of cultures flourishing through a process of intercultural dialogue for centuries among different cultures engaged in a permanent process of creative cross-fertilization?

Let me respond briefly in the form of short theses intended to spark future discussions:

In the first place, modernity is not the Enlightenment, and Kant's explanation of its character ("liberation from a state of immaturity and self-imposed guilt"[21]) is not sufficient. Modernity is an age of history inaugurated by Europe thanks to the discovery and dominion of the Atlantic Ocean (as a new geopolitical center) which enabled it to expand by sea and constitute commercial, military, and cultural empires, with Europe as their core. The European "I" (or *ego*) constituted other cultures as its colonies, subjected to its Will to Power, which encompassed nature as an exploitable set of objects that could serve as a form of mediation in order to obtain greater quantities of exchange value. This is an age characterized by huge technological advances, which reflected the demands of securing advantages among competing sources of capital and by scientific discoveries and the political organization of states in systems of representative democracy. It was imposed on other cultures up until the limits that we are seeing unfold today, which involve a civilizational crisis revealing the negative effects of its vast scale: the possibility that life on Earth might be extinguished.

Secondly, in the fullest sense, although there are historical antecedents—namely, the separation of science from religious faith in the philosophy of Córdoba reflected in thinkers such as Ibn Rush (often known by his Latinized name as Averroes); great technological, agricultural, and industrial discoveries in China; the invention of modern mathematics and heliocentric astronomy in Baghdad; etc.—modernity is European, unique, and is being imitated in part in the process of globalization, which is underway in other regions of the world. There are not several different modernities, although the extent and ways in which it is implanted may vary in diverse cultural contexts. If it was Calvinism which helped shape the initial development of capitalism (as Max Weber argued), at present it is neo-Confucianism which inspires the *suigeneris* versions of capitalism which have arisen in Southeast Asia and in China itself. This is the same modernity described above which has been imitated and expanded in certain respects.

Thirdly, we stand at the threshold of a *new age* of history given the exhaustion of the premises upon which modernity is founded. Ours is not a postmodern situation, but instead a moment characterized by radical transformations in the very cultural foundations of the modern *ethos*. It is upon the basis of these assertions that I therefore propose that *trans-modernity*, in the absence of another equivalent term, is the adequate description for the horizon that is opening up before our eyes. What is emerging is not a new stage of modernity but rather a *new world age* that lies beyond the assumptions of modernity, capitalism, Eurocentrism, and colonialism. A *new* age where the conditions necessary to sustain human life on Earth demand a transformation in our ontological attitudes regarding nature, work, property, and other cultures.

---

world Age, which is no longer Eurocentric, and which emerges from the Global South and includes the Global North and is thus truly planetary in character.

21. Immanuel Kant, "Beantwortung der Frage: Was ist Aufklärung?" (*Berlinische Monatsschrift* [December 1784]), in *Werke*, vol. 9 (Darmstadt: Wiss. Buchges., 1968), 53–61.

Fourth, in the context of trans-modernity, humanity will not be trapped in a *univocal universality* limited to a single culture, which would in turn be imposed to all of the rest in order to extinguish them, thereby producing a universality which is the fruit of an exclusionary process of identity. It will instead be a *pluriverse* where each culture will be in dialogue with all others from the perspective of a common "similarity," enabling each to continuously recreate its own analogical "distinction," and to diffuse itself within a dialogical, reciprocally creative space. It will be, as I have suggested here, an age which, as the result of new economic relations, will have succeeded in overcoming capitalism, given the imperative character of the demands of the environment and of the conditions necessary to make life possible for the majority of the Earth's population, which will have embraced a participatory form of democracy beyond the limits of liberalism, and which will no longer consent to the perpetuation of a system based upon the exploitation of those most vulnerable to the impact of increases in the rate of profit and to the commensurate increases in the poverty and inequality of citizens throughout the world.

All of this is a reasonable prognosis which can be argued upon an empirical basis, and which traces the outline of a future horizon which will at least attempt to overcome the substantial dominations which can be detected throughout our historical moment, because without this attempt, it is impossible to imagine today how we are going to overcome the inevitable dominations of the future, which will surely emerge because of the nature of our human condition.

BIBLIOGRAPHY

Collins, Randall. *The Sociology of Philosophies.* Cambridge, MA: Belknap/Harvard University Press, 1998.

Dussel, Enrique. "The Anti-Cartesian Meditations." *Poligrafi* 41–42 (2006): 5–60. http://www.enriquedussel.com.

Dussel, Enrique. *Politics of Liberation.* London: SCM Press, 2011.

Dussel, Enrique. "Transmodernity and Interculturality." Unpublished paper, 2004. http://www.enriquedussel.com.

Dussel, Enrique, Eduardo Mendieta, and Carmen Bohórquez, eds. *El Pensamiento Filosófico Latinoamericano, del Caribe y "Latino" (1300–2000): Historia, Corrientes, Temas y Filósofos.* México: CREFAL/Siglo XXI Editores, 2009.

Hinkelammert, Franz. *Crítica de la Razón Mítica.* San José, Costa Rica: DEI, 2009.

Kant, Immanuel. "Beantwortung der Frage: Was ist Aufklärung?" In *Werke,* vol. 9, 53–61. Darmstadt: Wiss. Buchges., 1968. Originally published in Berlinische Monatsschrift (December 1784).

Loewith, Karl. *Von Hegel zu Nietzsche.* Stuttgart: Kohlhammer, 1964.

Needham, Joseph. *Science and Civilisation in China.* 7 vols. Cambridge: Cambridge University Press, 1956–2012.

HUMAN ARCHITECTURE: JOURNAL OF THE SOCIOLOGY OF SELF-KNOWLEDGE
A Publication of OKCIR: The Omar Khayyam Center for Integrative Research in Utopia, Mysticism, and Science (Utopystics)
ISSN: 1540-5699. © COPYRIGHT BY AHEAD PUBLISHING HOUSE (IMPRINT: OKCIR PRESS) AND AUTHORS. ALL RIGHTS RESERVED.

Justice after the Law:
Paul of Tarsus and the People of Come

Eduardo Mendieta

State University of New York, Stony Brook

eduardo.mendieta@stonybrook.edu

Abstract: This is a commentary on "The Liberatory Event of Paul Tarsus" by Enrique Dussel (2009), a part of the third volume of Dussel's *Politics of Liberation*. The article's author seeks to show how Dussel reads Paul in a dialectical way, in what we can call a *prismatic hermeneutical* way, namely, first by attending to the *Sitz im Leben*, the historical-interpretative, context in which Paul produced his own texts, and how that existential and historical situation continues to disrupt the Pauline texts; second, by attending to ways in which this *Sitz im Leben*, has been excluded, concealed and negated when appropriating Paul's texts; third, by reading Paul against our own contemporary problems and questions. It is by reading Paul against and through his *Sitz im Leben*, the author argues, that Dussel is able to show how there are in Paul's letters a series of "critical categories"—to use the expression he uses in our text (Dussel 2009:115)—that can and must be recovered for the sake of a critical, liberatory political philosophy. In a third and final part, the author turns to Dussel's reading of Agamben, as is articulated in the text before us, in order to show that while Agamben is closer to Dussel than Dussel himself is willing to acknowledge, Agamben falls short of what Dussel's prismatic hermeneutics accomplishes—namely to show the way in which Paul can indeed be read in a philosophical-political way that does not retreat behind to a political-theological reading that closes off both Paul as a "sacred" text to innovative readings, nor closes off our political reality to a religious critique. The philosophical-political reading of a religious text can yield a religious critique of fetishized political institutions and ways of thinking that in turn may generate new critical categories. A philosophical-political reading of sacred texts may also yield a political-economic critique, as Marx so eloquently illustrated (see Dussel 2007 [1993]).

I. ON PRISMATIC HERMENEUTICS: HOW TO READ *SACRED* TEXTS IN ORDER TO SAVE THEM

The text before us "The Liberatory Event of Paul of Tarsus" (Dussel 2009) is part of a large project, the third volume of a *Politics of Liberation*, of which two have already appeared.

Volume one presented what is surely the first 'critical' world history of political philosophy. It is 'critical' because it places itself beyond the constitutive myths that

---

Eduardo Mendieta is professor of philosophy at the State University of New York, Stony Brook. He is the author of *The Adventures of Transcendental Philosophy* (Rowman & Littlefield, 2002) and *Global Fragments: Globalizations, Latinamericanisms, and Critical Theory* (SUNY Press, 2007). He is also co-editor with Jonathan VanAntwerpen of *The Power of Religion in the Public Sphere* (Columbia University Press, 2011), and with Craig Calhoun and Jonathan VanAntwerpen of *Habermas and Religion* (Polity, forthcoming), and with Stuart Elden of *Reading Kant's Geography* (SUNY Press, 2011). He is presently at work on another book entitled *Philosophy's War: Logos, Polemos, Topos*.

have guided the production of histories of political philosophy and the very thinking of the political in the 'West.' In his prologue to volume one of the *Politics of Liberation* (2007), Dussel enumerates seven conceptual limitations that have hobbled and blinded contemporary political philosophy: first, Hellenocentrism; second, Occidentalism; third, Eurocentrism; fourth, a self-serving periodization of world history that skews the perception of history in favor of the formation of Europe; fifth, an obfuscating secularism that distorts the role of religion in the emergence of modern societies, be they Western or non-Western; sixth, the occlusion and negation of the theoretical, philosophical and conceptual contributions that non-Western societies have made to the evolution of both political institutions and their theoretical conceptualization and understanding; seventh, the devaluing and suppression of the pivotal role that the discovery of the New World had in the emergence of the modern world, and in tandem, the devaluing of the contributions produced in the Americas to modern political thought (see my foreword to Dussel 2008 for further discussion).

This entire first volume, as well as the entire trilogy that makes up *Politics of Liberation*, is not simply a critique. It is also a positive contribution to the writing of a different kind of the history of political philosophy that departs from a different locus than that enabled by those seven blinders, limitations, ideological distortions. In this *critical world history* we can encounter the well known figures in the history of Western political thinking: Hobbes, Locke, Machiavelli, Schmitt, Rawls, Habermas, but also a whole series of figures that have been as important, even if they have been neglected, at best, and entirely ignored, at worst: Ginés de Sepúlveda, Bartolomé de las Casas, Francisco de Vitoria, Felipe Guamán Poma de Ayala. This history culminates with the presentation of a history of political thought in Latin American in five periods, from the Western "State of the Indies," through the colony, the early modern period, the period of "first Emancipation," the development of the new institutions and the emergence of the modern state, to the failure of the postcolonial state before the challenge of neo-imperialism. This history, thus, is a work that is suffused by prodigious generosity that is only matched by its critical reflexivity that prevents it from retreating to the safe theoretical bunkers of received ideological chronologies and self-serving histories.

For the moment, I want to foreground Dussel's critique of "secularism" as an ideological formation that has distorted the evolution of political thought in and outside the West. Even as *sui generis* as Dussel is among Latin American philosophers, he is part of a cohort of thinkers who have contributed to one of Latin America's most creative and generative religious and intellectual traditions, namely liberation theology. Dussel has contributed to the development of this tradition as a historian, as a philosopher, and as Marxologist of the first order. At the center of this movement, for it was and remains a social movement both within and outside the Catholic church, is the imperative to develop a religious critique of political systems of oppression while also developing a political critique of religion. Liberation theology means both the liberation of religious thinking and the religious thinking of liberation.

The religious critique of the world, about which the young Karl Marx wrote, was turned by liberation theologians into the theological, political and economic critique of neocolonial and neo-imperialistic servant states that pushed their military boots on the faces of the Latin American people. It would be a major mistake to think of Dussel's *oeuvre* as an appendage or extension of the liberation theology's corpus. But it would also be mistake not to see how that tradition and work has shaped some of Dussel's own orientations and problems. One of those is precisely the problem of how to approach the biblical texts that are source of the Christian faith. Secularism, as an ideology, is a way to cordon off, to isolate, to immunize Christian foundational texts from new, generative, transformative appropriation, and above all to render them ahistorical, or transhistorical. Secularism dehistoricizes the religious appropriation of sacred texts, and in this way, it also dehistoricizes the faith. By de-historizing the faith, the Christian doctrine, it closes off the future.

Secularism severs the umbilical cord that links a religious outlook, practice and form of life from its sacred texts. At the same time, secularism dissimulates and camouflages the ways in which these texts remain determining for the Western world. For this reason, to overcome secularism, to demystify its mythologies, means to approach the religious aspects of any culture in terms of its religious vitality, in terms of the ways in which "sacred" texts remain operative, generative, nourishing of that culture, while also recognizing the historicity of those very "sacred" texts. It may be said, then, that to overcome secularism is to be on the side of secularization, if by this latter term we understand a social, historical process that both secures and translates the religious meanings of a sacred corpus. It is secularization that has allowed the very preservation, protection and empowerment of sacred traditions, not against these very traditions, but for their own sake. If secularism may be conceived as anathema of religion, secularization may be thought as religion's offspring and protector; for it is secularization that shelters, while also empowering, the sources of a religious outlook. This is made most evident when we recognize that secularization is unleashed by the very relationship a faith or confession has to its texts and religious practices. Secularization is but the name of the process by which a religious tradition relates to its sources, its "sacred" texts.

Now, a "sacred" text becomes one, or rather it is so canonized, because it is thought to contribute to the elucidation of a faith's core vision. A religious experience is always a hermeneutical circle—there are no religious events, brute facts of revelation, or sacred happenings. There is always the exegesis and interpretation in light of what a community takes to be its faith, its belief, its proclamation, its confession. A "sacred" text, in other words, is never found as a sacred text; rather, it is so interpreted. A "sacred" text is always already an interpreted text. Every "sacred" text is the remnant of a series of interpretative practices. As a product of interpretative practices, "sacred" texts are always being read in different ways, from different angles, with different aims and finalities in mind. A "sacred" text is thus always already a sacred text, that is, one that begs to be read differently precisely because it is the product of a plurality of interpretative enactments. In other words, a "sacred" text is one that is always de-sacralizing itself so that it can remain "sacred."

A sacred text is thus a prismatic text—a refracted and refracting text. Sacred texts are the history of their production as "sacred" texts and history of their reception as "sacred." If, as the famous saying goes, the Western philosophy is one long footnote to Plato, then we could say that Christianity is one long history of the appropriation of "sacred" texts into sacred texts. Evidently, this applies *mutatis mutandis* to other faiths, even if they are not grounded on a book, or group of books. Even oral traditions are caught in this hermeneutical circle of the production of the religious text through acts of interpretation. I take it that it is from the standpoint of the critique of secularism, for the sake of secularization, that Dussel is engaging Paul of Tarsus. Indeed, the history of Christianity is the history of the different ways in which Paul the Apostle has been read, not just by Christians, but by many others as well (secular Christians, Jews, non-non-Christians, non-non-Jews).

In the following I want to show how Dussel reads Paul in a dialectical way, in what we can call a *prismatic hermeneutical* way, namely, first by attending to the *Sitz im Leben*, the historical-interpretative, context in which Paul produced his own texts, and how that existential and historical situation continues to disrupt the Pauline texts; second, by attending to ways in which this *Sitz im Leben*, has been excluded, concealed and negated when appropriating Paul's texts; third, by reading Paul against our own contemporary problems and questions. It is by reading Paul against and through his *Sitz im Leben*, I argue, that Dussel is able to show how there are in Paul's letters a series of "critical categories"—to use the expression he uses in our text (Dussel 2009:115)—that can and must be recovered for the sake of a critical, liberatory political philosophy. In a third and final part, I will turn to Dussel's reading of Agamben, as is articulated in the text before us, in order to show that while Agamben is closer to Dussel than Dussel himself is willing to acknowledge, Agamben falls short of what Dussel's prismatic hermeneutics accomplishes—namely to show the way in which Paul can indeed be read in a philosophical-political way that does not retreat behind to a political-theological reading that closes off both Paul as a "sacred" text to innovative readings, nor closes off our political reality to a religious critique. The philosophical-political reading of a religious text can yield a religious critique of fetishized political institutions and ways of thinking that in turn may generate new critical categories. A philosophical-political reading of sacred texts may also yield a political-economic critique, as Marx so eloquently illustrated (see Dussel 2007 [1993]).

II. The Paradox of Paul: The Critical Consensus of a People Divided Against Itself

Paul is a paradox, one that may reveal the truth of Christianity. Nietzsche's juxtaposition of Paul against Jesus articulates this paradox, but in the negative. Nietzsche's animus, diatribe, vile against Paul in his infamous *The Anti-Christ*, summarizes but also potentiates a whole interpretative tradition that thinks of Paul as the Jew that betrayed Jesus, the Jew that gave us the Catholic Church (Nietzsche 2005 [1888]). Nietzsche's Paul is the expression of exasperation with a paradox: Paul.

Paul's own letters, as well as the *Acts of the Apostles*, offer us ample material to sketch this paradox. For instance, in *Philippians* 3 we have Paul's own candid autobiography: "…circumcised on the eighth day, of the people of Israel, of the tribe of Benjamin, a Hebrew born of Hebrews; as to the law a Pharisee, as to zeal a persecutor of the church, as to righteousness under the law blameless."[1] This zeal to be a persecutor of the church is repeated in other places in Paul's letter, but also in the *Acts* 8, where it is written: "But Saul was ravaging the church, and entering house after house, he dragged off men and women and committed them to prison" (*Acts* 8.3). In *Galatians* 1.13 we have Paul's description of this zealotry in the following terms: "For you have heard of my former life in Judaism, how I persecuted the church of God violently and tried to destroy it; and I advance in Judaism beyond my own age among my people, so extremely zealous was I for the tradition of my fathers."

We could synoptically write that Paul or Saul of Tarsus came from the Jewish tribe of Benjamin, had been circumcised on the eighth day in accordance with Jewish tradition, and after a strict orthodox Jewish upbringing had joined the sect of the Pharisees. This means that Paul had been trained in the interpretation of the Jewish law and the Hebrew sacred texts. He thus knew Hebrew and very likely Aramaic. Additionally, born in Tarsus, capital of the Roman province of

---

1. When quoting from the New Testament, Paul and Acts, I am using *The New Oxford Annotated Bible with Apocrypha*, expanded edition of the Revised Standard Version (New York: Oxford University Press, 1973).

Cilicia, meant that Paul was a Roman citizen by birth, even if he later confesses to having bought Roman citizenship (*Acts*, 22.28-29). As Hans Küng put it, profiling the young Paul: "So we must imagine the young Paul as a reflective, deeply serious Pharisee of strict observance, influenced by contemporary Jewish apocalyptic, zealous for the law and the preservation of the traditions of the fathers. He was born probably at almost the same time as Jesus, but grew up in a Hellenistic environment in which Greek was the everyday language and therefore was his mother tongue" (Küng 2006:19).

Paul, very importantly, was not one of Jesus' direct apostles. He did not know Jesus in the flesh; nor was he directly related to any of the apostles who were charged by Jesus to bring the gospel to the world. As Paul confesses in *Galatians* 1.11: "For I would have you know, brethren, that the gospel which was preached by me is not man's gospel. For I did not receive it from man, nor was I taught it, but it came through a revelation of Jesus Christ." And then he adds after confessing his will to destroy the Church of God, "But when he who has set me apart before I was born, and had called me through his grace, was pleased to reveal his Son for me, in order that I might preach him among Gentiles, I did not confer with flesh and blood, nor did I go to Jerusalem to those who were apostles before me, but I went away to Arabia; and again I returned to Damascus." In *Acts* 9 we have the narrative of Paul's conversion, but also the confirmation that he was feared in the Christian communities because he was infamous for his zealous pursuit of the apostles and Christians. In fact, Anani'as responds to God's call to come to Saul thus: "Lord, I have heard from many about this man, how much evil he has done to thy saints at Jerusalem; and here he has authority from the chief priest to bind all who call upon thy name" (*Acts* 9.13—compare with *Acts* 22.1-22). The paradox of Paul, then, is that of a devout, doctrinaire Jew, a Pharisee, who becomes an apostle to the gentiles through revelation and conversion. Küng expressed this paradox in the following way: "Did he ever give up his Jewish faith? That is the question for Jews. And did he really understand Jesus of Nazareth rightly, or did he make something else of him? This is the question for Christians" (Küng 2006:17).

Whether Paul was either too much or too little Jewish or Christian is of relevance to Jews and Christian alike, but it is also to all those who are addressed as gentiles. It is from this paradox, this too much or too little, that Christian universalism is elucidated. But, just as importantly, it is from the standpoint of a devoutly, even zealous, observant of the law, a Pharisee, that we get the paradox of one who abolishes the law through its observance. The law as such is not negated by Paul, but is revealed to be burdened with what Franz Hinkelammert has called "a curse" (Hinkelammert, 1998, 35). While Jesus critiques the law through his actions (such as, healing on the Sabbath, failing to condemn in accordance with the law), it is Paul who announces that the law is subordinate to the life of the community. The law is for life, not life for the law. Hinkelammert has eloquently articulated the paradox of Christianity's critique of the law as is articulated in Jesus and Paul's preaching:

> Law is necessary for living. It consists in ceasing to treat the law as given for life. In legalistic terms, law destroys the human being when it eliminates human life as its source of discernment and reflexivity of law. This legalistic law is criticized by Jesus, which is followed in very faithful terms by Paul's critique of the law. According to Paul, a curse weighs over the law, which appears only when salvation is sought through the observance of the law. This curse makes the law kill. Law is violent, and behind the law threatens sin. It destroys the

human being and turns him into the great lie according to which the law saves as law of legalistic fulfillment. For this reason, when fulfilling the law an injustice is performed, and injustice is not itself the transgression of a law. Injustice is committed fulfilling the law. (Hinkelammert 1998:35)

Hinkelammert, Dussel, and Agamben coincide in focusing on this revolutionary, liberating, critical dimension of Paul's work, namely in seeing him as a critic of a legality that becomes necrophilic, but not so as to renounce the law, but to affirm the power of the law, so long as this never ceases to be guided by what Hinkelammert calls the source of its discernment and reflexivity. Agamben refers to this aspect of Paul's work in the following terms:

The caesura between constitutive and constituted power, a divide that becomes so apparent in our times, finds its theological origins in the Pauline split between the level of faith and that of *nomos*, between personal loyalty and the positive obligation that derives from it. In this light, messianism appears as a struggle, within the law, whereby the element of the pact and constituent power leans toward setting itself against and emancipating itself from the *entolê*, the norm in the strict sense. The messianic is therefore the historical process whereby the archaic link between law and religion (which finds its magical paradigm in *horkos*, oath) reaches a crises and the element of *pistis*, of faith in the pact, tends paradoxically to emancipate itself from any obligatory conduct and from positive law (from works fulfilled in carrying out the pact). (Agamben 2005:118-9)

The cut, or diremption between a constituted and constituting power, the abyss between an established order and a new order, is the pivotal issue of fetishized law—a law that has become "for life" unchanging and unchanging, which commands that it be fulfilled, even if the world should perish: "Fiat iustitia, et *pereat mundus*."

In Hinkelammert's terms: law for life (set in stone as a totem) is law against life. Law for life (at the service of life) is law that is guided by the life of the community. What is at stake is more than the conflict between legitimacy and legality, the norm and the law, authority and power, but precisely that there is a surplus, a remnant that is not encompass by the co-determination of one by the other: norm and law. Dussel gets at this problem more directly and clearly than Agamben when he focuses his analysis of Paul through a reading of *Romans* in terms of six fundamental themes (Dussel 2009:120): first, the meaning of "justification" as a criterion of legitimation; second, the legitimation of a certain order with reference to the law; third, the collapse of legitimation due to the fetishization of the law; fourth, the development of a "new" justificatory criterion; five, the constitution of a messianic community that irrupts into the establish order disrupting it; sixth, the creation of a new order beyond the defetishized law. The running thread in Dussel's analysis, however, is the ambiguity of the law; that is the inoperability and indiscernability of the law, or what Agamben calls the unobservability and unformulability of the law (Agamben 2005:105-6).

For Dussel, however, what is important in Paul is not simply the critique of fetishized law, but rather the project of developing a new "justificatory criterion." How do we discover that the law has become fetishized, if every practice in a given order is guided by the norm that finds itself embodied in the law? How can we see what is destroyed and killed if it is allowed to be seen by the law? We must be situated outside or beyond the law to see the nefarious consequences of a law blindly observed and performed. How is constituted power to be evaluated and judged if all that is legitimate is precisely what this constituted power permits to be said and seen? How is the law to be judge? This is what makes Paul so important for Christianity, for he lived by the law and from the law. A passage from *Romans* is key:

> What then shall we say? That the law is sin? By no means! Yet, if it had not been for the law, I should not have known sin. I should not have known what it is to covet if the law had not said, "You shall not covet." But sin, finding opportunity in the commandment, wrought in me all kind of covetousness. Apart from the law sin lies dead. I was once alive apart from the law, but when the commandment came, sin revived and I died. The very commandment which promised life proved to be death to me. (*Romans* 7.7-10)

What Paul may have meant when he wrote "that by the law he knew sin, that by the very commandment that promised life, death came to him" may be deciphered in *Acts* where we read that "Saul" approves of the execution of Christians (*Acts* 7.54-60-8.1). The law, as such, is not enough to guide us away from sin. The law may guard us, be our custodian, as Paul puts in *Galatians* 3, but now it is by faith that God's righteousness if manifested. "For we hold that a man is justified by faith apart from work of law" (*Romans*, 3.28-29). Or, as it is written in *Galatians* 3.23-27: "Now before faith came, we were confined under the law, kept under restraint under faith should be revealed. So that the law was our custodian until Christ came, that we might be justified by faith. But now that faith has come, we are no longer under a custodian; for in Christ Jesus you are all sons of God, through faith." For Dussel, as for Agamben, the operative phrase is "justified by faith." If law was our custodian, now we are free by faith—we experience God's justice through faith. We are justified in God's justice through faith. But what is this faith? What is faith for Paul? And why is specifically 'justified by faith' such a key critical concept for a "politics of liberation" in Dussel's analysis?

Faith, or *pistis* in Greek and *emunah* in Hebrew, refers to the credit one gives another, the confidence one places on another, and the trust that is placed upon someone or something. Faith, like trust, is relational. It has a passive and an active dimension, as well as a quasi-reciprocal aspect. To have faith, is a volitional act. I have faith. I place my confidence and trust. At the same time, I am at the mercy, at the disposition, of he on whom I have placed my faith. I am vulnerable before him on whom I place my faith. There is a potentiality to faith. It is a generation of power—a potentia, to use Dussel term (2008, paragraph 3.1.3). Faith expresses and generates a relational power. In faith, one grants a power, and by granting that power, one submits to it. There is power in faith. For this reason we say "by the power of faith," or "the power that faith grants us," and similar expressions. It is a power that emanates from this relational, even if not symmetrical, relation. Faith is a weakening strength, a disempowering power. It is an empowering vulnerability. A quote from Émile Benveniste can help us make clearer and stronger this tension in faith:

> The one who holds the *fidês* placed on him by a man has this man at this mercy. This is why *fidês* becomes almost synonymous with *dicio* and *potestâs*. In their primitive form these relations involved a certain reciprocity, placing one's *fidês* in somebody secured in return his guarantee and his support. But this very fact underlines the inequality of the conditions. It is authority which is exercised at the same time

as protection for somebody who submits to it, an exchange for, and to the extent of, his submission. (Benveniste 1973:97-98)

Here Benveniste links faith to *fidês* to rule, domain, authority, and thus to *potestâs*, to power and sovereign rule. What Benveniste points out, additionally, is that while the relationship is prima facie one of "a certain reciprocity," there is always a more fundamental inequality, asymmetry. The power we grant to the one on whom we place our faith can be betrayed. Yet, rather than foreground this asymmetry, I think we must underscore the proportionality of the power that is granted to that which one submits. Faith implies also "the extent" of one's submission, the power and depth of one's faith. This power, this *potestâs*, this "empowering vulnerability," is the transformative and liberatory dimension of faith. Faith liberates precisely because of the *potestâs* that it generates, grants, bestows and that returns augmented to the one that grants it. This is why Paul's "justification by faith" may be translated as "justified by the power that we entrust on the community of belief," justified by the "empower vulnerability" of the confidence and trust we place on each other. Faith is, thus, a relational *potestâs* of the community of belief, in which the community empowers itself towards something. Dussel articulates it this way:

> The messianic community, the *people*, confronting the immense power of the (Roman) empire, the temple (of Israel), and tradition (maintained by new Christians unable to overcome their ancient rites, customs, sacrifices, etc.) nevertheless dared to confront these powers from the *certainty* of possessing a conviction that can transform reality in its totality. That certainty—that *critical* consensus of the community itself—is what is called *emunáh* in Hebrew (הנומא) or *pístis* (πστις) in Paul's Greek, and which could be described as the enthusiastic certainty of the *critical* community (whose source is to be found in the people itself). (Dussel 2009:125)

Faith, then, is the name for that "*critical* consensus" of messianic community that stands against the extant consensus in the name of a new order, a new law, a new legitimacy. Here faith is a messianic power, a critical transformative power that inaugurates a new order of justification. Faith, the reflexive *potestâs* of the critical community, another way to think of the messianic community, is the construction of a new legality. It is for this reason that for Dussel faith can be translated as "mutual *confidence* that is continuous through time as the intersubjective fidelity of the members of such a community, convinced of their responsibility to create a new agreement, contract, Alliance, or Testament. This new agreement would legitimize or *justify* ("judge as just") the fearless praxis of the extreme danger of "messianic time" (of Walter Benjamin) as a source for the legitimation of the *future* system" (2009:125-6).

What would need to be commented on in Dussel's formulation is the "fearless praxis of the extreme danger" of messianic time. Why fearless and why extreme danger? It is fearless because it must face a formidable contender, itself, with all the tools of power, and authority, on its side. The messianic community is still part of a community. It is a part of the community that has become "critical" of the hegemonic order. Faith empowers the critical community to challenge, resist and transform the established consensus and order. In this project of messianic transformation there is great danger. How does the critical community, with its critical consensus, know and have confidence that it is establishing a *justified* ("judged as just") order? I will return to this question below; for it is in how this question is answered by Dussel and Agamben respectively that their differences flare up brilliantly.

Now we are able to return to our point of departure, that is why the task of elucidating Dussel's project of reading Paul as a philosophical-political thinker of the first order, from whose work we can rescue "critical categories" for a politics of liberation. Most specifically, our point of departure was to try to understand why Dussel must read Paul of Tarsus politically as he elaborates a *politics of liberation*. The third volume of the *politics of liberation* aims to articulate the "critical," "emancipatory," "liberating" categories of a political philosophy. Volume two elucidated the architectonic of political philosophy in terms of four key principles, which I am summarizing in the present way so as to advance to my main argument.

First, there is *potentia*, which is the power of a community, in its most raw and unmediated sense. This power is an expression of a will to live. The power of a community is expression of its will to live. It is grounded in the material, corporeal needs of a community of needing, suffering, thirsting, and vulnerable living beings who gather precisely to survive.

Second, this raw power becomes *potestas* when it is institutionalized. The will to live of a community now becomes a set of articulating, transmitting, augmenting, distributing institutions that act as conduits of the power of the community. All *potestas* thus is always delegated, lent, or borrowed, but never transferred or alienated. There are two manifestations of *potestas*: what Dussel calls *obedential power*, and what he calls fetishized power. If the former commands obeying (precisely because it commands only through delegation), the latter commands commanding (fetishizing its power to command as if it were the source of its power, and not the people).

Third, *potentia* become *potestas* through a process of legitimation that emerges from a consensus or process of deliberation. All potestas rests on some sort of legitimacy. A more just, well ordered, polity is one in which the legitimacy of its potestas is most reflexive of the source of its power. For Dussel, in fact, one of the greatest philosophical-political issues is that of the relationship between *potestas* and the participation of the political community in *obedential* power. The degree of justice of a polity is proportional to the way in which its legitimacy is reflexive of the will to live of the community.

Fourth, a potentia that through legitimacy takes on institutional form as *potestas*, is delegated to secure the life, preservation and growth of the life of the community. Political power has a futural dimension, but also an efficacy that is conditional on what can and must be accomplished. This securing, preserving and growing the life of the community is what Dussel calls feasibility. We can call it political efficacy. We can simplify these formulations with the following equation: a political community is organized for the sake of life, in order to guide its will to live, it must submit to some sort of deliberation, a process of justifying its decision about allocating resources, and the aims of its consensus have to be realistic, efficacious. In short: life, deliberative legitimation, and feasibility. A political community is not a suicide pact, but a life compact. A political community without some modicum of deliberation becomes either a tyranny or a regime of slavery. Finally, a political community that does not aim to secure its own ends in accordance with its wherewithal becomes an utopia, an anarchical community, or a tyranny.

There is no political community that is a perfect political community. Even an ideal *Kallipolis*, the beautiful, just city of Plato, is faulty, for even every imagined political community cannot but reflect the prejudices, interests, desires, needs, and wants of a particular community. But a particular community is never the entire human community. Even humanity as such is never itself completely. There is the supplement, the remnant of the humanity to come, the community to come. Most importantly, every political community that empowers a certain *potestâs* cannot not produce victims. Every political community produces its victims. Evidently some political communities produce more victims than others, and some victimize their victims more severely. There are degrees, for certain. These victims, who suffer the inevitable material privations produced by a certain community, whether as insiders or outsiders, challenge the established legitimacy, or deliberative consensus. Inasmuch as it continues to perpetuate these victims and not allow for their voices, their suffering, their exclusion, to be voiced and expressed in the legitimation of a new order, a new legitimacy, then the system is inefficacious.

This is where the task of a *politics of liberation* properly begins, namely in the formulation of those principles that would guide the transformation of a system that has been shown to be necrophilic, illegitimate, and inefficacious. Dussel articulates this point of departure in the following way:

> The discovery of the *non-truth* (as Adorno wrote), of the *non-legitimacy*, the *non-efficiency* of the system of domination is a moment of skeptical criticism with respect to that system, the moment of atheism toward the prevailing totality, as Marx correctly described it in accordance with prophets of Israel, who rejected the divinity of fetishes. (2008, paragraph 13.1.2)

By "non-truth" Dussel means that the hegemonic system negates life. Truth is practical. It is material. Truth is that which enables life. Its opposite is the negation of life. The non-truth of the system is discovered from the standpoint of the non-life of the victims of a system. They are the negation of the system, in the double sense that they are negated by the system, and in their negation, they negate the system. Those who discover themselves negated by the system, become the messianic community, the critical community that de-legitimates the established consensus. But in their negation of the establish consensus they prefigure, anticipate, decipher a new consensus, a new legitimacy, one that negate their negation. The critical community, which is part of the larger political community, sets itself apart and challenges the self-satisfied, self-enclosed, fetishized community. In setting itself a part the critical community unleashed a praxis of liberation: one that is fueled by the power of the certainty of the community in its righteous conviction. It believes justice is on its side. The justice of its project is shown by the extent of the injustice of the present system. This critical community with its critical consciousness of the non-truth of the system sets out to change the present order and establish a new one.

Dussel argues that this critical consciousness manifests itself as a *potentia* that gives birth to a new *potestas*. For this reason, the praxis of liberation has a deconstructive and a constructive moment. It deconstructs the hegemonic order, and gives birth to a new order. It is precisely in this transition between deconstructing and constructing a new order that Paul of Tarsus, the philosophical-political thinker becomes important for Dussel. For Dussel, Paul is the thinker of the new critical consensus that births new political orders. When Paul proclaims that we are justified by faith, and not by the law, or the flesh, or blood, or the apostles, he is proclaiming that we can establish a new order by virtue of the potestas we generate through belief, confidence, and trust in our conviction, in the justice of our judgment about the injustice of the present system. Justification by faith, then, means the inauguration of a new order after the law. Faith, the name of a political community's "empowering vulnerability" is what also names what comes after the law—a new justice, a new justified, that is judged to be just, order.

III. WHAT MAKES CRITIQUE CRITICAL? LIFE FOR LAW, LAW FOR LIFE.

At the V International Forum of Philosophy in Venezuela (July 7th-14th, 2010), at which Dussel received the *Premio Libertador al Pensamiento Critico* [Liberator of Critical Thought Prize] for volume two of the *Politics of Liberation*, I heard him explain some of these ideas with the following two formulations. First, "the people separates itself as a political agent from the larger political community in order to propose a new project that is articulated as a critique of the hegemonic community." And then he added, "This is the problem of faith. Where faith is when the people [pueblo] believes in the people, when the people opposes the law and anticipates a new legality. This is faith: the opposition to the extant law." Faith, thus, is not prophetic, but messianic. It is transformative in the here and now, by the agency of the power a critical community bestows on each other as members of a political community that is divided in its consensus. But what is the criterion of criticism? How do we know that the liberating praxis of a critical community is in fact "liberating"? Every critique is not always critical.

What makes critique critical? What makes faith liberating and not oppressive, transformative and not conservative? This is the question. Here Franz Hinkelammert can provide us with some guiding light, when he writes in his recent book *Toward a Critique of Mythical Reason* (2008):

> Every thought that critiques something is not for that reason critical. The critique of critical thought is constituted by a specific point of view, under which it is undertaken. This point of view is human emancipation, which is therefore the humanization of human relations and the relation with the whole of nature. Emancipation is humanization, humanization turns into emancipation. (267)

The new critical consensus of the political community that sets itself apart in the name of the community that is not yet, for its sake, is guided by a criterion: does the law kill, or does it grant life? For Jesus as for Paul, the fundamental guiding criterion is life: "…the *new* criterion is Life, which in turn provides the *ultimate* foundation for the Law. Life is the *content* of the law; its *inversion* is what Jeshúa and Paul of Tarsus criticize" (Dussel 2009:123). The new critical consensus is developed from the standpoint of the negation of the negation, the negation of the untruth of the system, that is, positively, in light of the practical, material, truth: law is at the service of life, not life at the service of the law. At this moment, we are now in a position to clearly discern the difference between Agamben and Dussel, notwithstanding their agreement on some key points.

Throughout, I have flagged where I think Dussel and Agamben agree, mostly due to the fact that they converge on key exegeses of Paul. As serious and thorough scholars, they cannot but agree on certain interpretations. I have signaled at least three such agreements: first, both agree that we must understand Paul's justification by faith as a reference to potestas, to a form of empowerment. Second, both agree that Paul's inchoate references to the messianic community elucidate a diremption within the people. For Agamben, in fact, it is this elucidation that marks out Paul's "political legacy." Agamben puts it this way:

> The people is neither the all nor the part, neither the majority nor the minority. Instead, it is that which can never coincide with itself, as all or as part, that which infinitely remains or resists in each division, and, with all due respect to those who govern us, never allows us to be reduced to a majority or a minority. This remnant is the figure, or the substantiality assumed by a

people in a decisive moment, and as such is the only real political subject. (2005:57)

It could be shown how Dussel and Agamben converge in understanding the people in the same way. For Dussel the *pueblo* is never itself, for the pueblo is always insurrected against itself, in the name of itself, itself in its mode of having been and not yet being. A people always has a messianic component, that which prevents it from ever being able to speak univocally in its name. Every avowal in the name of a "we the people" is always provisional and deferred. We the people—is something that can never be irrevocable and immediately intelligible. The people is always to come. When we thus speak in the name of the people we do so through delegation, or what Dussel calls "obedential power." Third, and finally, Dussel and Agamben coincide in challenging the interpretation that Paul's political inheritance has to do with universality. For Agamben, Paul's messianic vocation disrupts every separation in the name of a diremption that is not a negation of a positive (see Agamben's discussion, 2005:52-53). If for Agamben Paul is the philosopher of the diremption that qualifies every universal claim, for Dussel Paul is the political philosopher of a universality to come through a plurality of neutralizing divisions: victim-non-victim, orphan-non-orphan, widow-non-widow, gay-non-gay, etc. This universality is always deferred for we can only glimpse through the non-truth of its negations.

Where Dussel and Agamben differ substantively and tellingly, however, is on the criterion that guides the deconstruction and construction of the new order. Agamben uses Schmitt's concept of the "state of exception" to explain Paul' messianic *katargêsis*: the suspension and observance of the law (104-107). For Agamben, Paul's notion of *katargêsis* makes reference to three moments: the moment of the indistinction between the outside and inside the law. Like Schmitt's state of exception, this outside the law is inside the law—it is the enactment of the law. For Paul, in as much as the law is suspended and observed, the law becomes unobservable—its enactment leads to sin, but not observing it is itself sin. Thirdly, in this situation of indiscernibility or indistinction and unobservability, the law becomes unformulatable—there is no possibility of formulating a law.

Evidently, given the way I reconstructed Dussel's reading of Paul, with some help from Hinkelammert, it is clear that there is a justice that comes after the law that enables a political community to formulate a new law. The collapse of the law in light of its victims demands the establishment of a new order. After the collapse of the law, a new justice can be established. This justice to come is both discerned and established by and in the name of the people to come. Here we can use Agamben against Agamben, by showing how Dussel's reading is more insightful and consequent.

BIBLIOGRAPHY

Agamben, G. 2005. *The Time that Remains: A Commentary on the Letter to the Romans*. Stanford: Stanford University Press.

Benveniste, E. 1973. *Indo-European Language and Society*. Coral Gables, Florida: University of Miami Press

Dussel, E. 2007 [1993] *Las metáforas teológicas de Marx*. Caracas-Venezuela: Fundación Editorial el Perro y la Rana.

Dussel, E. 2007. *Política de la Liberación. Historia mundial y crítica*. Madrid: Editorial Trotta.

Dussel, E. 2008. *Twenty Theses on Politics*. Durham, NC: Duke University Press.

Dussel, E. 2009. "The Liberatory Event in Paul of Tarsus" *Qui Parle: Critical Humanities and Social Sciences*, Vol. 18, No. 1 (Fall/Winter 2009), 111-180.

Dussel, E. 2009a. *Política de la Liberación II. Arquitectónica*. Madrid: Editorial Trotta.

Hinkelammert, F. 1998. *El Grito del Sujeto: Del teatro-mundo del evangelio de Juan al per-*

ro-mundo de la globalización. San Jose-Costa Rica: DEI.

Hinkelammert, F. 2008. *Hacia una crítica de la razón mítica: el laberinto de la modernidad Materiales para discussion.* Caracas-Venezuela: Fundacion Editorial el Perro y la Rana.

Küng, H. 2006 (1994) *Great Christian Thinkers.* New York and London: Continuum.

Nietzsche, F. 2005 (1888) *The Anti-Christ, Ecce Homo, Twilight of the Idols. And other Writings.* Cambridge, UK: Cambridge University Press.

HUMAN ARCHITECTURE: JOURNAL OF THE SOCIOLOGY OF SELF-KNOWLEDGE
A Publication of OKCIR: The Omar Khayyam Center for Integrative Research in Utopia, Mysticism, and Science (Utopystics)
ISSN: 1540-5699. © COPYRIGHT BY AHEAD PUBLISHING HOUSE (IMPRINT: OKCIR PRESS) AND AUTHORS. ALL RIGHTS RESERVED.

Law, Globalisation, and Second Coming

Oscar Guardiola-Rivera

Birkbeck School of Law, University of London, UK

o.guardiola-rivera@bbk.ac.uk

Abstract: In the wake of the "war on terror" and the emergence of a global surveillance regime shrouded in secrecy during the first part of the 21st century, notions of "empire" and the "white man's burden" (including "saving" the global economy, or behaving as global protector) are in the process of being rehabilitated in social theory, public law, human rights and global economics. Meanwhile, such principles as universal access to justice and equality are relegated to the dustbin of history, as if they were dangerous remnants of a previous period of history in which genuine aspirations to global justice resulted in the pathologies of today. The work of social theorist and political philosopher Enrique Dussel, emerging from within the legacy of Latin American thought, is hereby marshalled to the aim of reconstructing such notions as "people", "justice" and "international" in relation to the need for political organisation and legal creativity, against new forms of imperialism today. Based on Dussel's reading of the liberatory event in Paulian theology and Latin American society's popular religiosity, this paper seeks to explore an alternative agenda for theorizing about legal and political principles and institutions from an internationalist perspective.

I. INTRODUCTION: FROM LAW AND GLOBALIZATION TO PEOPLES' GLOBAL JUSTICE

This article seeks to explore an alternative agenda for theorizing about legal and political principles and institutions from an internationalist perspective. It aims at creating reasonably comprehensive overviews of such phenomena as decisive legal transformation and political change taking place across borders, while emphasizing the need for international political organisation—emerging from the encounter (at times, "missed" encounter or mismatch) between peoples in movement and the normative principles of their actions—as the basis for creativity in law and politics, in economics as well as history.

In this respect, the article finds inspiration among the historical critiques of the "stages of growth" and modernization theories that developed in conversation with

---

Oscar Guardiola-Rivera is the award-winning author of *What If Latin America Ruled the World?* (Bloomsbury, 2010) and of the forthcoming *Story of a Death Foretold* (Bloomsbury, 2013). He teaches International Law, Rights and Political Philosophy at Birkbeck School of Law, University of London (UK).

critical dependency sociology in the 1960s and 1970s, critical geography, scholarly writing about law from a global (specifically, "southern") perspective, and more recent attempts to rehabilitate such notions as "earth", "world", "territory", "international" and "people(s)" in the wake of the rise and fall of globalization theory, growth economics, and the discourses and practices (economic, legal, philosophical) which conceived of freedom and everything designated by the term "public" as ruled by money and property.

Scholars writing about law from a global perspective have observed that although Western traditions of academic law and politics have a rich heritage, from a global standpoint they appear parochial, narrowly focused and even unempirical or, as Emeritus Professor of Jurisprudence at University College London William Twining put it, 'tending towards ethnocentrism'[1].

Furthermore, in the wake of the so-called "war on terror" and the merging of security and progress in public law, human rights and global economics, notions of "empire" and the "white man's burden" (including "saving" the global economy from the brink of disaster, or the emergence of a statutory and global surveillance regime shrouded in secrecy during the first part of the 21st century) are in the process of being rehabilitated. All the while, such crucial principles as universal access to justice and equality are being relegated to the dustbin of history, as if they were so many remnants of a previous period of history in which utopian aspirations to global justice resulted in the pathologies of today.

Sociologists concerned with the historical-comparative study of institutions, an interpretive approach that challenges the predominance of Rational Choice Theory in the social sciences, have observed that a similar set of problems stems from the persistent disavowal of objects ripe for historical comparative research across areas of the world, such as law and legal-political principles, in the richer sense of the term.[2] In turn, area and comparativist scholars, exploring legal conceptions and political institutions in non-Western parts of the globe, have noticed that certain epistemic disconnects, *idées fixes* and automatic reflexes add up to the basic constraints already faced by transnational commentators, 'truncating fuller debate about questions of law' in other parts of the world and displacing 'wider discussions over alternative policies, competing interests, and the distributional impacts of rules and institutions', privileging instead a narrow set of perspectives, positions, and prescriptions.[3]

Like the traditions it recognises as worthy predecessors, this article tends to favor a historical comparative perspective that allows for interpretive approaches, and argues for a more careful consideration of concrete locality and the sites in which so-called "free associations" have taken or can take place, vis-à-vis the prevalence of abstract (especially, probabilistic and choice theoretical) models in the social sciences. In accordance with such spirit, this article concerns itself with Latin America as a specific locality in which events of "free association" and people's creativity have been an can be set in motion, in relation to actual cases of legal transformation and political construction beyond current laws or the limitations of "the existing situation", as Frantz Fanon would've put it. However, this article does not intend to develop a full-blown case study of historical comparison between the countries of this region, or this region as a whole and some other global grouping.

This article shares with the aforementioned approaches the thesis that most processes of so-called "globalization" take

---

1. W Twining, *General Jurisprudence: Understanding Law from a Global Perspective* (2009) xi. See also *Human Rights, Southern Voices* (2009) 1-3.

2. J Mahoney & D Rueschemeyer, *Comparative Historical Analysis in the Social Sciences* (2003).

3. J Esquirol, 'Writing the Law of Latin America' (2009) 40 TGWILR 3, 694.

place at sub-global levels (e.g. regional, for instance Latin American) and that, as William Twining said, a healthy cosmopolitan discipline of law and political theory (here including political philosophy) should encompass all levels of social action and relations, as well as the principles prescribing the orientation of these actions and relations. Along these lines, the essay hopes to contribute to the critical review and extension of the so-called "Western" canon of jurisprudence and political philosophy beyond its limitations. It also hopes to contribute to the reconstruction of social, legal and political theory by taking into account not only some of the general and more specific problems of conceptualization, comparison and generalization, or the relationship between the local and the global, but more pointedly, by initiating a reflection on justice, law and globalization (in particular, global social justice) from within a specific legal and philosophical tradition that refuses to be reduced to this or that context (e.g., analytical or continental, common or civil)—in this case, Latin American thought.

II. EVENT AS PROBLEM: DUSSEL'S *KAIRÓS*

The work of social theorist and political philosopher Enrique Dussel, emerging from within the important legacy of Latin American thought, is appropriate to the aim of rehabilitating such notions as "people", "justice" and "international" in relation to the need for political organisation and legal creativity against new forms of imperialism today. In what follows I will be referring not so much to the more general significance of his contribution to Latin American thinking, but rather, to his specific presentation of the question of *kairós*, the event of radical turning and novelty, vis-à-vis more and less current understandings of law and planetary order as the normalization or mastering of contingency and time.

Way before notions of eventuality, situation, historical context, principled equality and the creativity of the people were recovered in contemporary European thought (from Fanon, among others, via Sartre and Foucault, or more recently Alain Badiou, Slavoj Zizek and Raymond Geuss) Dussel was developing his views on the problem of historical novelty in dialogue with radical currents of social theory and theology alive in the social and political movements of the Americas in the 1970s.

Such views contrasted with mainstream understandings of law and order as the normalization or mastering of contingency, backwardness and savage desires. Back in the '70s, such mainstream positions underpinned modernisation theory. Now, they inform the post-historical rediscovery of the empire-form in geopolitics, economic history, law and political theology.

On the one hand, I will be exploring Dussel's concern with the specific role that religion in general and Christianity in particular have played in the context of the totality of social relations and normative orders and principles in Latin America. On the other hand, as said before, this essay seeks to make a modest but honest contribution to the more general attempt to bring together theology, legal, political and social theory in order to further the aims of the emerging field of study of the concrete relationships between religion, politics and empire.

In this respect, following the example of the editors of the collection *Empire and the Christian Tradition*, I believe that no account of globalization and the hegemonic role played in that process by countries such as the United States, a country whose leaders 'often claim to represent the Christian tradition', or the counter-hegemonic role played by Latin American social and political movements that also claim to represent elements of the Christian worldview, would be complete without an exploration of the representatives and main conceptions of that religious heritage and its succession.[4]

One such element is the tension between conceptions of law and political institutions that see it as their task to normalize, manage, or master the contingency of time (e.g., the idea of the *katechon* as a Christian sovereign whose role is to defer the catastrophic end of times), on the one side, and on the other the crucial notion of "Final Judgement", as both the principle and the event or the act of bringing to an end the inequities of oppression and empire. I argue that the former—law and politics as the mastering of accidents and contingency—underpins current attempts to rescue the empire-form in geopolitics and history (against the onslaught of Third Worldism and egalitarianism in the 1960s and 1970s). The latter—the notion of "Final Judgment" or "the judgement of history"—has often been mobilized in support of a more radical view of spiritual liberation and decolonization with implications for legal, social political and economic institutions in the current situation. An example of such use was Fidel Castro's recourse to the judgment of history ("history will absolve me") during his defence in court after the assault against the Moncada barracks on 16 October 1963. Another was Salvador Allende's plea for a new "common orientation" or political purpose in his last radio broadcast on 11 September, 1973, as US-backed renegades among the Chilean military overthrew the constitutional government of that country.[5]

Within the framework of this set of questions, the following arguments will also consider the dynamic between 'critical' and 'therapeutic' understandings of the role of religion in Latin America and elsewhere.

III. Final Judgment and the Liberatory Event in Paul of Tarsus

I believe Dussel's position accurately responds to the concerns expressed by those in the "global north" who believe that "a just international order and a healthy cosmopolitan discipline of law need to include [non-Western] perspectives" as well as more nuanced views on the intellectual legacy of what is now called "the West", particularly in relation to the more complex histories of Christendom, Renaissance and the Enlightenment.[6] Given the global reach of his philosophical, historical and theological work, Dussel also strives to create a thoroughly original set of inter-cultural analytic concepts that critically reflect upon our stock of theories about justice, human rights, philosophy, legal pluralism, and crucially, comparative and global history.

His intellectual intervention amounts to nothing less than a reformation of thought. Building upon Dussel's insights, and some modest observations of my own, I will take his exemplary stance one step further and call for a wider and more encompassing reformation in relation to the substance of social relations and normative orders prevalent in Latin America, with consequences for the rest of the world. Toward this aim, let us consider Dussel's "The Liberatory Event in Paul of Tarsus", a text which he presents as a decisive contribution to "a very timely subject for political philosophy in recent years".[7] The argument developed by Dussel in this text is set in direct relationship with more and less recent European debates on the relation between religion (specifically, Christian theology) and the public use of reason (law and politics).

As he says in reference to the more re-

---

4. DH Compier, K Pui-Lan & J Rieger (eds.). *Empire & The Christian Tradition* (2007) xiii.

5. See O Guardiola-Rivera, *Story of a Death Foretold. The Coup Against Salvador Allende, 11 September 1973* (Bloomsbury, 2013).

6. W Twining, *Human Rights, Southern Voices* (2009) 1. See also B De Sousa Santos, 'A Non-Occidentalist West? Learned Ignorance and Ecology of Knowledge' (2009) 26 *TS* 7/8, 103-125, and T Ramadan *What I Believe* (2010).

7. E Dussel, *The Liberatory Event in Paul of Tarsus* (2009) 1.

cent debates on the place of religion in the public use of reason, "today, political philosophy has unexpectedly taken up a subject which had been ignored since the Enlightenment".[8] He is referring to the latest wave of writings on and around religion by commentators as diverse as Slavoj Zizek, Alain Badiou, Giorgio Agamben, Terry Eagleton, John Milbank, Jürgen Habermas, and Gianni Vattimo in Europe, or Franz Hinkelammert in the Americas, and in a more indirect way to some of the issues touched upon by "militant atheists" closer to the tradition of English evolutionism, such as Daniel Dennett, AC Grayling or Richard Hawkins.

It is crucial to understand that for Dussel the "new debate" on the role of religion in the public sphere is foreshadowed by a previous "older debate", harking back to Kant's *Conflict of the Faculties* and Hobbes's *Leviathan*. According to Dussel, in order to understand the new debates we must first acknowledge the stakes of the older one. At stake in this "older debate" was not only the question of how to read sacred texts (or "interpretation", according to Kant) but also, and most crucially, the question of "judgment", and thus of general jurisprudence in relation to the (economic, cultural and political) planetary crises at the time. This "relocation" of the object of such debates from "interpretation" to "judgment" opens up jurisprudence—in its more particular sense of the exploration of the activity of legislators, judges and precedents in bounded jurisdictions—to a much more general sense, one in which it also concerns itself with the beyond of jurisdictions (the "international") but also with "final judgment". The latter term refers to a specific kind of judgment: so-called chiliastic judgments. These are applied to the whole of history so far, and seek to transgress the present order in the sense of the radical overturning of established boundaries in time and space.

Passing judgment on the present order in order to subvert it, is a critical operation that seems to me parallel to what Kant termed "succession". Kant was referring to the way in which a tradition is inherited, reclaimed and thereafter "betrayed" or put to an original use that could not have been contemplated from the previous situation. This has to do with clearing the ground for the creation of what Kantians like Drucilla Cornell call "moral images" of freedom.[9] "Succession", as the activity of a community that receives and transforms its common heritage, and *kairós*, as both judgment and a turning of the page, allow for a powerful understanding of acts of rupture with/within imitation in history. Understanding them better may help us to achieve our aim: invoking a new thinking of history, sovereignty and independence in relation to what Dussel calls "the event of liberation".

Since the notion of "succession" is not used explicitly by Dussel, I will have to show that his conception of power as popular and communal requires it. Dussel's conception of power (which I understand to designate that which a people have "in common") refers to the capacity to open up politics and law to their exteriority—and pertains to the uses of imagination as a critical and regulatory element.

For now, it will suffice to say that Dussel's conception of power as communal, which is expressed in the injunction 'to govern while obeying' (*mandar obedeciendo*), includes an element of common memory and of the work of the community to recover such a memory while renewing it (as witnessing and testimony). This correlation between the memory of the community and the legitimacy of those who govern, the fact that they bear witness and give testimony to the living memory and future-oriented will of the community- makes it possible to open up the law so as to make it responsive to its surrounding environment. This constellation of time, memory and legitimacy through testimony is central to popular

---

8. Ibid.

9. Drucilla Cornell, *Moral Images of Freedom. A Future for Critical Theory* (Rowman & Littlefield, 2007).

practices and images of religiosity and narration in Latin America and elsewhere. It is a critical normative element in the construction of communities, and their projection beyond the present situation.[10]

That the stakes in the old and new debates on the relation between theology and politics are much higher than it may seem at first glance becomes clearer, as Dussel suggests, if we trace Hobbesian and Kantian motifs all the way up to the "political theology" of the 20th century. For instance, to the work of German jurist and transnational commentator Carl Schmitt, and to the constellation of 20th century thinkers that debated his positions on such issues as judgment (not just in the abstract sense, but also in the concrete sense of order and orientation in space and time), crisis (in geopolitical as well as global economic terms), and the jurisprudence of crisis and emergency.

As is well known, most of these debates followed the fall of the Weimar Republic in the 1930s and the political and economic upheavals that extended from that period into the 1940s and the rest of the twentieth century. They focused on the issue of political transformation, the rise of a global order in which the United States takes over "the *mission civilisatrice* of the West" (Mendieta 2007:1) and the nature of spatial division and newness in history.[11] Chief among the questions raised during these debates is that of the meaning of events of emancipation or "liberation" in the contemporary world of state-capitalist nations led by America.

Why is it that the names of relatively obscure political-theological thinkers such as Walter Benjamin or Jacob Taubes, and the classical archetypical figure of Paul of Tarsus, feature so prominently in these discussions? One must ask such a question since the connection between the normative order of religion and secular politics is not immediately apparent. After the Enlightenment, that connection tends to appear in two guises: on the one side, as a conservative advocacy of more or less benign forms of authoritarian paternalism and empire that can be traced back to Thomas Hobbes and the ultra-Catholic thinker Carl Schmitt in the twentieth century. On the other, the normative theological dimension is given a new lease of life under the cover of "Messianic" and prophetic power. The latter is often associated with a certain reading of crises and catastrophes as bringing an era of suffering and exile to an end, thereby opening the path of history towards the new and the unexpected—from tragedy to redemption and overturning, or the time of *kairós*—rather than bracketing history as "interregnum".[12]

The Hobbesian and Schmittian conception of history as "interregnum" closes history by introducing merely the possibility of its end. It sees history as a period marked by risk and uncertainty that needs to be mastered and managed, in which the absence or weakening of the authority of the political-religious leader increases the chances of some apocalyptic catastrophe to actually occur. The job of the paternalist leader at home and abroad is to avert or defer that possibility. To that aim, the leader exercises near-absolute power, which often takes the form of pre-emptive action and "exceptional" intervention in ever more catastrophic ways. The source of his authority is the particular and supposedly definitive act of a founding father, which the paternalist leader—functioning as the protector of the unity and homogeneity of the community—allegedly reproduces and continues. It is no surprise that in the versions of this conception closer to medieval Christian traditions,

---

10. E Dussel, *The Liberatory Event in Paul of Tarsus* (2009). On law's responsiveness to an exteriority, see the work of B Golder & P Fitzpatrick, *Foucault's Law* (2009) 99-131.

11. E Mendieta, *Global Fragments. Globalizations, Latinamericanisms, and Critical Theory* (2007) 1.

12. JA Gordon & LR Gordon, *On Divine Warning. Reading Catastrophe in the Modern Age* (2009) 117-120. See also D Cornell, *Moral Images of Freedom: A Future for Critical Theory* (2008) 137-149.

the political-religious leader is portrayed as a "retainer" or *kátechon*. This is the Christian prince whose pre-emptive action restrains evil by containing the archenemy of the community, thereby deferring the time of the coming of the Anti-Christ. According to this narrative, in doing so, in "deferring" time, the paternalist leader produces history.

These two "older" positions struggle over the meaning of modernity and enlightenment. In general, modernity can be defined as "the social order in which religion is no longer fully integrated into and identified with a particular life-form" but rather, acquires the ability to globalize itself.[13] However, the price religion has to pay if it is to become truly global is to be `reduced to a secondary epiphenomenon with regard to the secular functioning of the social totality`(ibid.). This means that in the "new" global order religion has two possible roles, invoked above: therapeutic or critical. It can either help individuals "function better in the existing order, or it can aim to assert itself as a critical agency articulating what is wrong with this order as such, as a space for the voices of discontent".[14]

The Hobbesian-Schmittian position, in trying to protect and reproduce the homogeneity of the community while at the same time projecting its crusading role into and against the future, is therapeutic in relation to the present order. The opposite position, which emphasizes the secular "messianic" powers of the community and the redemptive character of history, plays a critical role in relation to the present. Critics like Walter Benjamin or Jacob Taubes in the twentieth century, and Bartolomé de Las Casas, Thomas Müntzer or John Milton in the sixteenth and seventeenth centuries, took issue against the main tenets of Christian political theology—what would become galvanised in the Hobbesian-Schmittian position. Not only did they emphasize in various ways the secular powers of the community, they also associated this power to the coming into being (existence) of the community from an initial situation of persecution, inequality, anonymity, oppression, or in more general terms, of inexistence. In doing so, they linked the self-organizing power of the community to creativity and originality in history. And also, to the very question of how "new" history emerges and "old" history comes to pass.

In accordance with this position, new history emerges out of the opposition between two orders or epochs. In philosophical terms, between the present totality and its exteriority, situated as a concrete community of others that organize and project themselves beyond the prevailing coercive totality.[15] This is the moment of historical disruption and creativity that, in relation to the Paulian corpus of texts and the critical tradition it initiated, Dussel calls "*kairós*". In anthropological terms, *kairós* could be understood as the moment of recognition and memory in which the latter is deployed against prevailing cultural values, mores and ways of life. This is also the moment of the composition of a rational symbolic narrative against the present (imperial) order (of inexistence) in its very essence.

This means that such is the kind of narrative that shakes the very foundation "upon which the legitimation of the Roman state in its totality rested".[16] This narrative emerges also as a critique of other groups and interpretations within a common textual tradition from which the new (messianic) community slowly differentiates itself in a process of continuous division. Finally, and importantly, it opposes a form of legalism operative in the present or primitive community, or in certain groups within the primitive community, that failed to grasp "the novelty of the new position of the

---

13. S Zizek, *The Puppet and the Dwarf. The Perverse Core of Christianity* (2003) 3.
14. Ibid.

15. E Dussel, *The Liberatory Event in Paul of Tarsus* (2009) 7.
16. Ibid.

founding group" without contradicting the fact that this critique and division occur strictly within the confines of a common memory and tradition[17]. Thus emerging from within the order of the law (as its "zero" or lowest degree of impotence) this narrative stands against the very concept of Law as the foundation of the prevailing order or epoch. And, having borne witness to the collapse of the Law due to its insufficiency (or as Dussel says, invoking one of richest notions in the modern vocabulary of criticism and critique of religion, law, and economics, when it has become "fetishized") it brings forth a new justificatory criterion.

IV. *Kairós* and the Meaning of Heresy: On Religious Truth as Law's Critique and Exemplarity

To sum up the argument so far, the creative genius of Dussel's formulation of the Paulian *kairós* is to open a specific 'common' tradition or legacy to a superior form of commonality, schematized as a higher-order set of complimentary differences. The community of readers and interpreters receive a tradition while at the same time taking it into uncharted territories. In the process, an exemplary tradition comes to embody the very meaning of exemplarity itself. For Dussel, as well as for the critical tradition that he reinvents—from Las Casas and Milton to Benjamin and Taubes—Paul's writings are exemplary precisely in this sense: it is the very pliability of the exemplar or the classic (that is, of memory) or its unfixed quality, that is its essence. It makes itself at home wherever and whenever it finds itself, but in doing so it reinvents the very meaning of 'home' (which is why, seen from the standpoint of those comfortable in the present situation it would always seem 'unhomely' (*unheimlich*, violent and uncanny). It is the exemplar's ability (Paul's writings, in this case, as the operative basis for memory and action related to popular religiosity in Latin America) to be both antique and yet modern, 'its infinite—but never anarchic—plurality that categorizes it' as the embodiment of exemplarity itself.[18]

Any exploration of legality and politics in Latin America from a historical-comparative perspective would be incomplete without taking into consideration the role played by religious normative discourses and institutions, and in particular Christian religious discourse. This is due not only to the recognizable fact that a large majority of Latin Americans and Latinos leaving in the Americas and elsewhere declare themselves as practicing Christians, or that the practice of Christianity flourishes in the Americas while in Europe it languishes. This is no doubt an important fact. But it only tells one half of the story, if at all. Ditto, religion in modernity can play the role of critic or comforter (in Zizek's terms, "therapeutic" religiosity).

The fact that the overwhelming majority of the populations in Latin America assert their allegiance to Christianity gives religious institutions (in particular, the Roman Catholic Church) a huge sway over "secular" political and legal state institutions, and over political life in general. This has been true about Latin America for most of its his-

---

17. E Dussel *The Liberatory Event in Paul of Tarsus* (2009) 7-9.

18. As literary critic Frank Kermode observes, an exemplary text is a work that 'subsists in change, by being patient of interpretation'. Put simply, the antidote against fundamentalist word-worshipping is to keep on reading and writing. This means that every generation will read and understand received texts such as Paul's *Epistles* or the Qur'an differently, insofar as every generation is different from its predecessors. But every generation is also challenged to produce an interpretation that is not only satisfactory (i. e. that respects tradition by not presenting its own version of it as the 'final' version) but also categorically decisive and forward-looking (in the sense of adding to reality, rather than simply imitating). Kermodian categories of criticism are appropriate to introduce this aspect of Duseel's work to Anglo-Saxon audiences. See on this J Sutherland (21/08/2010)'Fierce Reading', *The Guardian*, , Review, 16. Also, F Kermode, *The Classic* (1983).

tory, and the justified cause of a great deal of criticism about the Church's role as a "comforter" and even an accomplice in many of the injustices visited upon the peoples of the Americas throughout its modern history. However, it is also true to say that in no other part of the world has the role of religious discourse as critique been developed as creatively as in Latin America—particularly as a critique of legal and political-economic institutions.

Although this is a well-known fact, few contemporary observers have explored its consequences for law and political economy in the context of wider processes of globalization. In fact, it is remarkable that the "new debates" about religion and politics in Europe seem to find no place for the implications of Liberation Theology and philosophy, which emerged in Latin America after the 1960s. Especially given that, as we will see, this is not only one of the most influential interpretations of the Christian tradition in recent times but it may also be the most universal; at least in its capacity to allow Christianity to subsist in the changing landscape of globalization and confront the challenge posed by major geopolitical shifts, by making its textual corpus "patient to interpretation".

The present situation of the globalized world is characterized by the decline in the capacities of all major states to run and regulate the international system. And after the 2008 Great Recession, also by major doubts about the persistence and the justification (the means-to-end nexus) of nation-state capitalism, underpinned by militarism, as the framework of globalization. In this situation, the central story is less a state (for instance, China) that is allegedly rising to take over the American position, but the likely consequence of the softening of power from the center. America will undoubtedly have to scale down its presence in global affairs as enforcer of the international system, both to rethink its role as "protector" and avoid being perceived once more as a "bully"; but its power is far from fading away. Pundits right and left of center who believe that the East (led by China) is on its way to replace a declining West (led by America) miss the point that there are no real rivals to the US. They also miss the fact that America is undergoing a major internal transformation driven by the increasing political and economic importance of its Latin American and Latino population, soon to become a majority. The United States is set to become the next Latin American country.

In both aspects of the story, religion, Christianity in particular, will be of central importance. The militant religious Conservatism that has become so outspoken and influential both at the level of high-end and grassroots politics in the US, threatens America's ability to rebrand itself internationally and to secure economic recovery and political stability at home. What it needs is precisely, a form of Christianity that can subsist—even with some conservative elements—in the rapidly changing world of globalization, while at the same time providing much needed energy and space for radical criticism and reform. Given their numbers and geographical location in the US, but also the dynamism of their religious practices, no other candidate seems to offer a better alternative to provide both elements than the popular religious beliefs of the US Latino and Latin American populations.

Abroad, the readiness of this framework of popular beliefs to relate to religious texts in a way that allows them to subsist "by being patient of interpretation" places this form of Christianity in a much better position than any nationalistic or expansive orthodoxy, Christian or not, in order to relate to and even inspire change among other text-based religious practices without violently dismissing them as backwards or heretic. At home, its firm opposition to established hierarchies that tend to impinge upon the weakest members of society, and to all forms of oppression and discrimination originating from the particular interests of a few in politics and the economy, will resonate with the militant core of those across party lines, race and class who believe that America must be rescued from such interests and that they should be tamed and overcome.

Add to this the fact that as America scales down its presence in global affairs, embraces its inner *Latinidad*, and looks for ways to secure its economic future, it is more rather than less likely to strengthen its ties with its closer neighbors, such as Mexico and Brazil. The latter two are already emerging as competitors of, say, other emerging (authoritarian) economies such as Russia and China, share a popular and historical commitment to democracy, a "melting pot" cultural legacy, and have shown the will and the capacity to play a mature role on the stage of global affairs. Indeed, the crucial point in this story is that the combined weight of the Americas will give any upstart nation with dreams of global hegemony a run for its money; and the catalyst of this combination might well be popular religion.

But the condition for this chemistry to occur, avoiding any major explosive effects, is that the popular religiosity of Latin Americans asserts itself as a force for change rather than an obstacle to it in the name of orthodoxy. This is to say that Latin American religiosity must go all the way through an inner reformation: it must fall (in a way that brings it closer to its Protestant siblings) on the side of heresy. Even if this means revising its ties with Rome, a center of power that has done everything it can to dismiss the fact that the special dynamism of Christianity in the Americas goes beyond anything that happens in Europe, and has actively misunderstood, discredited and even persecuted those who have emphasized the critical role of Christianity.

V. A Latin American Reformation?

What exactly means to say that Latin American religiosity, as a normative discourse, must go through a reformation? As suggested before, this is the case in which "religion as such *tends toward assuming the role of a heresy*".[19] This assertion helps clarify the critical role religion can play vis-à-vis law and politics in the contemporary world of "declining" state-capitalist nations. But it may not go far enough. It is symptomatic that in a recent debate between "radical orthodox" theologian John Milbank, whose work is one of the most important and influential sources driving the "one-nation" policies of the present Conservative British government, and liberation philosopher Enrique Dussel, who is in turn one of the most prestigious scholars of liberation theology and philosophy in the Americas, the former was forced to take out of the closet one of those old chestnuts of the medieval traditions of theology he so admires. Having exhausted all philosophically sound arguments and even some *ad hominem* attacks, which the Latin American philosopher rebutted and unpretentiously separated from—creating in the audience the effect known as "romance of the withheld". Milbank denounced Dussel with one word: "heretic".

We need to ask once more what is the normative significance of religion becoming heresy. The answer lies in the deeper meaning acquired by a "heretic" religious discourse: in the very act of a normative discourse being used by a specific sector of society to rise against the given order, to stand up against the law as it is in the name of the future, in the name of liberation. What is exactly at stake in this act? "Liberation is a concern about purpose", writes existential philosopher Lewis Gordon, "a concern about *ought* and *why*: Whatever we may be, the point is to focus energy on what *we ought to become*".[20] Accordingly, religion becomes heresy when it emphatically takes sides

---

19. S Zizek, *The Puppet and the Dwarf*, (2003) 3, my emphasis.

20. LR Gordon, *Existentia Africana. Understanding Africana Existential Thought* (2000) 6.

with those who remain invisible, as a residue, in the present order, question its justification, and having found all justifications wanting, reasonably conclude they ought to overcome it. To do so, and to avoid fallacious connections between what is and what to become, they appear in the world as a politically organized forward-looking group, rather than continuing to be defined as merely a series or a "cultural other".

It is not merely a case of religion making such sectors of society more visible, more "identical" to the rest of a society that ignores, serializes and devalues them. Rather, religion itself becomes located in the position of this otherness and rises against the bond of alterity that defines the social position of otherness: that is, being ignored, devalued and even demoted beneath the realm of humanity. When that happens, questions of "identity" (what am I? Am I other or identical, or something else? or what am I other than a problem or the very embodiment of insanity in this society?) become inseparable from the question of reason (or truth) and liberation. This is to say that such questions (and those who posit them) are now posed in a situation *before* symmetry.

In that situation, the struggle is to be in a position for truth and the ethical to emerge. This is also the answer to the question "what it means to struggle to be a human being, and to be reasonable, in the onslaught of the very denial of one's humanity and of existence?"[21]

Crucially, this position inevitably appears, from the perspective of the given order, as both mad and inhuman. There's no paradox here. What is at stake is the logic of the objectivity of an idea. Put otherwise, the issue here is how ideas gain concrete existence: they do so by affirming evidence that at first appears counter-intuitive (mad, inhuman). Or, as an internal criticism of given assumptions: the latter appear first as the very criterion of truth and justification, but then, in a second moment, as Dussel explains, the criterion collapses due to its insufficiency—it's shown to be inconsistent. However, in a third moment, rather than demanding that we do away with contradiction—or conversely, that we do away with consistency and logics—it is shown that consistency has to do with incompleteness and observation, and that a logical system of truth or justification is consistent only if it does not exclude its own problematic nature.

VI. Testimony, or Truthfulness in Action

This is precisely what is meant by the notion of action as testimony, or as "providing evidence". Such an account of human action "decisively marks its distance from assumptions about action as the successful assertion of will".[22] Action-as-willful-assertion-upon-others and nature is the common characteristic of fundamentalist word-worshipping and its apparent opposite, neo-humanitarian instrumentalist fear-mongering. These are the two sides of current debates about the role of religion vis-à-vis politics and science. Neo-humanitarians like Richard Dawkins seem to reduce the meaning of religion to its expansionist and violent drive, which allegedly follows from a deep-seated word-worshipping attitude, contrary to reason and Enlightenment values. There is, they seem to argue, a slippery slope from the logic of religious texts to the fundamentalist violence of Islamist suicide bombers and Jewish (Orthodox) or American (Evangelical) evolution-deniers and anti-abortionist murder justifiers.

There is much to learn from these and other strident critiques of Christianity and religion in general, such as Hannah Arendt's. However, all too often their strength

---

21. D Cornell, *Moral Images of Freedom* (2008) 107.

22. R Williams, Introduction to *Theology and the Political: The New Debate*. (Edited by Creston Davis, John Milbank and Slavoj Zizek) 2005: 1.

is diminished by a tendency to combine fear-mongering (against some fundamentalist "other", in the case of Dawkins) with a sound defense of the incompleteness of truth, evidence, and Enlightenment values.

This is problematic not necessarily because it goes too far, but rather, because it does not go far enough: on the one hand, it fails to recognize that neo-Humanitarianism can not only be described in terms that are merely apparently secular (as Tony Blair proved in the run-up to the Iraq War, through his discursive use of the singular character of "western" Enlightenment values—human rights and liberalism—before he "came out" as a Catholic) but can also be as violent and imperialistic as any religious fundamentalism, particularly in its fear-mongering and most "liberal" mode: that which has to do with the "virtues" and allegedly "scientific" assumptions of free-trade global capitalism. On the other, it is constantly at risk of simply replacing God with Human Will both when it does not distance itself sufficiently from a defense of science as the successful instrumentalization of nature or the external world to man's will, and also, when it seems unwilling to recognize that self-exposure to death isn't always some miscalculating, masochistic or mad attempt to seek atonement for non-existent sins committed by fictional characters.[23]

In fact, the category of martyrdom, when distinguished from all transcendent undertones (being "fast-tracked" to Paradise and so on) means, for Christians and others, a distinctive instance of testimony: it provides evidence that the Law, in the hands of political and religious meaning makers, has collapsed. This is the exact opposite of the "classical" (sacrificial) Greek, Semitic and Roman attitude toward the Law and Truth, which has passed into modernity in the sacrificial language and practice of imperialism and colonization (including its more "liberal" British and American contemporary versions), instrumentalist science and "free-market" economics. Testimony appears from this perspective as the enlightened opposite of persistent sacrificial attitudes in society, prejudiced beliefs that in turn allow inequality and injustice to persist. This is true in the sense that the death of an innocent and the destruction of nature function as evidence backing up the argument that condemns all forms of sacrifice, religious or secular, fundamentalist or liberal.

It is possible here to open up a dialogue between politics, theology, and science. On the one side, this dialogue can take place in the context of critical and post-Enlightenment questioning of sacrificial logics prevalent in even the most liberal and neo-humanitarian forms of globalism and expansionist behavior (Golub 2010:4-10) and in the capitalism of perpetual innovation and the enslavement of nature. On the other, the dialogue can continue in the context of careful consideration of the role of evidence vis-à-vis the Law and Truth, which is directly relevant to notions of Freedom, Autonomy and Liberation or independence. Among other things, this entails nuanced distinctions between Reason and Will, between Will-as-assertion and General Will, and between critiques of fundamentalism and instrumentalist fear-mongering (which is another form of will-assertion leading to sacrificial calculus). It also entails being careful not to render the category of "testimony" or evidence, in general, too optimistic. Monsignor Óscar Romero's death in El Salvador certainly testifies to the collapse of Law and Truth in the context of the establishment of financial liberalization and in-

---

23. This is how Richard Dawkins interprets Paul's writings in *The God Delusion* (2006). For an alternative interpretation of self-exposure to death see Rowan Williams' introduction to *Theology and the Political: The New Debate* (2005). Dussel shares Williams' understanding of Jesus Christ's death as martyrdom, rather than sacrifice, and thus as making evident to the new messianic community the fetishism of the Law. See E Dussel, op. cit. 10; and F Hinkelammert, *The Cry of the Subject: From the World Theater of the Gospel of John to the Dog Years of Globalization* (1998) 45.

terventionism in the Americas in the 1980s. But this does not make the fact of his assassination any less grotesque; it cannot be recovered as part of a "higher" narrative underlined by a superior purpose or a finalized and more perfect totality. His death was contingent, unnecessary. Much in the same way, evidence in science and the tribunal help us reflect upon the incompleteness and fragility of "natural" as well as "artificial" environments, of our truths about them, and our responsibilities toward them. No laws of necessity underpin such processes, particularly no man-made laws.

To sum up, the problem with "atheistic" responses in the "new debates" between theology and public reason is that they do not seem to draw all the consequences of the event of the death of God, as Slavoj Zizek has suggested: put simply, they're not atheistic enough. As suggested before, these responses cannot boil down to a defense of purely abstract (subjective or "negative') freedom, since the latter is indistinguishable from the actual struggles of specific peoples to be free and to bring themselves "out from beneath the despairing weight" of such real situations as racism, economic oppression, debt slavery, force displacement, land-grab, environmental destruction and colonization.[24]

The lack of a critique of "Capitalism as religion" remains a serious shortcoming in these critiques of religion. Particularly since the struggle referred to here is not to destroy but rather to edify, to build and to add more to reality. The action involved is not simply one of making visible what was masked or covered over, but rather, to bring into reality (thereby making visible) what was not there before. The issue is both ontological and political: it involves the fundamental question of existence and the classical problem of how an actuality emerges also from impotentiality.

In the "new debates" it is becoming clearer that, at its most fundamental, the question of existence involves more than solving the problem of what is it to be a human being in a situation in which one is not being seen as such by the rest of society. This is already the crucial problem for human rights discourse and practice. But in addition to that, those struggling against racism, economic oppression, debt, forced displacement, land-grab and the loss of sovereignty that leads to diminution of democracy and to the inability to decide one's own economic and political destiny, are realizing that their constraints are connected, in concrete ways, to the constraints being placed upon non-human environments by a form of "progress" that continues to pile catastrophe upon catastrophe and moves forward blindly, reaffirming the very limits of capitalism, of humanity, of nature.

This is why on April 22, 2010, in the context of the World People's Conference on Climate Change and the Rights of Mother Earth, the plight of the communities that are being most directly damaged by the environmental crisis brought about by a sacrificial model of capitalist consumption and production was turned into an argument to take the question of existence one step beyond the notions of symmetry and reciprocity that have traditionally informed international law and human rights discourse and advocacy.

In concrete terms, these peoples in struggle gathered in Cochabamba (Bolivia) for the Conference, proposed a Bill of Rights for Mother Earth and a climate tribunal to investigate those responsible for environmental damage. These proposals join the "leave resources in the soil" initiatives and the corresponding financial schemes developed by activists in the Amazon. Both actions have precedents in the long history of rights-based struggles, advocacy and institutional design: the thirteenth century Charter of the Forest, which together with Magna Carta constitutes the pillar of the Common Law tradition; the Law of Peace of the indig-

---

24. D Cornell, *Moral Images of Freedom* (2008) 106-7.

enous peoples of North and Central America, a component of the much more complex and living memory of the interrupted thought of the Amerindians; and the normative tradition of pretty much any religion with a long and venerable history in the face of the earth.

It is unsurprising that this extension of the fundamental question of existence has come to resonate strongly with the political theology developed with an eye on ancient sources and another in contemporary phenomena by thinkers such as Walter Benjamin, who also spoke of catastrophes piling upon catastrophes, of our blindness, and of the storm called progress, while bringing back the allure of the objects of the world, and in particular the images that best tell "history" nowadays, in the age of mechanical reproduction, of cinema and the internet. What might seem surprising to some is that Benjamin's political-theological reading of the fundamentals of existence resonates also with the least discussed and publicized feature of the 2010 Conference in Bolivia, the one ignored by contemporary "atheistic" critiques of religion: their call for an alternative polity, in the form of taking bold steps towards new and emancipatory ways of doing politics, decolonizing knowledge, and composing society (now including the non-human part of nature). In the Conference, this call took the normative form of an injunction to "live well". This injunction has also been enshrined in the Constitutions of countries like Ecuador, Bolivia or Colombia since at least 1991.

VII. The Meaning of Life, or Paul via Dussel (… and Monthy Python)

The normative injunction "Live well", and "Life" as its material basis, are among the most basic building blocks of the theses on politics developed by Dussel, of which his text on Paul constitutes a further development. The notions of "life" and "living well" are directly related to his understanding of the (liberatory) event he names *kairós*, referencing Paul of Tarsus.

They are also at the core of his reading of Paul's criticism of the concept of Law as foundation. According to this reading, the (religious) criticism of the Law has three moments:

First, the moment of justification, or "the subsumption of the concrete (the actor or the praxis) in the universal (the criterion according to which the evaluative judgment is based)".[25]

Second, an exploration of the deeper meaning of law. Since at least Paul's *Epistle*, law is the criterion held as valid for all in the justification of the agent or his or her praxis. Put otherwise, the law determines a framework for the will 'as a criterion to be able to judge by differentiating what is just' from what violates the law. This allows good to be discerned from evil, and thus to avoid moral error by moving from the justification of present evil as necessary (as in 'lesser' or necessary evil, or as inevitable 'costs' or the collateral result of 'hard choices) to a recognition of the insufficiency of such justifications and the positing of a future-oriented criterion of justice.

As Dussel observes, starting with the figure of the Egyptian goddess *Ma'at* all the way up to the *nómos physikón* of the Greek, Roman Law or the Jewish *Toráh*, the function of the law is to give consciousness of—or make visible—moral error and sin.[26] This function is also discernible in the structure of classical tragedy as the double aspect of truth, as truthfulness (prior to) truth, as what is known only in part and what is not known, for instance, in the cases of Osiris, Oedipus and Orestes. In this structure, only the composition of two contradictory testimonies—one looking backwards for self-referential justification in the prevailing totality (the given), the other projecting it-

---

25. E Dussel, *The Liberatory Event of Paul of Tarsus* (2009) 8. He cites Romans, 1, 17.

26. Ibid. Dussel cites Romans, 3, 20.

self beyond the given (prophetic or speculative)—allows for the passage from the present order to the new order, i.e., from given truth to truthfulness or reflective judgment in Kantian parlance.

This passage entails the analysis of the given as both catastrophe and farce, as an explanation of the collapse of the law due to its fetishization. As a phenomenon, 'fetishization' also has a double aspect: first, a critique of self-sufficiency as mere surface appearance or the result of the projection of forms of composite causality into a figure of necessity so as to make it appear as unconditional or sufficient reason, and second, a recognition of the composite and contingent nature of all purportedly necessary entities.

The result of this analysis is ontological (i.e., anti-dogmatism, based on the refusal of the principle of sufficient reason) and ethical or ethopoetic (the recognition of the fragility of everything that exists, and also the recognition of our collective responsibility to create future environments for all). Literary archetypes like Osiris, Oedipus, Orestes, Moses, Paul, Quetzalcoatl or 'the Founding Fathers' symbolize and embody, in their quest, the journey of the mind and the community through these distinctions, and from error (down below) to truth (up above).[27]

Third, there is the event. Here, it is recognized that the Law presupposes a time prior to its dictation (chaos and slavery), another time of hope (Abraham's first Alliance, in the Judeo-Christian narrative) and a time of the first Law (for instance, the law pronounced by Moses in the desert during exile from slavery). In the Judeo-Christian narrative, the event of the first Law established the order still prevailing during Paul's time. This foundational event and constitution must in turn be distinguished, according to Dussel, from what happens in the second event, following the collapse of the Law based on the foundational event.

This is the point where the apocalyptic writings of John and Paul's *Letters* emerge as cogent critiques of the Law. If, on the one hand, the Law appears as the criterion for the justification of the praxis carried out in any given order, on the other, the Law also emerges, after negative critique, as that which "can nevertheless become fetichized and corrupted, falling into contradiction even with itself, and thereby producing its own collapse".[28] This is the case when it can be shown that the Law has been affirmed as the single most basic foundation of justification of the present order, thereby becoming the ultimate cause of itself, and thus, absolutely necessary and dogmatic. Then and only then, can the Law be criticized from the standpoint of the future, understood in the sense in which John referred to early Christians as "being in the world" but not "of this world" (John 17, 14-17). For Dussel, this occurs when the Law is situated above Life.[29]

What does this mean? On the one side it means to say that the truly ethical act is the questioning, transgression or disobedience of the Law. Both Abraham, in refusing to sacrifice his son, and Jesus, in curing the

---

27. See on the priority of truthfulness over truth and on ethopoetic devices E Mendieta 'The Ethics of (Not) Knowing. Take Care of Ethics and Knowledge Will Come of Its Own Accord', in *Decolonizing Epistemologies. Latino/a Theology and Philosophy* (2012) 247-264.

28. E Dussel, *The Liberatory Event of Paul of Tarsus* (2009) 8.

29. Here Dussel follows F Hinkelammert, *The Cry of the Subject: From the World Theater of the Gospel of John to the Dog Years of Globalization* (1998), *Hacia Una Crítica de la Razón Mítica: El Laberinto de la Modernidad* (2008), and *Das Sujekt und das Gesetz: Die Ruckkehr des verdrangten Subjekt* (2007). In relation to this problematic, Dussel refers also to the distinction between foundation, justification and application developed in volume II of his *Política de la Liberación* (2007) 377 ff. This distinction is made in relation to Kant's analysis of future-oriented 'reflective judgment' as distinct from backward-looking 'determinate' or purely empirical judgment. This means that what Dussel calls 'fetichization' involves the elevation of the past and the given order to the level of an absolute and necessary order for all times and in all places. This is also the danger of 'globalization' discourses in relation to the law: that it becomes 'globalism'. I use the term 'globalism' in the sense of the ideological element present in the justificatory discourse about globalization.

blind man during Sabbath, in speaking against the laws of debt and proceeding to angrily "cleanse" the temple from the law of value, and especially when he observed that the law in its fetishized state would demand such a degree of application that it can even produce death, and moreover, in giving testimony of this demand by being crucified, deny the law its power of serving as the basis for justification.[30]

On the other, this is in contrast to the attitude toward the law (and truth) that was typical of classical Greek-Roman as well as Jewish legalism. In the latter, exemplified by the cases of Ifigenia in the *Oresteiad*, Socrates in Plato's *Apology* or the members of the tribunal that condemned Jesus to death in the *New Testament*, and later on also in the imposition of the Law of Christendom across the globe, after the imperialization (and intellectual Platonization) of Christianity, we must accept the Law (and truth as the whole truth) to its final consequences: that is to say, even if its application entails the death of the innocent, which is justified either as an abuse of the Law by those who apply it or as a necessary sacrifice in the altar of law, (whole) truth, order, national interest, self-righteousness or economic wisdom. What cannot occur to the legalistic "classical" mind or to its "modern" reinvention as economic wisdom and pragmatic calculus is the questioning and denunciation of the law itself and the order it founds as fatal and murderous. And yet, this is precisely what the death of Jesus and its apocalyptic interpretation by John and Paul entail: not sacrifice but scandal, the revelation that the law itself has become unjust and that "the wisdom of this world" has turned sacrificial mythology into economic calculus, which it calls "reason".

---

30. E Dussel, *The Liberatory Event of Paul of Tarsus* (2009) 10. See also F Hinkelammert, *The Cry of the Subject* (1998) 45. Dussel cites John 8, 40-44.

VIII. What If Latin America Ruled the World? The World Turned Upside Down

How do we turn this state of affairs on its head? The starting point is the recognition of the fragility of everything that exists. Call it "the meaning of life", in a reference to the brilliant pun on necessitarianism put together by philosophical comedians Monthy Python in *The Life of Brian*. From this standpoint, we start form absolute contingency rather than from the idea of mechanical patterns or rules that can be revealed through natural reason as, ultimately, the unconditioned reason of everything that exists and is efficiently moved forward in our images of nature. Another way to put this is to assert Nature (like in the 2010 Conference referred to above) as a living organism going through cycles underpinned by fragility, rather than some *machina mundi*. In the first conception, predictability, in the sense of a calculus of probabilities and costs attempting to derive some measure of necessity from within the manifold of accidents and phenomena, is seen as form of metaphysical dogmatism—in short, as ideology.

With no figure of necessity, no ultimately unconditioned set of rules or no big other in supply (neither as transcendent divinity nor as *deus ex machina*), the image of nature becomes a token of our radical freedom rather than the realm of determinism. This radical freedom is always here and now as well as future-oriented, present in our recognition of sociality as something in which we partake, and which is always beyond us, in fact a step toward recognizing, precisely, the specificity and universality of our common world. Our radical freedom lies in our acknowledged commonality, which can only grow out of our recognition that as embodied beings we will always speak to each other from different perspectives, and of the humility that arises when we actually confront the truth that we must live in a field of commonality that is the world and nature. Philosophically speaking, in Dussel the injunction to "live well" and the notion of the infinite fragility of nature (Life) vis-à-vis the bad infinity of our dreams of unending progress (which is the theme of his first theses in *Twenty Theses on Politics*), take us in a movement that goes from inter-subjectivity (language, reason, normative prescriptions) to the key problem of communication, understood ontologically in the sense of proximity and vicarious relationality between contingently existent and gathered entities (human and non-human assemblages and disassemblages). [31]

Another name for this process, one that has been coined and developed in the philosophies of existence of Caribbean writers and phenomenologists more than by Dussel himself, but one whose use he would surely endorse, is "creolization". The term often refers to phenomena of semio-semantic hybridization within or across cultures. It involves the inversion of a word from its negative meaning to something more positive, or the kind of proximity that does not entail imitation but achieves originality.

Examples of this phenomenon in history would include the Haitian revolutionaries of the 1800s singing La Marseillaise to occupation Napoleonic forces, or the case of the Yoruba religion of Africa being Christianized in the Americas while Christianity was refigured through the gods and goddesses of Yoruba African religiosity. Both religions changed, becoming perhaps unrecognizable to defenders of (European) orthodoxy, but in the process revealing the importance of the revaluing and affirmation of indigenous and original values and ideals. Put otherwise, the result of this kind of hybridization is a composite (a vicarious or creolized entity) of a higher order, a new reality that cannot be judged from the standpoint of its components and in fact would have seemed implausible or improbable (and may remain invisible) from the standpoint of the previous situation.

We're no longer talking about particular "identity" here, but rather, about "position". And we have moved from morality or ethics—the art of leading by precepts or example—to the fundamentals of existence: newness, originality in time and space, a priori causality or composition, and the autonomy of human and non-human nature, what philosophers call "ontology".

At stake is the issue of newness in history and reality in the most general sense. And this is what Enrique Dussel, no doubt having in mind Walter Benjamin and other writers embedded in the Miltonian-Kantian tradition, refers to when he speaks of a "liberatory event".[32]

Notice that vicarious communication, which opens up the set of options for communication and relationality (rather than merely choosing a form of communication between a given set of options) makes it possible to cross not only between cultures but also between the realms of the human and the non-human, allowing for richer and original relations between us humans and our conceptions of technological advancement so central to our present way of life, on the one hand, and nature on the other. The point is to disengage the mind and its capacity for technological advancement from what is empirical in examples of the relation between technology, production and consumption in the present situation, thus achieving exemplarity.

Only then, it begins to make sense to speak of the Earth or Nature as being entitled to (strictly non-reciprocal, or "post-human") rights. But not in the sense of some restorative project bringing back a purely emotive and non-technological union with

---

31. E Dussel, *Twenty Theses on Politics* (2008).

32. On the Miltonian-Kantian tradition, and the notions of 'the sublime' and 'succession' emerginf from that tradition, see S Budick, *Kant and Milton* (2010) 253-306. For the precedents of Latin American liberation philosophy originating at the end of the colonial period, in the late eighteenth century, among thinkers and activists who were engaged with the language and forms developed within the trans-Atlantic Lascasian-Miltonian-Kantian constellation, see O Guardiola-Rivera, *What If Latin America Ruled the World?* (2010) 107-179.

nature that in fact has never existed. Rather, in the sense of challenging the assumed intrasystemic consistency of the system and the way of life we usually call "capitalism" (which assumes a necessary connection between technological advancement and capitalist production/consumption, in which the former is dependent upon the latter) by raising systemic critique from within, from the standpoint of the real and contingent future as well as our responsibility to create future environments for all.

This would be a critique of "necessity" and of figures of necessity, in particular the dogma concerning the supposedly inevitable character of capitalist globalization and its correlative image of the world as a unity divided between nations that lead by precepts, permanent authority and example (recently couched in pseudo-humanitarian language) and peoples willing to be led by precepts and example. This was already the point highlighted by those participating in the "older debates" (Las Casas or Milton in the sixteenth and seventeenth century; the German Miltonians, Francisco de Miranda, Thomas Paine, Anna Barbauld, Olaudah Equiano and Simón Bolívar in the eighteenth and nineteenth centuries; W. E. B. Du Bois, Ernest Cassirer, Walter Benjamin, Jacob Taubes, Hans Jonas, Frantz Fanon and Roberto Fernández Retamar in the twentieth century).

This is also the point that needs to be recognized in the "new debates" about theology and politics: what about the peoples of the world not willing to be led by precepts, the permanent authority of a handful of nations, and their paternalistic example? What if, say, Latin America ruled the world? So far, these peoples have all too often been dismissed as "anti-modernist", "unorthodox" or "rogue"; in a word, as "heretic". These apparently blunt terms are in fact simplistic, particularly in their inability to help us understand the perverse complexity and allure of heresy: the peoples of the world not willing to be led by given precepts and example are in fact striving for and toward freedom. They do not offer just another choice, an alternative choice within the given dichotomy between "leaders" and "led" (or "developed" and "underdeveloped'). Rather, they seek to open up the set of available options and to move from given examples to exemplarity. They are transforming our image of the world, changing in the process the terms of language and communication: freedom and contingency rather than necessity; post-development rather than linear and inevitable orientation in geopolitics and global economics; human and non-human rights instead of the pure reciprocity and equivalence of "humanitarian" international relations underpinned by the alleged moral superiority of some; redemption in the present for the sake of the future, rather than austerity and pre-emptive action to avert announced catastrophes brought about by "monstrous" peoples or greed.

Refigured in such terms, religion ceases to be a normative discourse that mixes paradoxically the impatience of the crusader with the pacifying effect of the soldier-therapist. Notice how those who argue that saving modernity means abolishing religion and those who choose to respond in kind by seeking to abolish modernity provide the background noise of such confusing mixture. The bitter *Kulturkampf* that we seem to have witnessed in Britain and the USA (also addressing the Islamic world) in the first decade of the twenty-first century, between secular science on the one hand and religious social Conservatism on the other, can be understood precisely in such terms.

IX. CONCLUSION: LAW, GLOBALIZATION AND RELIGION'S SECOND COMING

As religion becomes more and more globalized in the contemporary world of state-capitalist nations, it has come to be seen merely as a set of ideas or an external state of affairs, which can be surgically separated from the public conduct of business and from the religious person like a potentially dangerous tumor. For this perspective there is a straight choice between political theology and political philosophy, including legal theory. Another perspective observes that we may have anachronistically misunderstood the Great Separation conflicts that took place in the West between 1550 and 1648 merely as wars of religion, in a way that serves to bolster our mythical understanding of the state and its legal and political institutions as both a "protector" and a "savior" from religious fanaticism. Furthermore, others add, it is possible to trace a line of continuity between the apocalyptic dimensions of Christianity and other religions and the modern political projects that in the West and elsewhere have aimed at radical and even violent transformations of human society. It follows that attempting to "abolish religion" by suppressing it from public conversation merely succeeds in repressing it, leading to its ever more violent return. They point out, however, that fully integrating the primary human need for religion in public life does not mean establishing any one religion as public dogma.

There is plenty of heat and some light in these "new debates". However, at least two important dimensions seem to have been hitherto ignored by the debaters: first, as political theologian William T. Cavanaugh suggests, the conflicts originated in the West between 1550 and 1648 had a more global dimension, related to the emergence and justification of modern imperialism. This is the dimension that the archbishop of Chiapas Bartolomé de Las Casas emphasized in the 1550 debates at Valladolid, Spain, concerning the status of Amerindians as "even bellow slavery", and the right of the Christian Spanish Crown to occupy and exploit the resources of the New World.[33]

These debates helped inaugurating modern international law and laid the groundwork for a truly cosmopolitan political philosophy. They also coincided with the emergence of a specifically global mercantilist/capitalist market, on the back of the Spanish (American) Silver Peso and the massive displacement of labor force from Africa and elsewhere. The language and arguments of these debates challenged from within a venerable tradition known as philosophical geography that was received in medieval Europe by such people as Albertus Magnus.

Mixing elements of theology, cosmology and philosophy from at least four cultural sources—Greek, Semite, Arabic and European—with elements of law's autonomy, it set the coordinates of our modern "secular" images of the world. Geopolitics, development economics and cartography, but also the languages of ethno- and Euro-centrism and the Atlantic bias of international relations owe much to the recovery of this ancient tradition at the very point of origin of modernity. These were the languages that Immanuel Kant continued to explore in his lectures on Geography and Anthropology at the University of Könisberg in the late eighteenth century.

Second, the new debates constantly miss how much they imitate the older debates: for instance, the point about fully integrating religion in public life without establishing any one religion, made in contemporary times by writers like John Gray, was well understood by the eighteenth century generation of liberationist thinkers in the Americas inspired by Las Casas.[34] For instance, in one of the most important episodes of the struggles for liberation in the late eighteenth and early nineteen centuries, Venezuelan Francisco de Miranda likely discussed the point with philosopher Moses Mendelssohn during an encounter in

---

33. WT Cavanaugh, *The Myth of Religious Violence: Secular ideology and the Roots of Modern Conflict* (2009).

34. J Gray, *Black Mass: Apocalyptic Religion and the Death of Utopia* (2007). For a useful survey of the virulent critiques of religion offered recently by Richard Dawkins, Daniel Dennett, Christopher Hitchens and others, see T Beattie, *The New Atheists* (2007).

Germany in 1758. He tackled the issue once again in his 1801 draft of a Constitution for the projected Great Colombia.

Similarly, the scientific secularism of Richard Dawkins or Daniel Dennett tends to imitate the French Positivists, whose views were central in the institutional design of modern Latin American nations such as Mexico and Brazil.

What is missing in the "new debates" is a form of repetition that is not mere imitation, but includes also a new wager and an original understanding of legality and history. If the "new debates" remind us of the Pascalian theology of the wager—which argued that theism is the rationally correct option because betting my life on the assumption that there is no God cannot benefit me if I win "and could be disastrous if I lose"—liberation philosophers and theologians like Dussel posit another argument that takes into account belief and communal experience in an original way. As theologian Michael Kirwan observes, this is the argument of a mutual wager between the poor and God. The poor trust in God as their champion, the one who will liberate them from their suffering, while God "wagers on humanity, by daring to enter, repeatedly, into political partnership (covenant) with human beings" and importantly, by handing over his son.[35]

The Christological frame of the discussion may seem obscure at first, but it matters: on the one hand, it indicates that in order to move beyond imitation the debate between theology and politics must emphasize a God who wholly became man and positioned himself among the oppressed and the excluded, those who don't count and remain invisible in the present order. On the other hand, this means that what matters is to draw all the consequences from the basic event in this symbolical narrative, the death of God and his passing over into the love that binds the "children of God".[36]

The exact meaning of what it is to be "children of God" constitutes the crucial problem. As Dussel, points out, this is where Paul's *Epistles* can be interpreted as offering political and legal categories of implicit philosophical importance: "Humanity watches impatiently (apokaradokía) waiting for what it is to be children of God to be revealed" (Romans 8, 19). This passage contains the interpretive key that clarifies both the Christological framework and advances the ultimate consequences of its basic event. "The meaning of "being children of God" enunciated for the slaves, the oppressed, and the excluded", Dussel says, "is the moment of "ransom", the payment of freeing the slave or "redemption", a subject suggested so clearly by Walter Benjamin".[37]

According to this contextual reading, the writings of Paul "must be situated in the political economic context of the Roman Empire during the stage of consolidation of the structure of slave-based domination" and inequality, which provoked "an immense clamor among the growing majority of oppressed and exploited masses" reduced to live in conditions of anonymity and inexistence—that they make themselves free and autonomous. This is the question of succession and liberation.

The notion of "succession" became explicit in the writings of a trans-national constellation of thinkers and political activists whose agency became globally significant during the revolutionary events of the late 18th and early 19th centuries. Immanuel Kant, who may have coined the term, was one of them. So was the group of German writers who introduced elements of the Semitic tradition into the conversation, such as Moses Mendelssohn, taking on board a number of observations on the nature of the sublime—

---

35. M Kirwan, *Political Theology: A New Introduction* (2008) xii.

36. S Zizek, *Living in the End Times* (2010) 34. See also S Zizek & J Milbank, *The Monstrosity of Christ* (2009) and E Dussel, *The Liberatory Event of Paul of Tarsus* (2009) 4.

37. E Dussel, *The Liberatory Event of Paul of Tarsus* (2009) 4, n. 18.

not only in its aesthetic but also in its political significance.

These meanings and languages were the common currency of a trans-continental debate often traced back to Edmund Burke's reaction to the events of the French Revolution, radical agitation and religious dissent in Britain, and anti-slavery or revolutionary struggle in Haiti and elsewhere in the Americas. Moses Mendelssohn and Lessing were among the German group. Thomas Paine, Joseph Priestley, Thomas Spence, Mary Wollstonecraft, Anna Barbauld, William Blake, Olaudah Equiano and the "Spencean Abolitionists", among others, were active in various and different ways in Britain and the Americas, and engaged both Burke and the Germans but also the French, and some writers from the Americas.

Latin American liberationist thinkers and activists such as Venezuelan Francisco de Miranda and others, came in contact with members of these circles at various points in their lives and exchanged similar meanings and languages, but also traced their traditions of thought back to early anti-slavery and anti-imperialist writers such as the Archbishop of Chiapas Bartolomé de Las Casas.

All of them shared, in different ways, a conception of the earth as common treasury, of history as contingent and punctured by original events of succession (or "sublime" occurrences in history), of self-determination as the decisive experience of the common, and of normative orders—including law and religious mores—as based upon such a experience of "inner communal conversion". It is no coincidence that the early example of John Milton and the significance of the context, language and memory invoked by his poetry, featured prominently in these global exchanges.

Ultimately, the idea of "succession" at the basis of these conversations constitutes an answer to the question of the just order of a political community which is not a community of believers gathered around a singular dogma imitating on earth the order and hierarchy of the heavens up above and organizing the multiplicity of the community (and nature) under the rule of the One, an identity of origin and a singular orientation (fate, character, destiny or necessity) expanding into time and space, flattening the geography and the history of the entire planet in its fatal and fated embrace. Succession and the sublime event of liberation (or independence) oppose and remain the answer to, precisely, such ideas of order, dogma, hierarchy, orientation in time and space and planetary expansion or diffusion.

This question of "the community of those who have nothing in common"—other than the renewal of the common is at the very heart of more or less recent explorations of the figure of Paul as archetype. It serves also as an entry point for arguments concerning the nature of law, order and justice in the global situation. For instance, notice how the opposition set up at the end of the previous paragraph calls for another distinction between two conceptions of order and legality: let us then distinguish between "the law of succession" on the one hand, and "the law of imitation" on the other.

I call "imitation" the procedure by means of which the order of the multiple (e.g. all existing objects and entities) is submitted to a single point of origin, efficiency and finality (e.g. God, dogma, self-correcting progress, or any other figure of necessity). The latter is said to sustain the former, while the former is said to participate in the latter. This paradoxical relation, it is argued, corresponds to the eternally paradoxical existence of the point of origin and singular orientation (or "God" as pure relationship of mastery over creation); normatively, this entails a relation of dependency. Also, the notion that one's given world is merely an inheritance; that it is proper and can be appropriated, but not created anew.

I call "succession" the procedure by means of which the order of the multiple or the finite is received and organized into actually infinite assemblages, or disassembled from existing ones, thereby adding to reality. Nothing, no law of necessity underpins this process. It isn't a matter of efficient or final causes but rather a matter of structural arrangements and compositions, in which the component elements are never completely absorbed within the resulting composition. Politics is also about entering into and withdrawing from relations without losing our capacity to move on or move out. The commonality which results from our acts of assembling and disassembling is never some all-encompassing whole. Relations within it and against it are not dependent but liberating, in the sense of adding existence and reality. The world as it is can thus be recreated anew, for it isn't submitted to fate or necessity. Similarly, who we are and who we become is not a question of fate or character, but rather, of freedom and responsibility.

It seems to me that Enrique Dussel's conception of the event as *kairós*—as liberating practice that gives meaning to life by bringing new and unexpected configurations out of inexistence and into existence—corresponds precisely to the truth-procedure of succession. As such, it partakes of the most enlightening tradition of critique while decisively renewing it.

BIBLIOGRAPHY

Budick, Sanford. *Kant and Milton* (Harvard University Press, 2010).
Beattie, Tina. *The New Atheists: The Twilight of Reason and the War on Religion* (Darton, Longman and Todd, 2007).
Cavanaugh, William T. *The Myth of Religious Violence: Secular Ideology and the Roots of Modern Conflict* (Oxford University Press, 2009).
Compier, D.H., Pui-Lan, K. & Rieger, J. (eds.). *Empire & The Christian Tradition: New Readings of Classical Theologians* (Fortress Press, 2007).
Cornell, Drucilla. *Moral Images of Freedom. A Future for Critical Theory* (Rowman & Littlefield, 2007).
De Sousa Santos, Boaventura. 'A Non-Occidentalist West? Learned Ignorance and Ecology of Knowledge' 26 *Theory, Culture & Society* 7/8, 103-125 (2009).
Dussel, Enrique. "The Liberatory event in Paul of Tarsus", *in Qui Parle: Critical Humanities and Social Sciences*, tans. By George Cicarello-Maher, vol. 18, no. 1 (Fall/Winter 2009), and "El Evento Liberador en Pablo de Tarso", manuscript on file with the author (2009).
Dussel, Enrique. *Twenty Theses on Politics* (Duke University Press, 2008).
Dussel, Emrique. *Política de la Liberación, Volumen II* (Trotta, 2007).
Esquirol, Jorge. "Writing the Law of Latin America" 40 *The George Washington International Law Review*, 693-732 (2009).
Golder, Ben & Fitzpatrick, Peter. *Foucault's Law* (Routledge, 2009).
Gordon, Jane Anna & Gordon, Lewis R. *On Divine Warning. Reading Catastrophe in the Modern Age* (Paradigm, 2009).
Gordon, Lewis R. *Existentia Africana. Understanding Africana Existential Thought* (Routledge, 2000).
Gray, John. *Black Mass: Apocalyptic Religion and the Death of Utopia* (Penguin, 2007).
Guardiola-Rivera, Oscar. *Story of a Death Foretold. The Coup Against Salvador Allende, 11 September 1973* (Bloomsbury, 2013).
Guardiola-Rivera, Oscar. *What If Latin America Ruled the World?* (Bloomsbury, 2010).
Hinkelammert, Franz. *Hacia Una Crítica de la Razón Mítica: El Laberinto de la Modernidad* (Desde Abajo, 2008)
Hinkelammert, Franz. *Das Sujekt und das Gesetz: Die Ruckkehr des verdrangten Subjekt* (Inst. fur Theologie und Pol. 2007).
Hinkelammert, Franz. *The Cry of the Subject: From the World Theater of the Gospel of John to the Dog Years of Globalization* (Exodus Publishers,1998 and 2001).
Kermode, Frank. *The Classic: Literary Images of Permanence and Change* (Harvard University Press, 1983).
Kirwan, Michael. *Political Theology: A New Introduction* (Augsbrug Fortress Publ. 2008 and 2009).
Mahoney, J. & Rueschemeyer, D. *Comparative Historical Analysis in the Social Sciences* (Cambridge University Press, 2003).
Mendieta, Eduardo. 'The Ethics of (Not) Knowing. Take Care of Ethics and Knowledge Will Come of Its Own Accord', in *Decolo-*

nizing Epistemologies. Latino/a Theology and Philosophy (Fordham University Press, 2012).

Mendieta, Eduardo. *Global Fragments. Globalizations, Latinamericanisms, and Critical Theory* (State University of New York Press, 2007).

Ramadan, Tariq. *What I Believe* (Oxford University Press, 2009 and 2010).

Sutherland, John. 'Fierce Reading', *The Guardian*, Review, 16 (21/08/2010).

Twining, William. *General Jurisprudence: Understanding Law from a Global Perspective* (Cambridge University Press, 2009).

Twining, William. *Human Rights, Southern Voices* (Cambridge University Press, 2009).

Williams, Rowan. "Introduction", in *Theology and the Political: The New Debate*. Edited by Creston Davis, John Milbank and Slavoj Zizek (Duke University Press, 2005).

Zizek, Slavoj & Milbank, John. *The Monstrosity of Christ* (The MIT Press, 2009).

Zizek, Slavoj. *Living in the End Times* (Verso, 2010)

Zizek, Slavoj. *The Puppet and the Dwarf. The Perverse Core of Christianity* (The MIT Press, 2003).

HUMAN ARCHITECTURE: JOURNAL OF THE SOCIOLOGY OF SELF-KNOWLEDGE
A Publication of OKCIR: The Omar Khayyam Center for Integrative Research in Utopia, Mysticism, and Science (Utopystics)
ISSN: 1540-5699. © COPYRIGHT BY AHEAD PUBLISHING HOUSE (IMPRINT: OKCIR PRESS) AND AUTHORS. ALL RIGHTS RESERVED.

Philosophy, the Conquest, and the Meaning of Modernity

A Commentary on "Anti-Cartesian Meditations: On the Origin of the Philosophical Anti-Discourse of Modernity" by Enrique Dussel

Linda Martín Alcoff

Hunter College and the Graduate School, C.U.N.Y.

lmartina@hunter.cuny.edu

Abstract: This is a commentary on the article "Anti-Cartesian Meditations: On the Origins of the Philosophical Anti-Discourse of Modernity" by Enrique Dussel published in this issue of the journal. According to the author, Dussel's Anti-Cartesian Meditations suggest the following conclusions for a revisioning of the discipline of philosophy: (1) If, as Rorty suggests, the meaning of philosophy is simply the history of philosophy or whatever philosophers discuss, then European philosophy does not understand what philosophy is because it does not understand its own history of philosophy; (2) Given that Descartes' skeptical reasoning "I" is produced through conquest, and the claim of comparative supremacy of the specific individual against its cultural others, this is hardly a good foundation for a truly rational modernity. Such a source of reasoning is neither sufficient nor reliable in terms of knowing one's self or knowing others, or certainly in knowing how one's own ideas and beliefs are related to or influenced by those of others; (3) The revision of the history of rationalism, modernity, and epistemology suggested in Dussel's account suggests a new way to understand the relationship and connection between secularism and rationalism, loosening the hold of the sometimes dogmatic assumption that secularism is the only route to rationalism; (4) Despite the intensity of Dussel's critique, his work also suggests that there may be a way to usefully distinguish the modern from Modernity, or in other words to separate a genuinely normative sense of the modern as a reflexive operation of critique from the colonialist Modernity with its legacy of self-justification and false consciousness. In this case, there may be a way to salvage philosophy after all.

In his "Anti-Cartesian Meditations: On the Origin of the Philosophical Anti-Discourse of Modernity" (see the version on www.enriquedussel.com used for page citations below; it also appears in this issue of the journal) Enrique Dussel makes a major

---

Linda Martín Alcoff is Professor of Philosophy at Hunter College and the Graduate School, C.U.N.Y. She is a past President of the American Philosophical Association, Eastern Division. Her writings have focused on social identity and race, epistemology and politics, sexual violence, Foucault, Dussel, and Latino issues in philosophy. She has written two books and edited ten, including: *Visible Identities: Race, Gender and the Self* (Oxford 2006), which won the Frantz Fanon Award for 2009; *Real Knowing: New Versions of the Coherence Theory* (Cornell 1996); *Feminist Epistemologies* co-edited with Elizabeth Potter (Routledge, 1993); *Thinking From the Underside of History* co-edited with Eduardo Mendieta (Rowman & Littlefield, 2000); *Identities* co-edited with Eduardo Mendieta (Blackwell, 2002); *Identity Politics Reconsidered* co-edited with Michael Hames-Garcia, Satya Mohanty and Paula Moya (Palgrave, 2006); and *Constructing the Nation: A Race and Nationalism Reader* co-edited with Mariana Ortega (SUNY 2009); She is originally from Panama, but lives today happily in Brooklyn. For more info go to www.alcoff.com

contribution to the developing work in post-colonial philosophy, an area or subfield within philosophy that is not yet recognized by any major philosophical association or research department. Because this area of philosophy remains unrecognized, there is the real danger that Dussel's critical text will go unrecognized, just as Felipe Guaman Poma's did for so many generations. The problems and obstacles that Dussel analyzes in the history of philosophy have not by any means been solved, and they continue to threaten to disable the reception of his own contributions. In this commentary, therefore, I want to think through the issue of how Dussel's historical revisions affect the doing of philosophy, its conditions of reproduction particularly in contemporary graduate departments, and its own self-understanding of its history and current disciplinary definition.

Even today, in the 21st century, there are no required courses in post-colonial philosophy in any department in the Americas, no comprehensive exams or advisory committees in this area, no associations, conferences, or journals, no compendiums of the major papers, nor encyclopedic overviews. Nor do the various programming committees of the major philosophical organizations recognize this as an area that merits its share of panels at the annual conventions, alongside, for example, early modern philosophy or ethics. Post-colonial philosophy exists only in the sense that there exists scholarly work that would fit within such a rubric, but it does not exist in the sense of being an acknowledged reality or recognized category. "Post-colonial philosophy" is like the categories "alternative medicine" or "racism" or "sexual harassment" in the not too distant past, categories with a referent (plenty of referents, actually), but no recognized reality or accepted linguistic usage. Let me begin, then, with a characterization of what the area of post-colonial philosophy concerns, and how it relates to other subfields within the discipline, as a way of placing Dussel's own analyses within a legible framework.

The term "post-colonial" is meant to refer not to a period after colonialism but to the analysis of colonialism in relation to the formation of the modern capitalist world system.[1] Although most formalized systems of colonial administration have been dismantled, neo-colonialism is alive and well, colonialism lingers, and what Anibal Quijano calls the coloniality of power—or the organization of power and status through social identities constructed within colonial relations of production—remains as strong as ever in literature as well as in the meta-narratives of culture, history and global political conflict, the representations of the West and its others, and so on. Another way to put this is that colonial ideologies remain strongly influential of new discourses and new theories even in the contemporary moment. The project of post-colonialism is to trace out these influences, to search them out, even where we might imagine them not to have much relevance, as Dussel does here and in his other work in the philosophical sub-field of epistemology.

As we might imagine, colonial narratives have had the most influence over the canonical histories of western philosophy, its periodizations, its ways of categorizing the major periods, and its organization of geographical borders. Still in graduate schools today the history of philosophy is grouped within the following categories: Ancient (meaning fourth century Greece), Early Modern (meaning 17th century northwestern Europe, excluding Spain), Modern (meaning the same area in the 18th century),

---

1. I'm going to set aside here the ongoing debates over whether using the term "post-colonial" is a good idea. Although critics of the term have made some good points (about the fact that it may be historically misleading, has emerged in the metropoles in some problematic ways, covers too diverse a set of projects and theoretical approaches, etc.), in my view the limitations of the concept are no greater than those of any other large and unwieldy and politically problematic category, such as "modernism" or even "Latin America."

and Nineteenth and Twentieth Century (including here England, Scotland, the U.S., Canada, Germany, Austria, and France). More recently the borders are opening up to include philosophy from the Netherlands, Italy and Poland (the latter for mostly Logic), but this is clearly still remarkably narrow. In fact, if anything, the last two decades have witnessed a further narrowing of philosophy graduate-level departments. Chinese and Indian Philosophy used to be commonly found but today these are rarely taught. Analytic philosophy has narrowed the arena of discussion to such an extent that the history of philosophy itself is no longer valued as a critical area to be covered in any department aiming for excellence.

Dussel's "Anti-Cartesian Meditations" provides a meta-philosophical argument made via the history of philosophy, and as such is doubly marginalized: marginalized because it takes up the history of philosophy as key to understanding the domain of philosophy proper, and marginalized because it goes outside the usual restricted areas included in that history. Dussel's analysis provides critical commentary on the field of philosophy itself by the means of a reclamation of important foundations of the field that lay outside its acknowledged geographical domain, as well as an argument that, to the extent the concept of modernity has normative force, its foundation also lies outside the domain identified as the "West." But this alteration of the history of philosophy has implications for the content of philosophy, and not simply for the way in which we teach its history.

There are two main meta-philosophical positions on how to define philosophy, and these contrasting positions correlate to alternative accounts of the relationship of the history of philosophy to philosophy proper.

The first view, held by such figures as Richard Rorty, holds that philosophy should be defined simply by the historical content of its conversations. That is, rather than hewing to an essential method or agreed upon formulation of the great issues, philosophy should be understood as a dialogue, a Socratic dialogue, where the content of that dialogue cannot be set out in advance. As Rorty puts this, "There is only the dialogue."[2] Importantly, such a minimalist formulation is put forward by Rorty precisely in order to remain critically alive to the possibility of altering philosophy's own method and formulations, to remain open to historical transformation and cross-cultural challenges, and as a way to avoid cultural narrowness. Any other, more substantive, definition of philosophy would fall into such narrowness by presupposing an objectivity, a rationality, a critical methodology, a notion of philosophical rigor, all defined and fixed prior to transcultural engagement. This road is bankrupt, Rorty declares, arguing specifically that "the traditional Western metaphysico-epistemological way of firming up our habits simply isn't working anymore."[3] And on his view, if we give up on the belief in such a "trans-cultural rationality," all that is left is our continuous dialogue called philosophy. Thus, philosophy is coterminous with its history; in fact, it is defined *as* its history.

The second, alternative meta-philosophical position on how to define philosophy is more substantive, and would define it via a specified set of questions. As Bertrand Russell defined these, philosophy "aims at knowledge which gives unity and system to the body of the sciences."[4] Philosophy is restricted to the search for knowledge in metaphysics, logic, ethics, aesthetics, and epistemology. Such aims invoke

---

2. Rorty, "Solidarity or Objectivity?" in *Post-Analytic Philosophy* edited by John Rajchman and Cornel West. New York: Columbia University Press, 1985, p. 15.

3. Ibid, p. 15. See also Dussel's critique of Rorty's position in chapter six of *The Underside of Modernity: Apel, Ricoeur, Rorty, Taylor, and the Philosophy of Liberation* edited and translated by Eduardo Mendieta. Atlantic Highlands, New Jersey: Humanities Press, 1996.

4. See chapter XV of Bertrand Russell's *Problems of Philosophy*. London: Simon and Brown, 2013.

precisely the sort of delimitation of the field that Rorty worried would be arbitrary and self-limiting, by conferring legitimacy on those who would close the conversation around pre-determined formulations of the great questions, such as those that aim for an analysis of justified true belief, not gnosis, understanding, or persuasion. The language game of philosophy can be justifiably distinguished from ethnophilosophies, wisdom traditions, cosmographies, or other conversations that (coincidentally?) occur outside of Europe. It might also be ideologically grounded in ways it has no power to reflect upon.

We then have two alternative meta-philosophical positions about how to define philosophy: one that defines it in terms of whatever kinds of dialogue philosophers have, and the other that defines it via a specified content. The first runs into a circularity problem: without defining what philosophy is, how are we to accredit dialogic interlocutors with the title 'philosopher'? The second runs the serious danger of dogmatism, a supremely unphilosophical end, by setting into stone either a method or a set of privileged topics. Dussel's work helps us to become more politically and philosophically reflective about each of these formulations.

The problem with the conversation idea is that it is a continuous conversation among a restricted set—how is it determined who is included? How has the conversation been structurally affected by conditions of power? Who has been allowed to speak? The problem with the more substantive idea is that it polices the border of the language game via certain crucial questions that may be conditioned by external considerations unknown to the participants, i.e. a colonial unconscious. Thus, both approaches to defining the domain of philosophy need a post-colonial critique.

I.

Dussel has correctly put his finger on the key element holding up western supremacist ideology, or the idea that the West deserves to control and lead the world, and that key element is the progressivist timeline embedded in a particular geographical movement. Success at overcoming other societies is itself taken as sufficient proof of merit. But such reasoning is no better than the reasoning that holds that a victim of torture is more likely to tell the truth, or that a woman with rocks tied to her ankles who does not float when thrown into a pond is thereby proved not to be a witch. Neither procedure has anything to do with truth, nor does the success of colonizing barbarities.

Yet the widespread assumption is that might, or success, does in fact make right in the sense that it establishes merit in the form of intellectual and cultural superiority. Hence we need not open the conversation, or rethink our tried and true formulations of the great philosophical problems.

One might plausibly hold that there is something natural about the phenomena of rising cultures—such as Spain was in the 16th century or England in the 18th—treating other cultures who are declining as cultural has-beens. Youth, in its firmness and strength, always has a tendency to disrespect the infirmities of old age. Yet the Incan civilization was actually not much older than the Spanish; its earliest period began around 1200 A.C.E., and its expansion into an Empire is dated only from the 1440s, a bare 50 years before the first European ships arrived. Its decline was not of its own making but the result of conquest. The progressivist teleology of Europe which sanctions its expansion by a belief in its own superiority is not the natural by-product of a culture on the rise but the result of false narratives, occluded histories, burned books, and murdered scholars.

Dussel analyzes some of the false narratives in some detail. The concept of "modernity" is the central protagonist here, the redemptive figure that justifies the unfortunate slaughters and redeems the weakened and scattered survivors of genocide and enslavement by their assimilation to a better world. In the narrative of modernity, though, there must be a "we" who are, or become, modern, constructed alongside a "they" who are not. Dussel suggests the "they" comes in two categories: the Orient, which consists of a competing rich culture but one that is in decadent decline, and another consisting of the "South of Europe" that has never at any time had anything intellectual to offer the world. Here he sometimes moves confusingly between time frames, from the 16th century when the "south of Europe" was indeed in mastery, to the 18th century when Spain and Portugal were now themselves consigned to the South. Today, clearly, the south of Europe is consigned to a pre-modern oblivion.

Given the restricted "we" of the modernist narrative, the protagonist of the story is exclusive and particular even while imagining itself as universal and unbounded. Thus we have Hegel's unabashed claim that "Man discovers America, its treasures and its people"(4). This is the irrational unconscious which produces a self-contradictory narrative separating the universal "Man" from a particular group of people, an impossible narrative that only a consciousness steeped in *mauvaise foi* can accept without questioning. The obviousness of the modernist fallacies manifest, Dussel interestingly suggests, a bad conscience: "a restless conscience toward the injustice committed"(19). It is the desperation of an unacknowledged guilt that directs an otherwise critical and sane reasoning faculty to accept claims with insufficient evidence and outright contradictions, but that can provide reasons to resign oneself to the daily crimes of colonial empires.

But the principal element that makes the modernist narrative operate effectively as a plausible truth is that the critique of the conquest has been ruled out of bounds since the 16th century, when Las Casas lost, in every material sense even if not in an intellectual sense, his debate with Sepulveda. Sepulveda's arguments, as convoluted as they were, became law and policy, while Las Casas's were lost to the oblivion of isolated scholars. From this point forward, Dussel holds, "the right of the modern Europeans (and North Americans of the 20th century) to conquer the Planet would never again be discussed"(16). It is true that slavery came in for some small debate, with predictable results, and the rights of other cultures also merited some discussion, but it is striking that these neglected passages in Locke and Kant were largely ignored for 200 years until very recently.

Dussel claims that Sepulveda's triumph established the concept of modernity, that is, its alibi. If modernity was thought to equal something like cultural advancement, a claim notably made in relative terms or in relation to other specified cultures, then modernity's acquiescence to the colonialism that made its supremacy possible formed the foundation for the developments of modernist philosophy. The fact that modernist philosophy was aware at some level of its foundation in colonialism is manifest in its very attempt to develop an *ethical* and *political* justification for itself, and not just a meta-theoretical justification. This is an interesting claim.

II.

Dussel seems to use the term "modernity" in his essay in two different senses: (1) as a normative or evaluative term, which distinguishes between better and worse modes of thinking, and (2) as a descriptive term denoting the historical period post-Conquest.

For example, when he claims in regard to Las Casas that "we are dealing with the most rationally-argued work of early Modernity—the first modern philosophy" (24), he is using both senses in the same sentence, to denote the historical time frame as well as the positive enactment of rational thought. We might keep these two meanings distinct by using "modernity" to refer to the historically and geographically bounded sense of the term, that which has the "restless conscience" and is the object of Las Casas's critique, and using "modern" to refer to the positive element of thought that Modernity has falsely allocated only to itself. The modern in this latter instance, as he uses it to describe Las Casas's arguments, is that which is, necessarily, directed against Modernity. But what, precisely, does Dussel mean by the normative sense of the term? What makes a thought, or a philosophy, modern? Merely that it is critical of Modernity?[5]

Dussel's recasting of Descartes' purported invention of modern philosophy can shed some light on this question. Descartes' pride of place in the history of philosophy cannot be underestimated. As if from a dream, Descartes is portrayed as jumpstarting modernity single-handedly, and that much of the rest of modern philosophy is an engagement with Descartes. Thus he is the Father, the *paterfamilia*, of all that develops from the point of his writing until now. His skeptical turn is credited with inaugurating epistemology, his individualism created the first discussions in philosophy of mind as well as founding liberal political philosophy, his ruminations of God and evil reinstated the integrity of the philosophy of religion from its long period of Scholastic dogmatism, and his dualist hypotheses instigated the development of metaphysics. Descartes is even credited with initiating the philosophy of science and of mathematics! Plato and Aristotle are important, to be sure, but it is Descartes that put philosophy on the firm ground of the individual's reasoning intellect and made of it a fit collaborator with the burgeoning empirical sciences.

In recent years there have been new and interesting interpretations of Descartes that consider what his dream arguments might mean on multiple levels, and that, against previous decontextualized readings, develop analyses that refer to his European social context as playing an explanatory role[6] Feminists continue to debate whether Descartes' mind/body dualism and rational individualism have more utility for feminists or anti-feminists. Derrida and Foucault famously debated the concept of madness Descartes uses, whether it was purely a rhetorical device with deconstructive effects on knowledge claims or had a referent in Europe's growing fascination with the mad which led to the eventual development of disciplinary techniques. Epistemologists continue to debate the adequacy of his refutation of skepticism, and what its ultimate failure teaches us.[7] Without a doubt, Descartes' rich discourses and meditations lend themselves to multiple readings, literary and psychological as well as philosophical.

---

5. In other works Dussel develops and elaborates on the concept "transmodern" as a way to avoid the progressivist, Eurocentric timeline that the historical term Modernity seems always to imply. Even the most transgressive post-modernists, as he points out, do not escape this teleology and thus do not avoid replicating Eurocentrism in their works. In contrast to modernity, 'transmodern' avoids connoting a center/periphery world structure and can more easily accommodate the idea that all parts of the colonial assembly line were involved in making modernity possible. 'Transmodern' enacts a simultaneity where 'modernity' lends itself to a backwards and forwards timeline and geographically exclusive center. (See Alcoff, "Enrique Dussel's Transmodernism" *Transmodernity: Journal of Peripheral Cultural Productions of the Luso-Hispanic World.* Vol. 1:3, 2012, pp. 60-68). In his "Anti-Cartesian Meditations...," Dussel is taking on the historical narrative of modernity but he is also, I am suggesting, using, as well as transforming the positive valence of the idea of the "modern." The latter is not a descriptive term involving history and geography and is therefore not replaceable by the term transmodern.

6. See e.g. Susan Bordo, *The Flight to Objectivity: Essays on Cartesianism and Culture.* New York: SUNY Press, 1987; and *Feminist Interpretations of Descartes* edited by Susan Bordo State College. PA.: Pennsylvania State press, 1999.

7. See e.g. Ernest Sosa *A Virtue Epistemology: Apt Belief and Reflective Knowledge.* Volume One New York: Oxford, 2011.

Dussel's claim against the authoritative treatments of Descartes's role in the history of philosophy is, again, both historical and substantive, and addresses issues that are generally still ignored in the mammoth secondary literature. The central point is that Descartes is not a thinker without influences but, unsurprisingly, emerges out of an intellectual tradition just as the rest of us. Given the genuine importance of Descartes' writings, then, that (largely invisible) intellectual tradition that spawned Descartes deserves analysis and scrutiny, or one might say it merits analysis for having influenced such a thinker. Yet it has received little, and this is principally because Descartes' influences hail from what is now lumped into the category of the "south of Europe."

Dussel's evidence for this claim is cumulatively persuasive. Descartes was educated by Jesuits within the Jesuit tradition in which students were counseled to perform as individuals, to use their critical minds rather than only their capacity for memorization. This tradition was barely formed when Descartes began his studies: the Jesuit order was founded only in 1536. It came to the New World a short 13 years later, in 1549, and thus the development of Jesuit practice and thought was indelibly linked to the profound experiences of missionary work as well as management and institution building that it oversaw on a wide scale throughout the Americas. Thus Descartes' association with the Jesuits links him securely both to Spain and to the New World. The flow of intellectual influences across the Atlantic was both enormous and intense in this period, and thus it was not at all odd that Descartes studied logic from a work written by the well known Mexican philosopher of that period, Antonio Rubio.

There is more than a hint of coincidence in the method of Jesuit teaching and Descartes' later philosophical ideas. The need for a thorough and sustained 'examination of conscience' championed by the Jesuits in which the individual is led to a path of self-reflection and self-examination maps easily onto the *Meditations on First Philosophy*, first published in 1641, in which Descartes provides an uncanny, and courageous for the times, reportage of his innermost doubts and debates.[8] Such self-examination is also clearly evident in Descartes' *Passions of the Soul*, a work published in 1646, devoted to a detailed account of the emotions.[9] Moreover, Dussel traces Descartes' formative influences back to Fonseca, the Portuguese philosopher who influenced a generation of Jesuits. Fonseca's milieu was known as the Coimbrian philosophers and their principal topic of discussion was the concept of method, identified as "the art of reasoning about whatever probable question"(15). Another important influence Dussel tracks is Francisco Sanchez, the prestigious Portuguese philosopher who proposed to find a way to arrive at certainty through a process of doubt. Descartes' most influential work, *Discourse on Method*, published in 1637, attempts to set out the best way to conduct one's reasoning toward dispelling doubt and reaching truth, and in this text he uses doubt or the dubitability of a claim as an epistemic device for assessing the justificatory status of belief.[10]

In standard intellectual histories Descartes' influences are listed along with the late works of Aristotle, the Stoic school of Greek philosophy, and St. Augustine. Notice the mainly secular status of these influences (and Augustine's influences are less theological than concerning his self-examining, reflexive practice and his logical approach to questions of time and reality). One

---

8. Rene Descartes, *Meditations on First Philosophy: In which the existence of God and the distinction of the soul from the body are demonstrated*, translated by Donald A. Cress 3rd edition. Cambridge MA.: Hackett Publishing Co, 1993.

9. Rene Descartes, *The Passions of the Soul: An English translation of Les Passions de L'Ame*, translated by Steven H. Voss. Cambridge MA.: Hackett Publishing Co, 1990.

10. Rene Descartes, *Discourse on Method and Related Writings*, translated by Desmond M. Clark. New York: Penguin Books 2000.

of the interesting implications of Dussel's contextualization of Descartes' ideas is that the move from religious to secular philosophy is not as sharp a break in philosophy as it is often made out to be. Descartes' own final capitulation to the ominipotent God who secures the reliability of our perceptual and rational capacities is often treated as if it was only written for the censors, and the Evil Demon he constructs to give structure to his doubts often gets revised as an entirely secular threat, a la the Matrix. Dussel suggests, by contrast, that Descartes' solipsistic consciousness—the unique individual that thinks—is founded in Christian theological traditions, a hypothesis that would be hard to assess fairly without knowing the Jesuit influences Dussel highlights. The focus here would not be on Descartes' stated theological commitments but on the praxis of a searching self-examination that puts one's amorphous thoughts and feelings to analysis, and not just one's beliefs.

So the link here between the secular epistemological focus on method and doubt, on the one hand, and the practice of self-examination within Christianity, on the other, is not made on the basis of accepted doctrine so much as it is a kind of analytical practice. And it is a practice which has the aim of reaching certainty, a value clearly spanning across the secular/religious divide to unite religious and scientific quests. This hypothesis might gain support from both Nietzsche and Foucault, who give symptomatic readings of the Christian tradition that reveal its central importance for the development of a heightened interiority, a sense of the infinite possibilities of the subjective self, as infinite as the universe beyond. Both Nietzsche and Foucault focus on the self-examinations instituted as requisite Christian practice since the Council of Trent that convened in Italy in the 16th century and promulgated the confessional as a central practice of the penitent.

If we were to add Descartes' formulation of epistemology into this narrative, we might then be motivated to explore anew the role of certainty and individual self-examination in western epistemology, and to question these as necessarily central to the theory of knowledge. The quest for certainty, as many have noted, can lead to sterile projects on inconsequential matters and dissuade us from embarking on larger, more important, but more speculative and risky inquiry. We are much more likely to achieve certainty on mundane matters than matters of consequence. The centrality placed on individual self-examination steers us away from the idea that collective processes of knowing might indeed be more reliable than individual ones. In particular, the possibility of ideological influences on our individual certainties are unlikely to be uncovered in a purely individual process of self examination; to uncover ideology, we need (speculative) social theory, as well as collectives of diverse knowers with whom we can compare notes.

Thus I see Dussel's revisionist recasting of Descartes' philosophy as not only historically important for improving the accuracy of the history of ideas—in which case philosophers would continue to cast this as a sideline issue of interest only to historians and not to philosophers. Rather, Dussel's revisions suggest new lines of philosophical inquiry into not only Descartes but also the various philosophical theories he is crediting with developing, from epistemology to the philosophy of mind. If we read these in the context of the Jesuit tradition, our mostly secular western philosophers of today might finally be persuaded that Descartes's legacy is more problematic than they usually perceive it to be. In any case, there is a need for a fresh look at his ideas to understand their true meaning.

If we accept the basic legitimacy of Dussel's arguments, arguments that bring in the scholarly work of numerous others, mostly working in Spanish, on the links between Descartes and the Spanish and Portuguese 16th century, Descartes need not be toppled from the throne of originator all the way to a plagiarist imitator who provided no independent thought. This is not the argument Dussel is making as I understand it. But we cannot even assess the originality his ideas achieved without considering them against the background of Descartes' formative, known influences. Descartes himself remains a formative influence on others, an institution, and thus his position as Father of Modern Philosophy may be historically false but philosophically accurate. What is perhaps only of biographical interest is the role that Descartes apparently played in creating this legacy himself, when he declines to mention his influences and claims to have "invented" a new method for the achievement of certainty. But this provides further evidence in favor of Dussel's claim that Descartes inaugurated the *ego conquir*, the I who conquers, and that the foundation of western epistemology is based in an experience of global conquest and the consequent fallacious self-aggrandizement that follows.

III.

Despite Descartes' obviously secure status as the formative influence on the developments of western philosophy after the 16th century, and Las Casas's equally obvious lack of influence, Dussel claims that Las Casas wrote the "first modern philosophy." Let us look again at these peculiar claims Dussel makes and how the concept of the modern might be reconstructed from his argument. Can we salvage the concept, retrieving something genuinely normative from its colonial legacy?

Dussel claims (1) that Las Casas wrote the first modern philosophy, and that (2) Las Casas wrote the first criticism of modernity, and that (3) it is on the basis of Sepulveda's effective defense of the Conquest that "Modern European Philosophy" was established. These three claims can be made consistent if we take the "Modern" in "Modern European Philosophy" to be the same as the modern of modernity. If this is the case, then "Modern European Philosophy" is not modern, or not wholly modern, to the extent it is marred by a "restless conscience," a lack of self knowledge together with the absence of any skills or methods that might lead to self-knowledge. It is blustery, aggressive word play that theorizes justice and truth in the netherworld of male elite interrelationships while the enormous servant class scurries about its feet, unseen, unknown, and unremarked upon. Truly, this is not the sort of picture we generally associate with the modern period, the flowering of a reflective, critical thought.

Las Casas, then, is modern in the sense that he goes against this ethereal, transcending mode of thought and perception, to the extent he notices the class of servants, and more than simply noticing their labor, he notices their condition, their state, perhaps the expressions on their faces and what this may indicate about the subjective experiences of their lives. He takes note also of their cultural practices and beliefs, arguing that their behavior is just as predictable and conventional within this context as any Spaniard's. To be modern in this normative sense is to be materially and culturally aware, and to take one's immediate material and cultural surroundings as a fit subject, perhaps *the* fit subject, for philosophical thought.

So what conclusions does Dussel's Anti-Cartesian Meditations suggest for a revisioning of the discipline of philosophy? Four spring to mind:

(1) If, as Rorty suggests, the meaning of philosophy is simply the history of philosophy or whatever philosophers discuss, then European philosophy does not understand what philosophy is because it does not understand its own history of philosophy.

(2) Given that Descartes' skeptical, reasoning "I" is produced through conquest, and the claim of comparative supremacy of the specific individual against its

cultural others, this is hardly a good foundation for a truly rational modernity. Such a source of reasoning is neither sufficient nor reliable in terms of knowing one's self or knowing others, or certainly in knowing how one's own ideas and beliefs are related to or influenced by those of others.

(3) The revision of the history of rationalism, modernity, and epistemology suggested in Dussel's account suggests a new way to understand the relationship and connection between secularism and rationalism, loosening the hold of the sometimes dogmatic assumption that secularism is the only route to rationalism.

(4) Despite the intensity of Dussel's critique, his work also suggests that there may be a way to usefully distinguish the modern from Modernity, or in other words to separate a genuinely normative sense of the modern as a reflexive operation of critique from the colonialist Modernity with its legacy of self-justification and false consciousness. In this case, there may be a way to salvage philosophy after all.

Thoughts on Dussel's "Anti-Cartesian Meditations"

Lewis R. Gordon

University of Connecticut at Storrs

lewis.gordon@uconn.edu

Abstract: This is a commentary on the article "Anti-Cartesian Meditations: On the Origins of the Philosophical Anti-Discourse of Modernity" by Enrique Dussel published in this issue of the journal. The author argues that Dussel's argument raises several important considerations in the study of the epistemic and normative presuppositions of European modernity.

The argument of Dussel's "Anti-Cartesian Meditations: On the Origin of the Philosophical Anti-Discourse of Modernity" (as appears in this issue of the journal, trans. by George Ciccariello-Maher) is as follows:

Modern philosophy preceded Descartes's seventeenth-century reflections on method, certainty, and the centering of the *Cogito* by more than a hundred years in the writings of the Latin American Jesuits (or those Spanish Jesuits who spent time in the New World) who inspired his thought. They include Francisco Suárez (1548–617) and Francisco Sánchez (1551–1623), as well as the Jewish philosopher Gómez Pereira (1500–1567), who wrote philosophical works on metaphysics, method, and doubt, printed in many editions by the time of Descartes's birth. The formulation of *Cogito, ergo sum* is not original in Descartes, as is known by any historian of philosophy who took the time to read St. Augustine's *City of God* (book XI, 26). Although Descartes claimed not to have been inspired by St. Augustine, the evidence, Dussel argues, suggests otherwise. In fact, Descartes seems to have offered his ideas as though they came to him willy-nilly, without the influence of his Jesuit teachers. Suárez's impact, for instance, led to the prioritizing of mathematics as a model of abstract reasoning. Descartes diverged from his teachers, however, who understood the importance of philosophical anthropology—that is, the human question—as the central concern of first philosophy. This divergence had the catastrophic consequence of offering models of science made supposedly rigorous through the expulsion of human elements. The dehumanization of the human world, marked by the disunity of soul (*cogito*) and body, became the model of this turn. This premise of disunity was al-

---

Lewis R. Gordon is Professor of Philosophy, Africana Studies, and Judaic Studies at the University of Connecticut at Storrs. His books include *An Introduction to Africana Philosophy* (Cambridge UP, 2008) and, with Jane Anna Gordon, *Of Divine Warning: Reading Disaster in the Modern Age* (Paradigm Publishers, 2009). His website is: http://www.lewisrgordon.com/

ready receiving concrete manifestation in the presupposition of the Christian European as reality purged of supposed embodied vices of emotion and passion in a philosophical anthropology of the truly human as this disembodied Christian European archetype. The first sustained critique of this view was issued by Bartolomé de las Casas (1484–1566), whose struggles on behalf of the Amerindians required also a philosophical anthropology that respected their humanity and, in so doing, raised the question of the human being anew in ways that responded to the de facto violence of the emergent modernity. As a critique of the dehumanizing elements of that modernity, Las Casas's arguments entailed a political philosophy in which legitimation emerged *from* the people instead of through a logic imposed on them. This legitimating practice brought into suspension the presuppositions of unquestioned truth and offered, in its stead, *critique*, including immanent critique. That the legitimating question posed by Las Casas required asking the Amerindian points of view require engaging the thought of such indigenous American thinkers as the Quechuas Felipe Guamán Poma de Ayala (1535–after 1616), who argued that the indigenous peoples of the Americas represented the better elements of Christian values than the European Christians who conquered them. There has, in other words, always been a critique from what Dussel calls the Underside of [European] Modernity, and it involves the challenge to the presuppositions of that modernity when the humanity of its underside is brought into focus.

Dussel's argument raises several important considerations in the study of the epistemic and normative presuppositions of European modernity.

I write *European modernity* to bring into question the presumption of modernity's only being European. Understood as a relational phenomenon, modernity could be read in terms of what human beings in a given region consider to be the future direction of humanity. In this sense, ancient Km.t, known today as Egypt, once represented the modern. So, too, did Babylonia, Athens, Rome, Holy Rome (Constantinople), Andalusia, Ottoman Turkey (Istanbul), and then "Europe." This story is complicated by unique convergences and transformations as the conquered fused with the conqueror often into something new. Thus, out of Greco and Roman conquest of West Asia and North Africa emerged Rabbinic Judaism and Christianity, which led to Christendom through Constantine's conversion in the 4th century, and a shift in thinking as the cyclical cosmology of the northern Mediterranean was fused with the eschatological one of West Asia. The Muslim conquests of Christendom represented its own future as a new modern until the "Reconquest" in 1492 shifted the terrain from the Mediterranean to the Atlantic and inaugurated the epistemic ruptures of which Dussel writes. This new development is a transition from a theological naturalism (Christendom) to a secular ethnos (Europe) with a new development.

The logic of an old metaphysics of substance was brought to bear on the new problematic of human difference outside of the framework of Christian, Muslim, and Jew. Along with this new problematic of constructing a philosophical anthropology attuned to experiences of unfamiliar (though ultimately not genuinely radical) difference was also a conception of time that marked *this* modernity in ways different from other modernities—namely, the notion of unfolding, linear, and progressive time. This temporal scheme needed to account for its normative outcome without its original source—namely, the benevolence or at least expectation of G-d. As singular and linear, the presupposition of uniqueness emerged, and the result is a shift from *a* modernity to *the* modern, to *modernity itself*, came about as presumably isomorphic with European reality. In effect, Europe became metonymic of modernity.[1]

A fallacy, however, is the presumption that indigenous peoples became frozen in a premodern condition from which they wait to be reawakened as either relics of the past or ghosts of the present as other-than-modern.[2] It is fallacious because it presumes a limbo status, a form of coma, of indigenous peoples and their thought. That they continue to fight and to think throughout makes them always *present* in this modernity. They are thus neither premodern nor postmodern but through-and-through modern. They exemplify, in a sense, what Paget Henry, drawing upon the thought of W.E.B. Du Bois, calls the potentiated double consciousness of humanity's global modernity.[3]

Double consciousness, according to Du Bois, had two stages. The first is the perception of the self through the eyes of the hostile or dominating Other. In Dussel's analysis, this would be the conception of Amerindians and Africans as posed by Ginés de Sepúlveda (1489–1573), who argued against their humanity. The acceptance of Sepúlveda's position, especially by indigenous peoples, would be the first form of double consciousness, since they would have been aware of the Spaniard's perspectives and theirs as the construction of the negative point of view. Potentiated double consciousness comes to the fore, however, from seeing the errors of those two initial perspectives, through subjecting them to critique and drawing out their contradictions. This, in effect, is what Las Casas and Guamán (among others) did: a Spaniard and a Quechuas both rejected the first stage of double consciousness through addressing the important missing premise—the humanity of indigenous peoples. Du Bois would also put it this way: the first form of double consciousness made indigenous people into problems. Potentiated double consciousness identified the problem of doing that and offered instead an understanding of the people as *facing problems instead of being them*. The obvious problem they faced was the assault on their humanity posed by conquest.

The critique of European modernity also required two additional elements, the first of which is addressed in Dussel's essay and the second of which only receives a hint of possibility through his evocation and questioning of Emmanuel Levinas. The first is the epistemic-metaphysical presuppositions that led to what Frantz Fanon called the attempted murder of man or, more properly, humanity. We could call this correlate of colonialism and conquest *epistemic coloni-*

---

1. This portrait emerges in a variety of ways in a broad spectrum of thinkers, in addition to Dussel. See, e.g., Hans Blumenberg, *The Legitimacy of the Modern Age*, trans. Robert M. Wallace (Cambridge, MA: MIT Press, 1985), Cedric Robinson, *An Anthropology of Marxism* (Aldershot, UK: Ashgate, 2001); Margaret R. Greer, Walter D. Mignolo, and Maureen Quilligan (eds.), *Rereading the Black Legend: The Discourses of Religious and Racial Difference in the Renaissance Empires* (Chicago: University of Chicago Press, 2007); Walter Mignolo, *The Darker Side of Western Modernity: Global Futures, Decolonial Options* (Durham, NC: Duke University Press, 2012); Nelson Maldonado-Torres, *Against War: Views from the Underside of Modernity* (Durham, NC: Duke University Press, 2008).

2. I offer a more detailed critique of this fallacy in Lewis R. Gordon, "On the Temporality of Indigenous Identity," in *The Politics of Identity: Emerging Indigeneity*, edited by Michelle Harris, Martin Nakata, and Bronwyn Carlson (Sydney, Australia: UTSePress, 2013), pp. 60–78; "Justice Otherwise: Thoughts on uBuntu," in *UBuntu: Curating the Archive*, edited by Leonhard Praeg (Scottsville, South Africa: University of KwaZulu Natal Press, 2013); see also my brief critique of primitivism and temporal displacement in my entry, "Race," in Mark Bevir and Naomi Choi (eds.), *Encyclopedia of Political Theory*, Vol. 3 (Thousand Oaks, CA: Sage Publishers, 2010), pp. 1133–1141.

3. See Paget Henry, "Africana Phenomenology: Its Philosophical Implications," *The C. L. R. James Journal* 11, no. 1 (2005): 79–112. For Du Bois's treatment, see 11W. E. B. Du Bois, *The Conservation of the Races* (Washington, DC: The American Negro Academy, 1898); *The Souls of Black Folk* (Chicago: A. C. McClurg & Co., 1903); *Dusk of Dawn: An Essay Toward an Autobiography of a Race Concept* (New York: Harcourt, Brace & Co., 1940); and *John Brown* (Philadelphia: G. W. Jacobs & Co., 1909), and for more discussion, see Lewis R. Gordon, *Existentia Africana: Understanding Africana Existential Thought* (New York: Routledge, 2000), chapter 4, "What Does It Mean To Be a Problem?," pp. 62–95.

zation, against which, with Dussel as inspiration, there emerges what Walter Mignolo and Nelson Maldonado-Torres call the *decolonial turn*.[4] The focus of that turn or, as Mignolo recently articulated it, *option*, is epistemic decolonization. The second consideration pertains to what I shall here call *normative decolonization*. It demands a radical critique of the normative presuppositions of Euro-global modernity.

To understand the second critique, in effect a form of decolonial critique of practical reason, consider these thoughts posed in the South African context, which, I hope will be evident, has much resonance for the Amerindian one. There is much discussion today about the normative term *uBuntu* used across the various indigenous ethnic groups of South Africa and now adopted, as well, among some of the post-apartheid people of European descent. The term is defined thus by P. Mabogo More:

> In one sense *ubuntu* is a philosophical concept forming the basis of relationships, especially ethical behaviour. In another sense, it is a traditional politico-ideological concept referring to socio-political action. As a moral or ethical concept, it is a point of view according to which moral practices are founded exclusively on consideration and enhancement of human well-being; a preoccupation with 'human'. It enjoins that what is morally good is what brings dignity, respect, contentment, and prosperity to others, self and the community at large. *uBuntu* is a demand for respect for persons no matter what their circumstances may be.
>
> In its politico-ideological sense it is a principle for all forms of social or political relationships. It enjoins and makes for peace and social harmony by encouraging the practice of sharing in all forms of communal existence.[5]

Read as an indigenous concept, discussions of *uBuntu* are often straitjacketed by discourses of authenticity, traditionalism, and even primitivism. Yet a brief interrogation of More's definition reveals its peculiar relevance to *modern* debates, including a unique challenge to the metanormative status of certain dominating concepts of Euro-modern thought. For example, the claim of the universal translatability of the English word *justice* is an extraordinarily presumptive one. Is *justice* as John Rawls and many of us in the English language use it really identical to the ancient Greek word δίκη (*dikē*) or, when engaged philosophically, δικαιοσύνη (*dikaiosune*)? Or how about the Km.t or ancient Egyptian word 𓐙 (*maat* or *ma'at*)? As we offer the variety of normative concepts with which to examine the proper ordering of a society, why couldn't one bring to the table the normative ideals, that to which to aspire at the societal level, from the elements of a society that reaches out and attempts to speak to the rest of humanity? In other words, what might emerge from the question not of the justice of *uBuntu* or whether *uBuntu* is a form of justice but the *uBuntu* (or other Amerindian concept) of justice?[6]

This rather unusual formulation to some should rightfully suggest a point of

---

4. See Maldonado-Torres, *Against War* and Mignolo, *The Darker Side of Western Modernity*.

5. P. Mabogo More, "South Africa under and after Apartheid," in Kwasi Wiredu (ed.), *A companion to African Philosophy* (Oxford, Blackwell Publishing, 2006), 149 and 156-157. A variety of expanded definitions are offered in Drucilla Cornell and Noyoko Muvangua (eds.), *Law in the Ubuntu of South Africa* (New York: Fordham University Press, 2012).

6. For a brilliant study of this question in the context of Amerindians in Colombia, especially with regard to challenges of human rights, see Julia Suárez Krabbe, "At the Pace of Cassiopeia Being, Nonbeing, Human Rights and Development" (Roskilde, Denmark: Roskilde University School of Intercultural Studies Doctoral Thesis, 2011).

continuity and differentiation. For it would be correct to say there are points of normative convergence of justice and *uBuntu* (and varieties of other indigenous concepts in Africa and the Americas), but the extent to which they are identical should occasion pause. I say this for the same reasons of consideration with *'dikē'* and *'ma'at'* (although *ma'at* is closer to *uBuntu* than *dikē* because of its significance also for *truth*). Here, I am drawing on an insight from the famed Ghanaian philosopher Kwasi Wiredu, who in his excellent and underappreciated *Cultural Universals and Particulars*, argued simultaneously for universality and specificity through focus on the human capacity for communication.[7]

Although not all cultural concepts are translatable—that is, there isn't complete linguistic isomorphism across human languages—it doesn't follow that their meanings cannot be *learned*. Anyone who has acquired language can in principle learn a concept from another language *in its own terms*. Thus, the significance of *uBuntu* is not so much a matter of definition, although that intellectual exercise is not short of importance, but of *understanding*. If this is correct, then a question posed to patrons and matrons of justice is this: could they not be defending a concept offered as universal when it is in fact particular? If so, this may mean that some of the indigenous concepts as continued critiques of Euro-modern normativity—like the challenge of potentiated double consciousness—is broader in scope, more universal, than justice. This is not to say that justice does not offer its necessary conditions in the arena of normative human life; it is to say that while necessary, it may be insufficient precisely because it is blind to its own hegemonic conditions. It is possible, for instance, to talk about justice without once prioritizing the humanity of the subjects to whom it has been historically misapplied. That is why modern European conquest and colonization could assert themselves ironically often *in the name of justice*. To respond that such efforts were false justice is, in many ways, to beg the question of justice's scope. There may be a point at which a different term is needed to evaluate justice, and that one may require attunement to the human reality by which that critique could emerge. We see here, then, the human question coming to the fore with the normative question.

Dussel's closing lamentation—"Levinas remains inevitably Eurocentric, despite discovering the irrationality of the totalization of modern subjectivity, since he could not situate himself in the exteriority of metropolitan, imperial, and capitalist Europe"—could also be formulated as an encomium on what needs to be done when justice is not enough. The radicality of this additional decolonial turn, which will no doubt point to the political actions needed to address the human being who continues to suffer under the weight of a profoundly and inhumanly imposed system of justice, demands interrogation into the normative when justice is, at the end of the day, not enough but beyond which waits the better underside of human life.

---

7. Kwasi Wiredu, *Cultural Universals and Particulars* (Bloomington, IN: Indiana University Press, 1996).

HUMAN ARCHITECTURE: JOURNAL OF THE SOCIOLOGY OF SELF-KNOWLEDGE
A Publication of OKCIR: The Omar Khayyam Center for Integrative Research in Utopia, Mysticism, and Science (Utopystics)
ISSN: 1540-5699. © COPYRIGHT BY AHEAD PUBLISHING HOUSE (IMPRINT: OKCIR PRESS) AND AUTHORS. ALL RIGHTS RESERVED.

The Structure of Knowledge in Westernized Universities
Epistemic Racism/Sexism and the Four Genocides/Epistemicides of the Long 16th Century

Ramón Grosfoguel

U.C. Berkeley

grosfogu@berkeley.edu

Abstract: This article is inspired by Enrique Dussel's historical and philosophical work on Cartesian philosophy and the conquest of the Americas. It discusses the epistemic racism/sexism that is foundational to the knowledge structures of the Westernized University. The article proposes that the epistemic privilege of Western Man in Westenized Universities' structures of knowledge is the result of four genocides/epistemicides in the long 16th century (against Jewish and Muslim origin population in the conquest of Al-Andalus, against indigenous people in the conquest of the Americas, against Africans kidnapped and enslaved in the Americas and against women burned alive, accused of being witches in Europe). The article proposes that Dussel's argument in the sense that the condition of possibility for the mid-17th century Cartesian "I think, therefore I am" (ego cogito) is the 150 years of "I conquer, therefor I am" (ego conquiro) is historically mediated by the genocide/epistemicide of the "I exterminate, therefore I am" (ego extermino). The 'I exterminate' is the socio-historical structural mediation between the idolatric 'I think' and the 'I conquer.'

I. INTRODUCTION

The work of Enrique Dussel, liberation theologian and liberation philosopher, is fundamental for anybody interested in the decolonization of knowledge and power. He has published more than 65 books. His titanic effort has been dedicated to demolish the philosophical foundations and world-historical narratives of Eurocentrism. He has not only deconstructed dominant knowledge structures but also constructed a body of work in Ethics, Political Philosophy and Political Economy that has been internationally very influential. His work embraces many fields of scholarship such as Political-Economy, World-History, and Philosophy, among others.

Ramón Grosfoguel is Associate Professor of Ethnic Studies at the University of California, Berkeley, and a Senior Research Associate of the Maison des Sciences de l'Homme in Paris. He has published many articles and books on the political economy of the world-system and on Caribbean migrations to Western Europe and the United States.

This article has been inspired by Dussel's critique of Cartesian philosophy and by his world-historical work on the conquest of the Americas in the long 16th century.[1] Inspired by Dussel's insights, the article adds another dimension to his many contributions by looking at the conquest of the Americas in relation to three other world-historical processes such as the Conquest of Al-Andalus, the enslavement of Africans in the Americas and the killing of millions of women burned alive in Europe accused of being witches in relation to knowledge structures.[2] As Dussel focused on the genocidal logic of the conquest, this article draws the implications of the four genocides of the 16th century to what Boaventura de Sousa Santos (2010) calls "epistemicide," that is, the extermination of knowledge and ways of knowing. The focus of this article is fundamentally on the emergence of modern/colonial structures of knowledge as the foundational epistemology of Westernized universities and its implications for the decolonization of knowledge.

The main questions addressed are the following: How is it possible that the canon of thought in all the disciplines of the Social Sciences and Humanities in the *Westernized university* (Grosfoguel 2012) is based on the knowledge produced by a few men from five countries in Western Europe (Italy, France, England, Germany and the USA)? How is it possible that men from these five countries achieved such an epistemic privilege to the point that their knowledge today is considered superior over the knowledge of the rest of the world? How did they come to monopolize the authority of knowledge in the world? Why is it that what we know today as social, historical, philosophical, or Critical Theory is based on the socio-historical experience and world views of men from these five countries? When one enters any department in the Social Sciences or the Humanities, the canon of thought to be learned is fundamentally founded on theory produced by men of the five Western European countries outlined before (de Sousa Santos 2010).

However, if theory emerges from the conceptualization based on the social/historical experiences and sensibilities as well as world views of particular spaces and bodies, then social scientific theories or any theory limited to the experience and world view of only five countries in the world are, to say the least, provincial. But this provincialism is disguised under a discourse about "universality." The pretension is that the knowledge produced by men of these five countries has the magical effect of universal capacity, that is, their theories are supposed to be sufficient to explain the social/historical realities of the rest of the world. As a result, our job in the Westernized university is basically reduced to that of learning these theories born from the experience and problems of a particular region of the world (five countries in Western Europe) with its own particular time/space dimensions and "applying" them to other geographical locations even if the experience and time/space of the former are quite different from the latter. These social theories based on the social-historical experience of men of five countries constitute the foundation of the Social Sciences and the Humanities in the Westernized universities today. The other side of this epistemic privilege is epistemic inferiority. Epistemic privilege and epistemic inferiority are two sides of the same

---

1. The Long 16th Century is the formulation of French historian, Fernand Braudel, who has influenced the work of world-system scholar, Immanuel Wallerstein (1974). It refers to the 200 years that covers the period between 1450-1650. This is the period of the formation of a new historical system named by Wallerstein as the Modern World-System, or the European World-Economy, or the Capitalist World-Economy. The historical process that formed this new system covers the 200 years of the long 16th century. I will use Long 16th Century to refer to the long durée processes that cover the initial formation of this historical system and use the term 16th century to refer to the 1500s.

2. I believe that the best hommage to an intelectual is to take his/her work seriously to bring new aspects provoked by their work.

coin. The coin is called epistemic racism/sexism (Grosfoguel 2012).

In Westernized universities, the knowledge produced by other epistemologies, cosmologies, and world views arising from other world-regions with diverse time/space dimensions and characterized by different geopolitics and body-politics of knowledge are considered "inferior" in relation to the "superior" knowledge produced by the few Western men of five countries that compose the canon of thought in the Humanities and the Social Sciences. The knowledge produced from the social/historical experiences and world views of the Global South, also known as "non-Western," are considered inferior and not part of the canon of thought. Moreover, knowledge produced by women (Western or non-Western) are also regarded as inferior and outcast from the canon of thought. The foundational structures of knowledge of the Westernized university are simultaneously epistemically racist and sexist. What are the world-historical processes that produced structures of knowledge founded on *epistemic racism/sexism*?

To answer these questions, we need to go back several centuries and discuss the formation of racism/sexism in the modern world and its relation to the long durée of modern structures of knowledge. Since the Cartesian legacy has been so influential in Western structures of knowledge, this article begins in the first part with a discussion on Cartesian philosophy. The second part is on the Conquest of Al-Andalus. The third part is on the conquest of the Americas and its implications for the population of Muslim and Jewish origin in 16th century Spain as well as for African population kidnapped in Africa and enslaved in the Americas. The fourth part is on the genocide/epistemicide against Indo-European women burned alive by the Christian Church accused of being witches. The last part is on Enrique Dussel's project of transmodernity and what it means to decolonize the Westernize university.

II. Cartesian Philosophy

We need to begin any discussion of the structures of knowledge in Westernized universities with Cartesian philosophy. Modern philosophy is supposed to have been founded by Rene Descartes (2013).[3] Descartes' most famous phrase "I think, therefore I am" constitutes a new foundation of knowledge that challenged Christendom's[4] authority of knowledge since the Roman Empire. The new foundation of knowledge produced by Cartesianism is not anymore the Christian God but this new "I." Although Descartes never defines who this "I" is, it is clear that in his philosophy this "I" replaces God as the new foundation of knowledge and its attributes constitute a secularization of the attributes of the Christian God. For Descartes, the "I" can produce a knowledge that is truth beyond time and space, universal in the sense that it is unconditioned by any particularity—"objective" being understood as equal to "neutrality" and equivalent to a God-Eye view.

To make the claim of an "I" that produces knowledge equivalent to a God-Eye view, Descartes makes two main arguments: one is ontological and the other epistemological. Both arguments constitute the condition of possibility for the claim that this "I" can produce a knowledge that is equivalent to a God-Eye view. The first argument is ontological dualism. Descartes claims that the mind is of a different substance from the body. This allows for the mind to be undetermined, unconditioned by the body. This way Descartes can claim that the mind is

---

3. I said "supposed" because as Enrique Dussel (2008a) has demonstrated in his essay Anti-Cartesian Meditations, Descartes was highly influenced by the Christian philosophers of the Spanish conquest of the Americas.

4. Notice that I make a distinction between Christianity and Christendom. Christianity is a spiritual/religious tradition, Christendom is when Christianity becomes a dominant ideology used by the state. Christendom emerged in the 4th century after Christ when Constantine appropriated Christianity and turn it into the official ideology of the Roman Empire.

similar to the Christian God, floating in heaven, undetermined by anything terrestrial and that it can produce a knowledge equivalent to a God-Eye view. The *universality* here is equal to Christian God's universality in the sense that it is not determined by any particularity, it is beyond any particular condition or existence. The image of God in Christendom is that of a White, old, bearded man with a cane sitting in a cloud, watching everybody and punishing anybody who misbehaves.

What would happen to the "God-Eye view" argument if the mind is of a similar substance to the body? The main implication would be that the claim that a human "I" can produce a God-Eye view falls apart. Without ontological dualism, the mind would be located in a body, would be similar in substance to the body and, thus, conditioned by the body. The latter would mean that knowledge is produced from a particular space in the world and, thus, there is no unsituated knowledge production. If this is the case, then it cannot be argued anymore that a human "I" can produce a knowledge equivalent to a God-Eye view.[5]

The second argument of Descartes is epistemological. He claims that the only way the "I" can achieve certitude in knowledge production is through the method of solipsism. How can the "I" fight skepticism and be able to achieve certitude in knowledge production? The answer given by Descartes is that this could be achieved through an internal monologue of the subject with himself (the gender here is not accidental for reasons that will be explained later). With the method of solipsism, the subject asks and answers questions in an internal monologue until it reaches certitude in knowledge. What would happen if human subjects produce knowledge dialogically, that is, in social relations with other human beings? The main implication would be that the claim about an "I" that can produce cer-

5. For a very interesting discussion on this question see Enrique Dussel (1995) and Donna Haraway (1988).

titude in knowledge isolated from social relations with other human beings falls apart. Without epistemic solipsism, the "I" would be located in particular social relations, in particular social/historical contexts and, thus, there is no *monological, unsituated* and *asocial* knowledge production. If knowledge is produced in particular social relations, that is, inside a particular society, then it cannot be argued that the human "I" can produce a knowledge equivalent to a God Eye view.

Cartesian philosophy have been highly influential in Westernized projects of knowledge production. The unsituatedness of Descartes' philosophy inaugurated the ego-politics of knowledge: an "I" that assumes itself to be producing a knowledge from no-where. As Colombian philosopher, Santiago Castro-Gomez (2003) argues, Cartesian philosophy assumes a point zero epistemology, that is, a point of view that do not assumes itself as a point of view. The importance of Rene Descartes for Westernized epistemology can be seen in that after 370 years, Westernized universities still carry the Cartesian legacy as a criteria of validity for science and knowledge production. Even those who are critical of Cartesian philosophy, still use it as criteria for what differentiates science from non-science. The "subject-object" split, "objectivity" understood as "neutrality," the myth of an EGO that produces "unbiased" knowledge unconditioned by its body or space location, the idea of knowledge as produced through an internal monologue without links with other human beings and universality understood as beyond any particularity are still the criteria for valid knowledge and science used in the disciplines of the Westernized university. Any knowledge that claims to be situated in body-politics of knowledge (Anzaldúa 1987; Frantz Fanon 2010) or geo-politics of knowledge (Dussel 1977) as opposed to the myth of the unsituated knowledge of the Cartesian ego-politics of knowledge is discarded as biased, invalid, irrelevant, unserious, that is, inferior knowledge.

What is relevant to the "Western men tradition of thought" inaugurated by Cartesian philosophy is that it constituted a world-historical event. Prior to Descartes, no tradition of thought claimed to produce an unsituated knowledge that is God-like or equivalent to God. This *idolatric universalism* of "Western men tradition of thought" inaugurated by Descartes (2013) in 1637, pretends to replace God and produce a knowledge that is God-like. The Dusselian questions are: What are the political, economic, historical, and cultural conditions of possibility for someone in the mid-seventeenth century to produce a philosophy that claims to be equivalent to God's Eye and to replace God? Who is speaking and from which body-politics of knowledge or geo-politics of knowledge is he speaking from?

Enrique Dussel (2005) responds to these questions with the following argument: Descartes' "I think, therefore I am" is preceded by 150 years of "I conquer, therefore I am." The *ego conquiro* is the condition of possibility of Descartes's *ego cogito*. According to Dussel, the arrogant and idolatric God-like pretention of Cartesian philosophy is coming from the perspective of someone who thinks of himself as the center of the world because he has already conquered the world. Who is this being? According to Dussel (2005), this is the *Imperial Being*. The "I conquer" that began with the European men colonial expansion in 1492, is the foundation and condition of possibility of the "I think" that secularizes all the attributes of the Christian God and replaces God as the new foundation of knowledge. Once European men conquered the world, God is disposable as a foundation of knowledge. After having conquered the world, European man achieve "God-like" qualities that gave them epistemic privilege.

However, there is a missing link between the "I conquer, therefore I am" and the "I think, therefore I am." There is no inherent necessity to derive from the "I conquer, therefore I am" the "idolatric universalism" (the God-Eye view) nor the "epistemic racism/sexism" (the inferiority of all knowledges coming from human beings that are classified as non-Western). What links the "I conquer, therefore I am" (*ego conquiro*) with the idolatric, God-like "I think, therfore I am" (*ego cogito*) is the epistemic racism/sexism produced from the "I exterminate, therefore I am" (*ego extermino*). It is the logic of genocide/epistemicide together that mediates the "I conquer" with the epistemic racism/sexism of the "I think" as the new foundation of knowledge in the modern/colonial world. The *ego extermino* is the socio-historical structural condition that makes possible the link of the *ego conquiro* with the *ego cogito*. In what follows, it will be argued that the four genocides/epistemicides of the long 16th century are the socio-historical condition of possibility for the transformation of the "I conquer, therefore I am" into the epistemic racism/sexism of the "I think, therefore I am." These four genocides/epistemicides in the long 16th century are: 1) against Muslims and Jews in the conquest of Al-Andalus in the name of "purity of blood"; 2) against indigenous peoples first in the Americas and then in Asia; 3) against African people with the captive trade and their enslavement in the Americas; 4) against women who practiced and transmitted Indo-European knowledge in Europe burned alive accused of being witches. These four genocides/epistemicides are frequently discussed as fragmented from each other. The attempt here is to see them as interlinked, inter-related to each other and as constitutive of the modern/colonial world's epistemic structures. These four genocides were at the same time forms of epistemicide that are constitutive of Western men epistemic privilege. To sustain this argument we need to not only go over the history but also explain how and when racism emerged.

III. THE CONQUEST OF AL-ANDALUS: GENOCIDE/EPISTEMICIDE AGAINST MUSLIMS AND JEWS

The final conquest of Al-Andalus in the late 15th century was done under the slogan of "purity of blood." This was a proto-racist discourse against Muslim and Jewish populations during the Catholic Monarchy colonial conquest of Andalusian territory to destroy the sultanate of Granada which was the last Muslim political authority in the Iberian Peninsula (Maldonado-Torres 2008a). The practice of ethnic cleansing of the Andalusian territory produced a physical genocide and cultural genocide against Muslims and Jews. Jews and Muslims who stayed in the territory were either killed (physical genocide) or forced to conversion (cultural genocide). This ethnic cleansing was achieved through the following genocide (physical) and epistemicide (cultural):

1- The forced expulsion of Muslims and Jews from their land (genocide) led to the repopulation of the territory with Christian populations from the North of the Iberian Peninsula (Caro Barojas 1991; Carrasco 2009). This is what in the literature is called today "settler colonialism."
2- The massive destruction of Islamic and Judaic spirituality and knowledge through genocide, led to the forced conversion (cultural genocide) of those Jews and Muslims who decided to stay in the territory (Barrios Aguilera 2009, Kettami 2012). By turning Muslims into Moriscos (converted Muslims) and Jews into Marranos (converted Jews), their memory, knowledge and spirituality were destroyed (cultural genocide). The latter was a guarantee that future descendants of Marranos and Moros will be born fully Christians without any memory trace to their ancestors.

The Spanish state discourse of "purity of blood" was used to surveil the Muslim and Jewish populations who survived the massacres. In order to survive and stay in the territory, they were forced to convert to Christianity (Galán Sánchez 2010). Those populations that were forced to convert or that had Jewish or Muslim ancestry, were surveilled by the Christian monarchy in order to assure that they were not faking conversion. "Purity of blood" was a discourse used to surveil the converts or descendants of the converts. It referred to the "family tree" of the population. The "family tree" provided to state authorities the information needed in order to know if the ancestry of an individual or a family was "purely" Christian or "non-Christian" in the case they were Christian converts. The discourse of "purity of blood" did not question the humanity of the victims. What it aimed was to surveil those populations with non-Christian ancestry in terms of how far or close they were to Christianity in order to confirm if the conversion was real or not. For the Castillian Christian Monarchy, Muslims and Jews were humans with the "wrong God" or "wrong religion." They were perceived as a "fifth column" of the Ottoman sultanate in the Iberian Peninsula (Martín Casares 2000; Carrasco 2009; Galán Sánchez 2010). Thus, the old European Medieval religious discriminatory discourses such as the old anti-semite discourses (judeophobic or islamophobic) were used against Jews and Muslims in the conquest of Al-Andalus.

It is important to emphasize that since the possibility of conversation was still open, the old anti-semitic European Medieval religious discrimination of the Castillian Christian Monarchy (at the end of the 15th century) was not yet racial and included among semitic people both Muslims and Jews[6]. As long as the Muslims and Jews con-

---
6. It is the recent Western European, North American and Israeli Zionist orientalist literature that after Second World War excluded Arabs from semite people and reduced the definition of

verted to Christianity, the doors for integration were open during the Medieval Spanish Monarchy conquest of Al-Andalus (Galán Sánchez 2010; Dominguez Ortiz 2009). The humanity of the victims was not in question. What was in question was the religious identity of the social subjects. The social classification used at the time was related to a theological question about having the "wrong God" or the "wrong religion" to stratify society along religious lines.

In sum, what is important here is that the "purity of blood" discourse used in the conquest of Al-Andalus was a form of religious discrimination that was not yet fully racist because it did not question in a profound way the humanity of its victims.

III. The Conquest of the Americas in Relation to the Conquest of Al-Andalus: Genocide/Epistemicide Against Indigenous Peoples, Marranos, Moriscos, and Africans

When Christopher Columbus presented for the first time the document known as "The Indian Enterprise" to the King and Queen of the Castilian Monarchy, their response was to accept it and postpone it until after the conquest of all the territory known as Al-Andalus. They ordered Columbus to wait until the final conquest over the "Kingdom of Granada," the last sultanate in the Iberian Peninsula. The idea of the Castilian Christian Monarchy was to unify the whole territory under its command by the rule of "one state, one identity, one religion" in contrast to Al-Andalus where there were multiple Islamic states (sultanates) with recognition of rights to the "multiple identities and spiritualities inside their territorial boundaries" (Maíllo Delgago 2004; Kettami 2012).

The project of the Castillan Christian Monarchy to create a correspondence between the identity of the state and the identity of the population within its territorial boundaries, was the origin of the idea of the nation-state in Europe. The main goal that the Queen and the King expressed to Columbus was the unification of the whole territory under the power of the Christian Monarchy as a first step before going abroad to conquest other lands beyond the Iberian Peninsula.

The final conquest over Muslim political authority in the Iberian Peninsula was finalized in January 2, 1492 with the capitulation of Granada's Nazarí emirate. Only nine days later, on January 11, 1492, Columbus met again with Queen Elizabeth. But this time the meeting was held in Granada's Alhambra Nazarí Palace where Columbus got the royal authorization and resources for his first voyage overseas. Only ten months later, on October 12, 1492, Columbus arrived at the shores of what he named "Indias Occidentales" (West Indies) because he wrongly believed that he had arrived to India.

The relationship between the conquest of Al-Andalus and the conquest of the Americas has been under-researched in the literature. The methods of colonization and domination used against Al-Andalus were extrapolated to the Americas (Garrido Aranda 1980). The conquest of Al-Andalus was so important in the minds of the Spanish conquerors that Hernan Cortés, the conqueror of Mexico, confused the Aztecs' sacred temples with Mosques.

In addition to the genocide of people, the conquest of Al-Andalus was accompanied by epistemicide. For example, the burning of libraries was a fundamental method used in the conquest of Al-Andalus. The library of Cordoba, that had around 500,000 books at a time when the largest library of Christian Europe did not have more than 1000 books, was burned in the 13th century. Many other libraries had the same destiny during the conquest of Al-Andalus un-

---

anti-semitism to racial discrimination against Jews. The latter is part of a perverse Zionist strategy to conflate Arab-Muslims' critique to Zionism as equivalent to anti-semitism (Grosfoguel 2009).

til the final burning of more than 250,000 books of the Granada library by Cardenal Cisneros in the early 16th century. These methods were extrapolated to the Americas. Thus, the same happened with the indigenous "códices" which was the written practice used by Amerindians to archive knowledge. Thousands of "códices" were also burned destroying indigenous knowledges in the Americas. Genocide and epistemicide went together in the process of conquest in both the Americas and Al-Andalus.

A similar process happened with the methods of evangelization used against indigenous people in the Americas (Garrido Aranda 1980; Martín de la Hoz 2010). It was inspired in the methods used against Muslims in the Iberian Peninsula (Garrido Aranda 1980). It was a form of "spiritualicide" and "epistemicide" at the same time. The destruction of knowledge and spirituality went also together in the conquest of both Al-Andalus and the Americas.

However, it is fundamental to also understand how the conquest of the Americas affected the conquest of "Moriscos" (converted Muslims) and "Marranos" (converted Jews) in the Iberian Peninsula in the 16th century. The conquest of the Americas was at the center of the new discourses and forms of domination that emerged in the long 16th century with the creation of the modern/colonial world-system. Here the contribution of Nelson Maldonado-Torres is crucial when he said that the 16th century transformed the ancient forms of imperial social classification that existed since the 4th century when with Constantine, Christianity became the dominant ideology of the Roman Empire. As Maldonado-Torres (2008a) said:

> ... the conceptual coordinates that defined the 'fight for the empire' and the forms of social classification of the 4th century and of later centuries prior to the "discovery" and conquest of the Américas change drastically in the 16th century. The relationship between religion and empire would be at the center of a dramatic transformation from a system of power based on religious differences to one based on racial differences. It is for this reason that in modernity, the dominant episteme would not only be defined by the tension and mutual collaboration between the idea of religion and the imperial vision of the known world, but, more precisely, through a dynamic relation between empire, religion, and race. Ideas about race, religion, and empire functioned as significant axes in the imaginary of the emergent modern/colonial world ... (p. 230)

If the military and evangelization methods of conquest used in Al-Andalus to achieve genocide and epistemicide were extrapolated to the conquest of indigenous people in the Americas, the conquest of the Americas also created a new racial imaginary and racial hierarchy that transformed the conquest of Moriscos and Marranos in 16th century Iberian Peninsula. The conquest of the Americas affected the old forms of Medieval religious discrimination against Moriscos and Marranos in 16th century Spain. The first point to emphasize in this history is that after months of navigation through the Atlantic Ocean, the moment Columbus stepped out of the ship he wrote in his diary the following on October 12, 1492:

> ... it seemed to me that they were a people very poor in everything. All of them go around as naked as their mothers bore them... They should be good and talent servants, for I observed that they quickly took in what was said to them. And I believe that they would easily be made Christians, as it appeared to me that they had no sect. (my own translation)

This statement by Christopher Columbus opened a debate for the next 60 years (1492-1552). As Nelson Maldonado-Torres (2008a) argues, in the late 15th century, Columbus' notion of "people without sect" ("people without religion") meant something new. To say "people without religion" today means "atheist people." But in the Christian imaginary of the late 15th century, the phrase "people without religion" had a different connotation. In Christian imaginary, all humans have religion. They could have the "wrong God" or "wrong Gods," there could be wars and people could kill each other in the fight against the "wrong God," but the humanity of the other, as a trend and as a form of domination, was not yet put in question. What was being questioned was the theology of the "other." The latter was radically modified after 1492 with the conquest of the Americas and the characterization of indigenous peoples by Christopher Columbus as "people without religion." An anachronistic reading of this phrase might lead us to think that Columbus referred to "atheist people." But not having religion in the Christian imaginary of the time was equivalent to not having a soul, that is, being expelled from the realm of the human. As Nelson Maldonado-Torres (2008a) said:

> To refer to the indigenous as subjects without religion removes them from the category of the human. Religion is universal among humans, but the alleged lack of it among natives is not initially taken to indicate the falseness of this statement, but rather the opposite, that there exist subjects in the world who are not fully human. ...Columbus' assertion about the lack of religion in indigenous people introduces an anthropological meaning to the term. In light of what we have seen here, it is necessary to add that this anthropological meaning is also linked to a very modern method of classifying humans: racial classification. With a single stroke, Columbus took the discourse on religion from the theological realm into a modern philosophical anthropology that distinguishes among different degrees of humanity through identities fixed into what would later be called races. (p. 217)

Contrary to the contemporary common sense, "color racism" was not the first racist discourse. "Religious racism" ("people with religion" vs. "people without religion" or "people with soul" vs. "people without a soul") was the first marker of racism in the "Capitalist/Patriarcal Western-Centric/Christian-centric modern/colonial world-system" (Grosfoguel 2011) formed in the long 16th century. The definition of "people without religion" was coined in late 15th and early 16th century Spain. The debate provoked by the conquest of the Americas was about whether the "people without religion" found in Columbus' voyages were "people with a soul or without a soul." The logic of the argument was as follows: 1) if you do not have religion, you do not have a God; 2) if you do not have a God, then you do not have a soul; and 3) if you do not have a soul, you are not human but animal-like.

The debate turned "people without religion" into "people without a soul." This colonial racist debate produced a boomerang effect that redefined and transformed the dominant imaginary of the times and the Medieval religious discriminatory discourses. The concept of "purity of blood" acquired a new meaning. "Purity of blood" was not any more a technology of power to surveil persons that have a Muslim or Jewish ancestry in the family tree in order to make sure he/she is not faking conversion as in 15th century conquest of Al-Andalus. The meaning of "purity of blood" after the conquest of the Americas with the emergence of the concept of "people without a soul" shifted from a theological question about having the "wrong religion" into a question about the humanity of the subject practicing the "wrong religion."[7]

As a result, the great debate in the first five decades of the 16th century was about whether "Indians" have a soul or not. In practice, both the Church and the Spanish imperial state were already massively enslaving indigenous people assuming the notion that "Indians" have no soul. State racism is not a post-18th century phenomenon, but a phenomenon that emerged following the conquest of the Americas in the 16th century. However, there were critical voices inside the Church questioning this idea and proposing that "Indians" have a soul but were barbarians in need of Christianization (Dussel 1979; 1992). They claimed that since the "Indians" have a soul, it is a sin in the eyes of God to enslave them and the job of the Church should be to Christianize them using peaceful methods. This debate was the first racist debate in world history and "Indian" as an identity was the first modern identity.

The category of "Indian" constituted a new modern/colonial identity invention that homogenized the heterogeneous identities that existed in the Americas before the arrival of the Europeans. It is also important to remember that Columbus thought he had arrived in India and, thus, leading to the use of the term "Indian" to name the populations he encountered. Out of this eurocentric geographical mistake, emerges "Indian" as a new identity. But to question if "Indians" have a soul or not was already a racist question that referred directly to the question of their humanity.[8]

In 16th century Christian imaginary, this debate had important implications. If "Indians" did not have a soul, then it is justified in the eyes of God to enslave them and treat them as animals in the labor process. But if they had a soul, then it was a sin in the eyes of God to enslave, assassinate, or mistreat them. This debate was crucial in the mutation of the old European medieval religious discriminatory discourses and practices. Until the end of the 15th century, the old islamophobic and judeophobic discourses were related to having the "wrong God," the "wrong theology," and to the influence of Satan in the "wrong religion," without questioning the humanity of their practitioners.[9] The possibility of conversion was available for the victims of these discriminatory discourses. But with the colonization of the Americas, these old medieval discriminatory religious discourses mutated rapidly, transforming into modern racial domination.

Even though the word "race" was not used at the time, the debate about having a soul or not was already a racist debate in the sense used by scientific racism in the 19th century. The theological debate of the 16th century about having a soul or not had the same connotation of the 19th century scien-

---

7. It is important to remember that Latin was the written language of 16th century Europe. Since the Christian church was the authority of knowledge through Christian theology, the debates about the conquest of the Americas in Spain travelled to other European territories through the Church networks. Thus, the debates about Columbus and the Spanish Christian theologians on the New World and the subjects found there were read with particular attention in other parts of Europe.

8. This skepticism about the humanity of other human beings is what Nelson Maldonado-Torres (2008b) called "misanthropic skepticism."

9. I refer to the social classification of the social system. As Maldonado-Torres argues, there were already individuals articulating discourses that could be identified as racialist from a contemporary point of view. However, the social classification of the population in Medieval Europe was not based on racial classification, that is, it was not organized around social logics related to a radical question about the humanity of the social subjects. The social classification of the population based on racist social logics was a post-1492 process with the formation of the "Capitalist/Patriarchal Western-centric/Christian-centric Modern/Colonial World-System" (Grosfoguel 2011). Thus, in this article the argument about the emergence of racism is related to a post-1492 global social system and not to individual statements before 1492.

tificist debates about having the human biological constitution or not. Both were debates about the humanity or animality of the others articulated by the institutional racist discourse of states such as the Castilian Christian monarchy in the 16th century or Western European imperial nation-states in the 19th century. These institutional racist logics of "not having a soul" in the 16th century or "not having the human biology" in the 19th century became the organizing principle of the international division of labor and capitalist accumulation at a world-scale.

The debate continued until the famous Valladolid trial of the School of Salamance in 1552. Since Christian theology and church was the authority of knowledge at the time, the Spanish Christian imperial monarchy put in the hands of a tribunal among Christian theologians the question about whether "Indians have a soul or not." The theologians were Bartolomé de las Casas and Gines Sepúlveda. After 60 years (1492-1552) of debate, the Spanish imperial Christian monarchy finally requested a Christian theological tribunal to make a final decision about the humanity or lack of humanity of the "Indians."

As is well-known, Gines Sepúlveda argued in favor of the position that "Indians" are "people without a soul" and, therefore, they are animals that could be enslaved in the labor process without being a sin in the eyes of God. Part of his argument to demonstrate the inferiority of the "Indians" below the line of the human was the modern capitalist argument that "Indians" have no sense of private property and no notion of markets because they produce through collective forms and distribute wealth through reciprocity.

Bartolomé de las Casas argued that "Indians" have a soul but were in a barbarian stage in need of Christianization. Therefore, for Las Casas it was a sin in the eyes of God to enslave them. What he proposed was to "Christianize" them. Both Las Casas and Sepulvera represent the inaguration of the two major racist discourses with long lasting consequences that will be mobilized by Western imperial powers for the next 450 years: biological racist discourses and cultural racist discourses.

The biological racist discourse is a 19th century scientificist secularization of Sepúlveda's theological racist discourse. When the authority of knowledge passed in the West from Christian theology to Modern Science after the 18th century Enlightenment Project and the French Revolution, the Sepulveda theological racist discourse of "people without soul" mutated with the rise of natural sciences to a biological racist discourse of "peoples without human biology" and later "peoples without genes" (without the human genetics). The same happened with the Bartolomé De Las Casas discourse. The De Las Casas theological discourse of "barbarians to be Christianized" in the 16th century, transmuted with the rise of the social sciences into an anthropological cultural racist discourse about "primitives to be civilized."

The outcome of the Valladolid trial is also well known: although Sepúlvedas' view won in the long run, in the short run Las Casas won the trial. Thus, the Spanish imperial monarchy decided that "Indians" have a soul but are barbarians to be Christianized. Therefore, it was recognized that it was a sin in the eyes of God to enslave them. The conclusion seemingly meant the liberation of "Indians" from the Spanish colonial rule. But this was not the case. The "Indians" were transferred in the international division of labor from slave labor to another form of coerced labor known as the "encomienda." Since then it became institutionalized in a more systematic way the idea of race and institutional racism as an organizing principle of the international division of labor and capitalist accumulation at a world-scale.

While "Indians" were placed in the "encomienda" under a coerced form of labor,

Africans who were already classified as "people without a soul" were brought to the Americas to replace "Indians" in slave labor. Africans were perceived at the time as Muslims and the racialization of Muslims in 16th century Spain was extended to them. The decision to bring captives from Africa to enslave them in the Americas was directly related to the conclusion of the 1552 Valladolid trial. Here begins the massive kidnapping and captive trade of Africans that is going to be enforced for the next 300 years. With the enslavement of Africans, religious racism was complemented with or slowy replaced by color racism. Since then, anti-black racism became a foundational constitutive structuring logic of the modern/colonial world.

The kidnapping of Africans and their enslavement in the Americas was a major and significant world-historical event (Nimako and Willemsen 2011). Millions of Africans died in the process of being captured, transported and enslaved in the Americas. This was a genocide at a massive scale. But as with the other cases outlined above, the genocide was inherently epistemicide. Africans in the Americas were forbidden from thinking, praying or practicing their cosmologies, knowledges and world views. They were submitted to a regime of epistemic racism that forbade their autonomous knowledge production. Epistemic inferiority was a crucial argument used to claim biological social inferiority below the line of the human. The racist idea in late 16th century was that "Negroes lack intelligence" which turned in the 20th century to "Negroes have low IQ levels."

Another consequence of the debate about the "Indians" and the Valladolid tribunal was its impact on the Moriscos and Marranos in 16th century Spain. The old islamophobic and judeophobic medieval religious discriminatory discourses against Jews and Muslims were transformed into racist discrimination. The question was not any more about whether the religiously discriminated population have the wrong God or wrong theology. The anti-indigenous religious racism that questioned the humanity of the "Indians" was extrapolated to the Moriscos and the Marranos questioning the humanity of those who pray to the "wrong God." Those who prayed to the "wrong God" were conceived as not having a soul, as "soul-less subjects" ("sujetos desalmados"), non-humans or sub-humans. Similar to indigenous people in the Americas, they were expelled from the "realm of the human" being described as "animal-like" (Perceval 1992; 1997). The latter represented a radical transformation that goes from the inferiority of non-Christian religions (Islam and Judaism) in Medieval Europe to the inferiority of the human beings who practiced these religions (Jews and Muslims) in the new emerging Modern Europe. Thus, it is as a result of the impact of the conquest of the Americas in the 16th century that the old European islamophobic and judeophobic anti-semitic religious discrimination going back to the crusades and before, turned into racial discrimination. This is the boomerang effect of colonialism coming back to hunt Europe.

The entanglement between the religious Christian-centric global hierarchy and the racial/ethnic Western-Centric hierarchy of the "capitalist/patriarcal Western-centric/Christian-centric modern/colonial world-system" created after 1492, identified the practitioners of a non-Christian spirituality with being racialized as an inferior being below the line of the human. Contrary to Eurocentric narratives such as Foucault (1996), that situates the transmutation from religious anti-semitism to racial anti-semitism in the 19th century with the emergence of scientific racism, anti-semitic racism emerged in 16th century Spain when the old medieval anti-semitic religious discrimination was entangled with the new modern racial imaginary produced by the conquest of the Americas. The new racial imaginary mutated the old religious anti-semitism into racial anti-semitism. Contrary to Foucault, this anti-semitic racism of the 16th century was already institutionalized as state biopolitical racism.[10]

The concept of "people without a soul" was not extended to Moriscos immediately. It took several decades in the 16th century to be extrapolated to Moriscos. It was after the mid-sixteenth century and, specifically, during the Alpujarras[11] trial that Moriscos where called "souless people" ("sujetos desalmados"). Moreover, after mid-16th century, as a consequence of being classified as "souless people," Moriscos were massively enslaved in Granada. Despite the Christian church prohibition to enslave Christians and people baptized as Christian, Moriscos (Muslims converted to Christianity) were still enslaved (Marín Casares 2000).

Now, "purity of blood" was related to "souless people" making irrelevant the question about how assimilated they were to Christianity. Their being was itself in question making their humanity suspicious. Thus, from then on they were not considered truly Christians nor equal to Christians. Anti-Morisco racism would be intensified during the later part of the 16th century until their mass expulsion from the Iberian Peninsula in 1609 (Perceval 1992, 1997; Carrasco 2009).

In sum, the conquest of the Americas in the 16th century extended the process of genocide/epistemicide that began with the conquest of Al-Andalus to new subjects such as indigenous people and Africans, while simultaneously intensified through a new racial logic the genocide/epistemicide against Christians from Jewish and Muslim origin populations in Spain.

IV. THE CONQUEST OF INDO-EUROPEAN WOMEN: GENOCIDE/EPISTEMICIDE AGAINST WOMEN

There is a fourth genocide/epistemicide in the 16th century that is not frequently related to the history of the three genocides/epistemicides outlined before.[12] This is the conquest and genocide of women in European lands who transmitted Indo-European knowledge from generation to generation. These women mastered indigenous knowledge from ancient times. Their knowledge covered different areas such as astronomy, medicine, biology, ethics, etc. They were empowered by the possession of ancestral knowledge and their leading role inside the communities organized around commune-like forms of economic and political organization. The persecution of these women began from the late Medieval era. However, it became intensified in the 16th and 17th century (long 16th century) with the rise of "modern/colonial capitalist/patriarchal" power structures.

Millions of women were burned alive, accused of being witches in the Early Modern period. Given their authority and leadership, the attack against these women was a strategy to consolidate Christian-centric

---

10. Scientific racism in the 19th century was not, as Foucault argued, a resignification of the old European "race war" discourse but a secularization of the old Christendom religious theological racism of "people without a soul" in the 16th century. The old discourse of "race war" inside Europe was not the foundation of scientific racism as Foucault insisted on with his "genealogy of racism." The foundation of scientific racism was the old religious racism of the 16th century with roots in the European colonial conquest of the Americas. Foucault is blind towards the conquest of the Americas, colonialism and Spain's 16th century.

11. These were the trials against Moriscos that uprose in the Alpujarras mountains outside the city of Granada after the mid-16th century.

12. The seminal work of Silvia Federici (2004) is one of the few exceptions. Although Federici's work does not link these four processes in relation to genocide/epistemicide, she at least links the witch hunt of women in the 16th/17th century with the enslavement of Africans and the conquest of the Americas in relation to global capitalist accumulation, in particular, the early formation of capitalism, that is, "primitive accumulation." Her work is focused on political-economy rather than structures of knowledge. However, her contribution is crucial for the understanding of the relation between the genocide/epistemicide of women and the other genocide/epistemicides of the 16th century.

patriarchy and to destroy autonomous communal forms of land ownership. The Inquisition was at the forefront of this offensive. The accusation was an attack to thousands of women whose autonomy, leadership and knowledge threatened Christian theology, Church authority and the power of the aristocracy that turned into a capitalist class transnationally in the colonies as well as in European agriculture.[13]

Silvia Federici (2004) argues that this witch hunt intensified between 1550 and 1650. Her thesis is that the witch hunt against women in European territory was related to primitive accumulation during the early capitalist expansion in the formation of the labor reserve for global capitalism. She linked the African enslavement in the Americas with the witch hunt of Women in Europe as two sides of the same coin: capital accumulation at a world-scale in need of incorporating labor to the capitalist accumulation process. In order to achieve this, capitalist institutions used extreme forms of violence.

Contrary to the epistemicide against Indigenous people and Muslims where thousands of books were burned, in the case of the genocide/epistemicide against Indo-European women there were no books to burn because the transmission of knowledge was done from generation to generation through oral tradition. The "books" were the women's bodies and, thus, similar to the Andalusian and Indigenous "books" their bodies were burned alive.

V. Consequences of the Four Genocides/Epistemicides for Global Structures of Knowledge: The Formation of Epistemic/Sexist Structures and the Hope for a Future Transmodern World

The four genocides/epistemicides of the long 16th century discussed before created racial/patriarchal power and epistemic structures at a world scale entangled with processes of global capitalist accumulation. When in the 17th century Descartes wrote "I think, therefore I am" from Amsterdam[14], in the "common sense" of the times, this "I" could not be an African, an indigenous person, a Muslim, a Jew nor a woman (Western or non-Western). All of these subjects were already considered "inferior" along the global racial/patriarchal power structure and their knowledge was considered inferior as a result of the four genocides/epistemicides of the 16th century. The only one left as epistemically superior was the Western man. In the hegemonic "common sense" of the times, this "I" was that of a Western male. The four genocides/epistemicides are constitutive of the racist/sexist epistemic structures that produced epistemic priviledge and authority to Western man's knowledge production and inferiority for the rest. As Maldonado-Torres (2008b) affirms, the other side of the "I think, therefore I am" is the racist/sexist structure of "I do not think, therefore I am not." The latter expresses a "coloniality of being" (Maldonando-Torres 2008b) where all of the subjects considered inferior do not think and are not

---

13. For an analysis of the transformation of the European aristocracy into a capitalist class in relation to the formation of the modern world-system see the work of Immanuel Wallerstein, specially his Modern World-System, Vol. 1 (New York: Academic Press).

14. It is important to say that when the Dutch defeated the Spaniards in the 30 years war, the new center of the new world-system created after 1492 with Spain expansion to the Americas shifted from the Iberian Peninsula to North-Western Europe, that is, Amsterdam. Dussel's characterization of Descartes philosophy as one produced by someone who is geopolitically thinking from the center of the world-system, the imperial being, is not metaphorical.

worthy of existence because their humanity is in question. They belong to the Fanonian "zone of non-being" or to the Dusselian "exteriority."

Westernized universities internalized from its origin the racist/sexist epistemic structures created by the four genocides/epistemicides of the 16th century. These eurocentric structures of knowledge became "commonsensical." It is considered normal functioning to have only Western males of 5 countries to be producing the canons of thought in all of the academic disciplines of the Westernized university. There is no scandal in this because they are a reflection of the normalized racist/sexist epistemic structures of knowledge of the modern/colonial world.

When the Westernized university transformed in the late 18th century from a Christian theological university into the secular Humboldtian university, it used the Kantian anthropological idea that rationality was embodied in the White man north of the Pyrenees mountains classifying the Iberian Peninsula within the realm of the irrational world together with Black, Red and Yellow people. The people "lacking rationality" were epistemically excluded from the Westernized university knowledge structures. It is from this Kantian assumption that the canon of thought of the contemporary Westernized university was founded.

When the center of the world-system passed from the Iberian Peninsula to North-Western Europe in the mid-17th century after the Thirty Years War when the Dutch defeated the Spanish armada, the epistemic privilege passed together with the systemic power from the empires of the Iberian Peninsula to North-Western European empires. Kant's anthropological racist view placing the Pyrenees mountains as a dividing line inside Europe to define rationality and irrationality is just following this 17th century geopolitical power shift. Kant applied to the Iberian Peninsula in the 18th century the same racist views that the Iberian Peninsula applied to the rest of the world during the 16th century. This is important in order to understand why Portuguese and Spaniards are also out of the canon of thought in the Westernized university today despite being at the center of the world-system created after 1492. Since the late 18th century, it is only men from five countries (France, England, Germany, Italy and the USA) who are the ones monopolizing the privilege and authority of canons of knowledge production in the Westernized university.

In the face of the challenge represented by Eurocentered modernity and its epistemic racist/sexist colonial structures of knowledge, Enrique Dussel proposes Transmodernity as the project to fulfill the unfinished project of decolonization. The "Trans" of Transmodernity means "beyond." What does it mean to go beyond Eurocentered modernity?

If the Western colonial project of genocide/epistemicide was to some extent successful in particular spaces around the world, it was a huge failure in its overall results in most of the world. Critical Indigenous, Muslim, Jewish, African and women thought as well as many other critical knowledges from the Global South are still alive. After 500 years of coloniality of knowledge there is no cultural nor epistemic tradition in an absolute sense outside to Eurocentered modernity. All were affected by Eurocentered modernity and even aspects of Eurocentrism were also internalized in many of these epistemologies. However, this does not mean that every tradition is in an absolute sense inside and that there is no outside to Western epistemology. There are still non-Western epistemic perspectives that have a *relative exteriority* from Eurocentered modernity. They were affected by genocide/epistemicide but not fully destroyed. It is this *relative exteriority* that according to Enrique Dussel, provides the hope and possibility for a Transmodern world: "a world where many worlds are possible" to use the Zapatista slogan.

The existence of epistemic diversity provides the potential for struggles of decolonization and depatriarchalization that are not centered anymore in Western-centric epistemologies and world views. To move beyond Eurocentered modernity, Dussel proposes a decolonial project that takes seriously the critical thinking of the epistemic traditions of the Global South. It is from these diverse traditions that we can build projects that will take different ideas and institutions appropriated by Eurocentred modernity and to decolonize them in different directions. In Eurocentric modernity, the West kidnapped and monopolized the definition of Democracy, Human Rights, Women liberation, Economy, etc. Transmodernity implies redefining these elements in different directions according to the epistemic diversity of the world towards a pluriverse of meaning and a pluriversal world.

If people from the Global South do not follow the Western hegemonic definition, they are immediately denounced and marginalized from the global community, being accused of fundamentalism. For example, when the Zapatistas talk about democracy they are not doing it from a Western-centric perspective. They propose a project of democracy that is quite different from liberal democracy. They redefine democracy from the indigenous perspective of "commanding while obeying" with the "Caracoles" as the democratic institutional practice. However, to use a different concept of democracy in Eurocentered modernity is denounced as a form of fundamentalism. The same with the concept of feminism. If Muslim women develop an "Islamic feminism" they are immediately denounced by Eurocentered Western feminists as patriarchal and fundamentalist. Transmodernity is an invitation to produce from the different political-epistemic projects existing in the world today a redefinition of the many elements appropriated by Eurocentered modernity and treated as if naturally and inherently European, toward a decolonial project of liberation beyond the "Capitalist/Patriarchal Western-centric/Christian-centric Modern/Colonial World-System." As Dussel states:

> When I speak of *Trans-modernity*, I am referring to a global project that seeks to transcend European or North American Modernity. It is a project that is not post-modern, since post-Modernity is a still-incomplete critique of Modernity by European and North America. Instead, *Trans-modernity* is a task that is, in my case, expressed philosophically, whose point of departure is that which has been *discarded, devalued,* and judged *useless* among global cultures, including colonized or peripheral philosophies… (Dussel 2008b: 19-20)

Moreover, Transmodernity calls for inter-philosophical political dialogues to produce pluriverses of meaning where the new universe is a pluriverse. However, Transmodernity is not equivalent to a liberal multiculturalist celebration of the epistemic diversity of the world where the power structures are left intact. Transmodernity is a recognition of epistemic diversity without epistemic relativism. The call for epistemic pluriversality as opposed to epistemic universality is not equivalent to a relativist position. On the contrary, Transmodernity acknowledges the need for a shared and common universal project against capitalism, patriarchy, imperialism and coloniality. But it rejects a universality of solutions where one defines for the rest what "the solution" is. Uni-versality in European modernity has meant "one that defines for the rest." Transmodernity calls for a pluriverse of solutions where "the many defines for the many." From different cultural and epistemic traditions there will be different responses and solutions to similar problems. The Transmodern horizon has as a goal to produce pluriversal concepts, meanings and philosophies as well as a pluriveral world. As Dussel states, Transmodernity is

> ...oriented towards a *pluriversal future global philosophy*. This project is necessarily *trans-modern*, and thus also trans-capitalist... For a long time, perhaps for centuries, the many diverse philosophical traditions will each continue to follow their own paths, but nonetheless a global analogical project of a ***trans-modern* pluriverse** (other than universal, and not post-modern) appears on the horizon. Now, 'other philosophies' are possible, because 'another world is possible'—as is proclaimed by the Zapatista Liberation Movement in Chiapas, Mexico. (Dussel 2008b:20)

VI. Conclusion

This discussion has enormous implications for the decolonization of the Westernized university. So far, the Westernized university operates under the assumption of the uni-versalism where "one (Western men from five countries) defines for the rest" what is truthful and valid knowledge. To decolonize the structures of knowledge of the Westernized university will require among other things to:

1) acknowledge the provincialism and epistemic racism/sexism that constitute the foundational epistemic structures as a result of the genocidal/epistemicidal colonial/patriarchal projects of the 16th century;
2) break with the uni-versalism where one ("uni") defines for the rest, in this case, the one is Western man epistemology;
3) bring epistemic diversity to the canon of thought to create a pluri-verse of meanings and concepts where the inter-epistemic conversation among many epistemic traditions produce new re-definitions of old concepts and creates new pluriversal concepts with "the many defining for the many" (pluri-verse) instead of "one for the rest" (uni-verse).

If Westernized universities assume these three programmatic points, it would stop being Westernized and a Uni-versity. It will turn from a Westernized Uni-versity into a Decolonial Pluri-versity. If Kant's and Humboldt's Eurocentered modern racist/sexist epistemic projects became the epistemic foundation of the Westernized university since the late 18th century as a result of three hundred years of genocide/epistemicide in the world, Enrique Dussel's Transmodernity is the new epistemic foundation of the future Decolonial Pluri-versity whose knowledge production will be at the service of a world beyond the "Capitalist/Patriarchal Western-centric/Christian-centric Modern/Colonial World-System."

Bibliography

Anzaldúa, Gloria (1987) *Borderlands/La Frontera: The New Mestiza*. (San Francisco: Spinsters/Aunt Lute).

Barrios Aguilera, Manuel (2009) *La suerte de los vencidos: Estudios y reflexiones sobre la cuestión morisca*. (Granada: Universidad de Granada).

Caro Baroja, Julio (1991) *Los moriscos del Reino de Granada* (Madrid: Ediciones Istmo).

Carrasco, Rafael (2009) *Deportados en nombre de Dios: La explusión de los moriscos cuarto centenario de una ignominia*. (Barcelona: Ediciones Destino).

Castro-Gomez, Santiago (2003) *La Hybris del Punto Cero: Ciencia, Raza e Ilustración en la Nueva Granada (1750-1816)* (Bogotá: Editora Pontífica de la Universidad Javeriana).

Crenshaw, Kimberlé (1991) "Mapping the Margins: Intersectionality, Identity Politics, and Violence against Women of Color." *Stanford Law Review* 43, 1241-1279.

De Sousa Santos, Boaventura (2010) *Epistemologias del sur*. Mexico: Siglo XXI.

Descartes, Rene (2013) *Discours de la Méthode* (Cambridge: Cambridge University Press).

Dominguez Ortiz, Antonio (2009) *Moriscos: la mirada de un historiador*. (Granada: Universidad de Granada).

Dussel, Enrique (1977) *Filosofía de Liberación*. (México: Edicol).

Dussel, Enrique (1979) *El episcopado latinoamericano y la liberación de los pobres (1504-1620)* (Mexico: Centro de Reflexión Teológica, A.C.).

Dussel (1992) *Historia de la Iglesia en América Latina: Medio Milenio de Coloniaje y Liberación* (Madrid, Spain: Mundo Negro-Esquila Misional).

Dussel, Enrique (1995) *The Invention of the Americas*. New York: Continuum.

Dussel, Enrique (2008a) "Anti-meditaciones cartesianas: sobre el origen del anti-discurso filosófico de la modernidad." *Tabula Rasa* No. 9: 153-197.

Dussel, Enrique (2008b) "A New Age in the History of Philosophy: The World Dialogue Between Philosophical Traditions." *Prajñā Vihāra: Journal of Philosophy and Religion*, Vol. 9, No. 1: 1-21.

Fanon, Frantz (2010) *Piel Negra, Máscara Blancas* (Madrid: AKAL).

Federici, Silvia (2004) *Caliban and the Witch: Women, The Body and Primitive Accumulation* (New York: Autonomedia).

Foucault, Michel (1996) *Genealogía del racismo*. La Plata, Argentina Colección Caronte Ensayos.

Galán Sánchez, Ángel (2010) *Una sociedad en transición: Los granadinos de mudéjares a moriscos*. (Granada: Universidad de Granada).

Garrido Aranda, Antonio (1980) *Moriscos e Indios: Precedentes Hispánicos de la Evangelización de México* (México: Universidad Nacional Autónoma de México).

Grosfoguel, Ramon (2009) "Human Rights and Anti-Semitism After Gaza" *Human Architecture: Journal of the Sociology of Self-Knowledge*, Vol. VII, issue No. 2 (Spring): 89-101

Grosfoguel, Ramón (2011) "Decolonizing Post-Colonial Studies and Paradigms of Political-Economy: Transmodernity, Decolonial Thinking and Global Coloniality" *Transmodernity: Journal of Peripheral Cultural Production of the Luso-Hispanic World* Vol. 1, No. 1: 1-38 http://escholarship.org/uc/item/21k6t3fq

Grosfoguel, Ramon (2012) "The Dilemmas of Ethnic Studies in the United States: Between Liberal Multiculturalism, Identity Politics, Disciplinary Colonization, and Decolonial Epistemologies" *Human Architecture: Journal of the Sociology of Self-Knowledge*, Vol. X, No. 1: 81-90. http://www.okcir.com/WEB%20Pdfs%20X%20Winter%2012/Grosfoguel.pdf.

Haraway, Donna (1988), "Situated Knowledges: the Science Question in Feminism and the Privilege of Partial Perspective," *Feminist Studies*, 14, 575-99.

Kettami, Ali (2012) *El resurgir del Islam en Al-Ándalus* (Barcelona: Abadia Editors)

Maíllo Salgado, Felipe (2004) *De la desaparición de Al-Ándalus* (Madrid: Abada Editores).

Maldonado-Torres, Nelson (2008a) "Religion, Conquête et Race dans la Fondation du monde Moderne/Colonial." In *Islamophobie dans le Monde Moderne*, 205-238. Edited by Mohamed Mestiri, Ramon Grosfoguel and El Yamine Soum. Paris: IIIT.

Maldonado-Torres, Nelson (2008b) *Against War* (Durham and London: Duke University Press).

Martín Casares, Aurelia (2000) *La esclavitud en la Granada del Siglo XVI*. (Granada: Universidad de Granada y Diputación Provincial de Granada).

Martín de la Hoz, Juan Carlos (2010) *El Islam y España* (Madrid: RIALP).

Nimako, Kwame and Willemsen, Glenn (2011) *The Dutch Atlantic: Slavery, Abolition and Emancipation* (London: Pluto Press).

Perceval, Jose María. (1992). "Animalitos del señor: Aproximación a una teoría de las animalizaciones propias y del otro, sea enemigo o siervo, en la España imperial (1550-1650)" en *Areas: Revista de Ciencias Sociales* (Universidad de Murcia), No. 14: 173-184.

Perceval, José María. (1997). *Todos son uno. Arquetipos, xenofobia y racismo. La imagen del morisco en la monarquía española durante los siglos XVI y XVII*. Almería: Instituto de Estudios Almerienses.

Wallerstein, Immanuel (1974) *The Modern World-System*, Vol. 1 (New York: Academic Press).

Exploring Pluriversal Paths Toward Transmodernity

From the Mind-Centered Egolatry of Colonial Modernity to Islam's Epistemic Decolonization through the Heart

Dustin Craun

craund@gmail.com

Abstract: This paper explores the intersections between the decoloniality/transmodernity school of thought and Islamic spirituality, popularly known as Sufism. Beginning with an in depth study of the egolatry of Western epistemology which places white Western man and the mind on a false god like pedestal, this work explores two modes of being. One that is centered in coloniality/modernity what is called here the pyramidal construction of man, versus a decolonial process centered in the seat of human perception/ consciousness centered in the heart as understood in Islamic/sufi epistemology, called here the pyramidal construction of the human. As these pyramids clearly demonstrate, needed is a shift from the ego/nafs/self at the top or center of Man's onto-epistemological existence, to the ego/nafs/self being placed in a state of spiritual peace at the bottom of one's existence where the ego/nafs/self is placed last. To make this shift in the geo-politics of knowledge in the context of Islam, he argues that what is needed is a shift away from Descartes and Western modernity's centering of human consciousness in the mind, to a re-centering of consciousness in the spiritual heart (*qalb*). This in turn requires a shift back to a *Tassawuf* (Islamic Sufism) and thus a heart (*qalb*) centered understanding of Islam in relation to modernity. Since the Islamic spiritual science of *Tassawuf* has been de-centered and scapegoated in relation to Islamic discourses such as "modern revivalist Islam" (Wahabism/Salafism) and secular modernists, in this paper the author seeks to show that as it relates to the Muslim world, Islamic Sufism can make an important epistemological contribution to the perspective of decoloniality. Pulling from the decoloniality/transmodernity thinkers such as Enrique Dussel, Walter Mignolo, Nelson Maldonado-Torres, and Ramon Grosfoguel, this paper also engages the work of Fanon, Cesaire, Laura Perez, and the Muslim thinkers Abu Hamid al-Ghazali, Ibn Arabi, and Sherman Jackson.

I. INTRODUCTION

In his major work *Ethics of Liberation* (2013), Enrique Dussel's "point of departure is a world system of globalized exclusion," which can be placed against his imagining of what he calls "the Transmodern" (xv), i.e., to move beyond modernity to a pluraversality of existence. Similarly, according to Sylvia Wynter, "The struggle of our new millennium will be one between the ongoing

---

Dustin Craun is a writer, community organizer, and digital strategist who has worked with more than twenty-five different social movement organizations over the last twelve years in the U.S., and throughout the world. Dustin works on the clergy organizing team for the PICO National Network building Muslim Community organizing into the largest faith based community organizing network in the United States. His writings have been featured in a number of blogs and publications such as *Adbusters*, and he is working on publishing his first two books titled *White Benevolent Innocence: Race, Whiteness and the Genocidal Mentality of Colonial Modernity* and *Decolonizing the Heart in an Upside Down World*. He has a Masters degree from the College of Ethnic Studies at San Francisco State University and a Bachelors in Ethnic Studies from the University of Colorado-Boulder. Beyond this he has also studied the classical Islamic sciences with some of the world's leading Muslim scholars at Zaytuna College.

imperative of securing the well-being of our present ethnoclass (i.e., Western bourgeois) conception of the human, Man, which over-represents itself as if it were the human itself, and that of securing the well-being, and therefore the full cognitive and behavioral autonomy of the human species itself/ourselves."[1] If so, then to move towards an actual theorization of the human, we must first shatter and expose the "overrepresentation of Man"[2] as it has been molded into marble, bronze, and the psyche of peoples throughout the world as the normative construction of a universalized Western/white male being.

In imagining the human, the images that instantly come to mind are those of this overrepresentation, from global images of a supposed white/blue eyed Jesus, the anthropomorphic rendering of the elderly white bearded Christian God as painted in the *Sistine Chapel* creating Adam, Michelangelo's *David*, statues of Christopher Columbus pointing West, Santa Claus and his rosy red cheeks, George Washington's angel-like representation emblazoned atop the rotunda in the United States capitol building, and today, that of the lifestyle branded white male celebrity jet setting across the planet to "save" children in Africa at one moment, then wearing the latest Giorgio Armani suit at his movie premier the next. While these altruistic images are central to the construction of "egology,"[3] which sits atop the pyramidal construction of Man, it is primarily on its epistemological and ontological basis that I will focus my attention here. To properly understand, and to expose the "clay feet" of these false gods of what W.E.B. DuBois called "the religion of whiteness,"[4] we must shift the study to focus on what Walter Mignolo terms the "geo-politics of knowledge" —that is, the epistemological and ontological roots of the overrepresentation of a false universal Western Man, rooted in Renaissance and Enlightenment epistemology and ontology. To make this decolonial move it is necessary to ally my critique with that of the modernity/coloniality school of thought, to first properly understand the discourses of modernity, and also to privilege epistemologies of the South—which help us in shattering the falsely-universalized conception of Man—in order to move towards the transmodern understanding of the Human.

In this paper I will follow the line of thought of key decolonial theorists as I attempt to map what I have termed the pyramidal construction of Man, and the inverted pyramid as constructing the Human. Placed together with the pyramid representing the logic of modernity at the top, and the inverted pyramid as representing the logic of coloniality at the bottom, this visualization of these theoretical matrixes will help us in understanding the processes that are necessary to create an "epistemic geo-political move"[5] to a politics of what Nelson Maldonado-Torres terms, "epistemological decolonization."[6] As these pyramids clearly demonstrate, needed is a shift from the ego/*nafs*/self at the top or center of Man's onto-epistemological existence, to the ego/*nafs*/self being placed in a state of spiritual peace at the bottom of one's existence where the ego/*nafs*/self is placed last.

To make this shift in the geo-politics of

---

1. See: Sylvia Wynter, "Unsettling the Coloniality of Being/ Power/ Truth/ Freedom: Towards the Human, After Man, Its Overrepresentation—An Argument," CR: *The New Centennial Review*, 3:3, (Fall 2003): 260.

2. Ibid, 262.

3. This term was first used by Walter Mignolo. He defines "egology," as "a frame of knowledge having "ego" instead of "theo," as the center and point of reference." See: Walter Mignolo, *The Idea of Latin America* (Malden, MA: Blackwell, 2005):10.

4. See: W.E.B. Dubois, *Darkwater: Voices from Within the Veil* (New York: Schocken, 1999): 18.

5. Mignolo describes this as a, "a move that shifts the geo-politics of knowledge." Walter Mignolo, *The Idea of Latin America*: 39.

6. See: Nelson Maldonado Torres, "Lewis Gordon: Philosopher of the Human," *The CLR James Journal* (The Caribbean Philosophical Association: Volume 14. Number 1. Spring 2008b): 124.

knowledge in the context of Islam, I argue that what is needed is a shift away from Descartes and Western moderniy's centering of human consciousness in the mind, to a re-centering of consciousness in the spiritual heart (*qalb*). This in turn requires a shift back to a *Tassawuf* (Islamic Sufism) and thus a heart (*qalb*) centered understanding of Islam in relation to modernity. Since the Islamic spiritual science of *Tassawuf* has been de-centered and scapegoated in relation to Islamic discourses such as "modern revivalist Islam" (Wahabism/Salafism) and secular modernists, in this paper I will show that as it relates to the Muslim world Islamic Sufism can make an important epistemological contribution to the perspective of decoloniality.

In his classic decolonial manifesto, *Discourse on Colonialism*, Aime Cesaire writes that "a poison has been distilled into the veins of Europe."[7] The poison Cesaire speaks of is a poison that has been spread to the planet starting in 1492, when Christopher Columbus' march of death and genocide came to the Americas in full force, and then spread swiftly to the rest of the world atop piles of bodies and enslaved millions. While the papal bulls of the crusades and the conquest of the Americas set the legal stage for Western colonization, a genocidal Christian supremacism spread colonization to the far reaches of the earth.[8] While the logic of conquest and enslavement began with Western religious fanatics, it would become further racialized and move to an epistemological level with the Renaissance and Enlightenment philosophers led by Rene Descartes. Descartes' philosophical move was to replace the conception of the Christian God-centered soul as eternal, to an understanding of the mind in the place of the soul as what is eternal. Descartes' famous dictum, 'Cogito ergo sum'/ 'I think, therefore I am' would ultimately have the effect of shifting the center of Western thought away from the sacred, and would create Western white Man as the supreme being at the center of the universe. From Descartes' moment on, the idea of Western thought as 'objective' or 'unbiased' and as 'rational' and 'scientific,' became the most explicit form of racism that still lives with us today. This is an epistemological racism that universalizes Western knowledge as applicable to all people in the world, while also delegitimizing other knowledge forms as 'unscientific' or 'pre-modern.'

This philosophical stand is a spiritual poison that has deeply infected the white West. It's attribution of Godhood to its Western self has caused epistemological, cultural, and planetary ecological destruction which we are only now beginning to understand. This desacralization of the European self, life worlds, and the accompanying status of 'non-being' given to colonized bodies of Third World peoples, can leave our spiritual hearts dead and void of almost any connection to the sacred. In the American Indian Scholar/ Activist Vine Deloria Jr's final book titled *The World We Used to Live In*, he writes that "The secularity of the society in which we live must share considerable blame in the erosion of spiritual powers of all traditions, since our society has become a parody of social interaction lacking even an aspect of civility. Believing in nothing, we have preempted the role of the higher spiritual forces by acknowledging no greater good than what we can feel and touch."[9]

To make this critique which I have briefly sketched above, I will start by looking at how Nishitani Osamu and Nelson Maldonado-Torres understand the process of constructing Modernity/Man in its current state of "egology." After this I will look at the work of Joseph Massad to show the ways in

---

7. See: Aime Cesaire, *Discourse on Colonialism* (New York: Monthly Review Press, 2005): 36.

8. See: Robert Williams Jr, *The American Indian and Western Legal Thought: The Discourses of Conquest* (Oxford: Oxford University Press, 1992): 3-58.

9. See: Vine Deloria, Jr. *The World We Used to Live In: Remembering the Powers of the Medicine Men*. (Golden, CO: Fulcrum Publishing, 2006): xviii.

which this normalization of the Western overrepresentation of Man has been internalized by Muslim/Arab populations in the secular-progressive/neo-conservative call for reforms throughout the Muslim world. Finally in my attempt to theorize an epistemic geo-political move, I will look at the work of Timothy Winter (Shaykh Abdul Hakim Murad) and Sherman Jackson who have been two of the central Muslim scholars in the West calling for a shift back to a *Tassawuf* (Islamic Sufism) centered understanding of Islam in relation to modernity. Since the Islamic spiritual science of *Tassawuf* has been decentered and scapegoated in relation to Islamic discourses such as "modern revivalist Islam"[10] (Wahabism/Salafism) and secular modernists, I will show that as it relates to the Muslim world Sufism can make an important epistemological contribution to the decolonial perspective.

II. *HUMANITAS* AND THE STRUGGLE FOR RECOGNITION

The self-deception of Europe, the delusion of US patriotism, the bad-faith of Euro-American whiteness, and the Westernized mind are in a global crisis—a global crisis which has dehumanized humanity, and in its hybrid form of neoliberal multiculturalism[11] continues its global ravages at a breakneck speed. With its placement of Man at the center of modernity, the West has taken its discourses of supremacism—and what Enrique Dussel calls the *ego conquiro*[12]—to their heights by creating secular-

---

10. This term is used by Abdul Hakim Murad, in the article Abdul Hakim Murad, "Islamic Spirituality: the Forgotten Revolution," (Masud, UK, no date given), Available at: http://www.masud.co.uk/ISLAM/ahm/fgtnrevo.htm. I should note here that the British convert to Islam Timothy Winter who is a professor at Cambridge University, in Cambridge, England, is also Abdal-Hakim Murad, the Shaykh of the Cambridge Mosque and a prominent Islamic thinker in the West. He seems to publish under the name Timothy Winter when publishing in Western academic presses, and the name Abdal-Hakim Murad when publishing articles strictly related to the traditional Islamic sciences. What is often referred to as the "traditional Islamic sciences" refers generally to the religious study (ilm in Arabic) of the Quran, *Tafsir* (Qur'an Commentary), *Aqida* (Theology), Hadith (the sayings of the Prophet Muhammad), Seerah (the life of the Prophet Muhammad), *Fiqh* (Islamic Law), Usul al-fiqh (Legal Theory), Arabic grammar, and Tassawuf (Sufism).

11. I use the term "neoliberal multiculturalism" here as Jodi Melamed defines it in her article, "The Spirit of Neoliberalism: From Racial Liberalism to Neoliberal Multiculturalism." She writes that, "Multicultural reference masks the centrality of race and racism to neoliberalism. Race continues to permeate capitalism's economic and social processes, organizing the hyperextraction of surplus value from racialized bodies and naturalizing a system of capital accumulation that grossly favors the global North over the global South. Yet multiculturalism portrays neoliberal policy as the key to a postracist world of freedom and opportunity. Neoliberal policy engenders new racial subjects, as it creates and distinguishes between newly privileged and stigmatized collectivities, yet multiculturalism codes the wealth, mobility, and political power of neoliberalism's beneficiaries to be the just desserts of "multicultural world citizens," while representing those neoliberalism dispossesses to be handicapped by their own "monculturalism" or other historico-cultural deficiencies. A language of multiculturalism consistently portrays acts of force required for neoliberal restructuring to be humanitarian: a benevolent multicultural invader (the United States, multinational troops, a multinational corporation) intervenes to save life, "give" basic goods or jobs, and promote limited political freedom." See: Jodi Melamed, "The Spirit of Neoliberalism: From Racial Liberalism to Neoliberal Multiculturalism," *Social Text*, 89 Vol. 24, Number 4, (Winter 2006), Duke University Press: 1.

12. Following Dussel, according to Maldonado-Torres, the *ego conquiro* is a central attitude in the construction of modernity, "what was born in the sixteenth century was something more pervasive and subtle than what at first transpires in the concept of race: it was an attitude characterized by a permanent suspicion. Enrique Dussel states that Hernan Cortes gave expression to an ideal of subjectivity that could be defined as the *ego conquiro*, which predates Rene Descarte's articulation of the *ego cogitio*. This means that the significance of the Cartesian *cogito* for modern European identity has to be understood against the backdrop of an unquestioned ideal of self expressed in the notion of the *ego conquiro*. The certainty of the self as a conqueror, of its tasks and missions, preceded Descartes' certainty about

ized bodies and rational thought in the form of Descartes *ego-cogito* ('Cogito ergo sum'/ 'I think, therefore I am') that create the Western white Man as the supreme being at the center of the universe.

Through this desacralization[13] of the European self, life worlds, and the accompanying status of 'non-being' given to colonized bodies of Third/Fourth World[14] peoples, the Western world has spread its physical, epistemological and ontological conquests throughout the planet. The identitarian logic of this genocidal violence of the 'West' versus the 'non-West' started with the first crusade, and the absolute annihilation of the Muslim population of Jerusalem. It then re-mapped Western conceptions of reality and was globalized at the outset of modernity in 1492. While our moment is one that is often theorized as being 'post-colonial,' the legacies of genocide, colonialism, and the resulting historical trauma, and systemic hierarchies still live with us today. The best theorization of these legacies have been put forth by the Modernity/Coloniality research project[15] led by Anibal Quijano[16], Enrique Dussel[17], Walter Mignolo[18], Ramon Grosfoguel[19], Nelson Maldonado-Torres[20],

---

the self as a thinking substance (*res cogitans*) and provided a way to interpret it." Nelson Maldonado-Torres, "On the Coloniality of Being: Contributions to the Development of a Concept," *Cultural Studies*, Vol. 21, Nos. 2-3 March/ May 2007: 245.

13. The term desacralization was first used by the Islamic/perennialist philosopher Seyyed Hossein Nasr. See his seminal work: Seyyed Hossein Nasr, *Knowledge and the Sacred* (New York: SUNY Press, 1989): 1.

14. The Fourth World refers to the indigenous "nations forcefully incorporated into states which maintain a distinct political culture but are internally unrecognized." Richard Griggs, "Background on the term "Fourth World,"" *Center for World Indigenous Studies*, Available at: http://cwis.org/GML/background/FourthWorld/

15. For an overview of this project, and a listing of the work by its primary contributors see Walter Mignolo, "DELINKING: The Rhetoric of Modernity, the Logic of Coloniality and the Grammar of De-coloniality," *Cultural Studies* Vol. 21, Nos. 2-3 March/ May 2007: 449-450 and especially the end notes numbers 1 and 2 on pages 500-502.

16. See Anibal Quijano, "Colonialidad y modernidad/ racionalidad," *Los Conquistados. 1492 y la poblacion indigena de las Americas*, Heraclio Bonilla (editor). (Ecuador: Libri Mundi, Tercer Mundo Editores, 1992) for his original articulation of the idea in Spanish, and the translation into English of the same article see: Anibal Quijano, "Coloniality and Modernity/ Rationality," *Cultural Studies*, Vol. 21, Nos. 2-3 (March/ May 2007).

17. See: Enrique Dussel, "Beyond Eurocentrism: The World-System and the Limits of Modernity," Fredric Jameson and Masao Miyoshi (editors). *The Cultures of Globalization*. (Durham: Duke University Press, 1998). For Dussel's philosophy of liberation see: Enrique Dussel, *Philosophy of Liberation*, Translated by Aquilina Martinez and Christine Morkovsky. (Maryknoll, N.Y.: Orbis Books, 1985). For the best summation of Enrique Dussel's thought, and particularly his ideas of "philosophy of liberation" see generally Nelson Maldonado-Torres, *Against War: Views from the Underside of Modernity* (Durham: Duke University Press, 2008a). While Dussel is discussed in relation to the thought of Levinas and Fanon throughout the text, the specific chapters on Dussel are on pages 162-236.

18. Walter Mignolo's major contributions to this field of thought include his books: Walter Mignolo, *Local Histories/ Global Designs: Coloniality, Subaltern Knowledges, and Border Thinking* (Princeton, N.J.: Princeton University Press, 2000); And Walter Mignolo, *The Darker Side of the Renaissance: Literacy, Territoriality, and Colonization*. 2nd Ed. (Ann Arbor: University of Michigan Press, 2003); And most recently his article: Walter Mignolo, "DELINKING."

19. See the volume he edited: Ramon Grosfoguel, (editor), *Latin@s in the World-System: Decolonization Struggles in the Twenty-First Century U.S. Empire*, (Boulder: Paradigm Publishers, 2005); and his article Ramon Grosfoguel, "World-Systems Analysis in the Context of Transmodernity, Border Thinking, and Global Coloniality," *Review: Fernand Braudel Center*. Vol. XXIX. Number 2, 2006.

20. His article on the coloniality of being is especially important, see: Nelson Maldonado-Torres, "On the Coloniality of Being"; He is also the only author to thus far theorize secularism as it relates to coloniality/ modernity, see: Nelson Maldonado-Torres, "Secularism and Religion in the Modern/Colonial World-System: From Secular Postcoloniality to Postsecular Transmodernity." Mabel Morana, Enrique Dussel, and Carlos A. Jauregui (editors). *Coloniality at Large: Latin America and the Postcolonial Debate*. (Durham, NC: Duke University Press, 2008c). And most recently his book length project: Nelson Maldonado-Torres,

and Maria Lugones.[21] Starting with Quijano's idea of "colonialidad de poder" (the coloniality of power), this idea has been expanded to include the concepts: the coloniality of knowledge, the coloniality of being, and perhaps most importantly de-coloniality. Grosfoguel, expanding upon Quijano, has theorized the complexity and scale of the coloniality of power. He writes that,

> The sixteenth century initiated a new global colonial power matrix that by the late nineteenth century covered the whole planet…I conceptualize the coloniality of power as an entanglement of multiple and heterogeneous hierarchies ("heter-archies") of sexual, political, epistemic, economic, spiritual, linguistic, and racial forms of domination and exploitation where the racial/ethnic hierarchy of the European/non-European divide transversally reconfigures all other global power structures. What is new in the "coloniality of power" perspective is how the idea of race and racism becomes the organizing principle that structures all of the multiple hierarchies of the world-system.[22]

As the heter-archies of the coloniality of power have been constructed over the last five hundred years, it is important to recognize as the modernity/coloniality research project does, the centrality of modernity's philosophical roots in Renaissance and Enlightenment thought. The basis of the pyramidal construction of Man, is Rene Descartes' "first philosophy," as a break from a theo centered episteme to an ego centered one, where Man displaces God as the center of existence. Descartes' first philosophy, coupled with Hegel's understanding of the struggle for recognition, construct the perspective of modernity where Western Man as the egolatrous being is placed at the top of existence for all others to look towards for recognition. Here I will look at the work of Osamu and Maldonado-Torres to gain a perspective on how this standpoint of what Maldonado-Torres calls the "Imperial Man" takes shape.

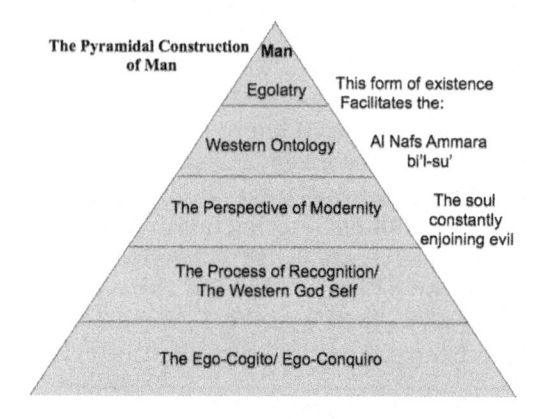

The Pyramidal Construction of Man
- Man
- Egolatry — This form of existence Facilitates the:
- Western Ontology — Al Nafs Ammara bi'l-su'
- The Perspective of Modernity — The soul constantly enjoining evil
- The Process of Recognition/ The Western God Self
- The Ego-Cogito/ Ego-Conquiro

Maldonado-Torres has written of the centrality of Descartes to the West's "first philosophy" when he states that,

> Following Rene Descarte's legacy modern Western philosophy has been highly invested in figuring out the extent and limits of the powers of the mind in general and of perception in particular in a context where revelation has lost a high degree of legitimacy. In this context, epistemology becomes *philosophia prima*. This epistemology, as Descartes also made clear, presupposes an anthropology and an ontology that are both well expressed in the Cartesian split of *res extensa* (matter) and *res cogitans* (thinking sub-

---

Against War.

21. For the most important contribution made thus far that engages ideas pertaining to Gender and Coloniality see: Maria Lugones, "Heterosexualism and the Colonial/ Modern Gender System," *Hypatia*, vol. 22, no. 1 (Winter 2007).

22. Ramon Grosfoguel, "World-Systems Analysis in the Context of Transmodernity, Border Thinking, and Global Coloniality,": 172.

stance).[23]

It is in this context of the West's thinking substance of rationality, that it would philosophically move away from Christianity as an organizing principle towards one that would similarly see itself as the only proper form of existence—but here organized around the epistemological foundations of a 'rational' Western 'civilization.' From this foundation Nishitani Osamu writes about *Humanitas* and *Anthropos* as the "two terms that signify "human being" within European languages.[24] *Humanitas* here represents the terms "human being" or "human nature"[25] while *Anthropos* is always an object of Western study. While keeping these categories central to his argument, Osamu states that the first interpretation of the Other was through the lens of "the Greek code of barbarian." In time the salvation narrative of Christianity was added on top of this, with the discourse eventually shifting to secularism and the "progress of civilization" that would ultimately be reinforced by Darwin's theory of evolution.[26]

According to Osamu this "discovery of difference," beyond being spatiotemporally located, is also central to the consciousness of modernity and its onto-epistemological existence where,

> ...humans who possess "civilization" are *"humanitas"* never "anthropos." These two designations, moreover, are not selected according to the differing contexts of the same object, nor do they create a simple oppositional binary within a genre called human being. Rather, there exists an inextricable and fundamentally asymmetrical relation between the two. That asymmetry performs a systemic function related to the regime of modern "knowledge" itself (for that very reason, this distinction is made automatically whenever people speak "knowledgeably"), a function that constitutes the "double standard" of modern human, or humanistic, knowledge. In other words, "*anthropos*" cannot escape the status of being the object of anthropological knowledge, while *"humanitas"* is never defined from without but rather expresses itself as the subject of all knowledge.[27]

The key idea here as Walter Mignolo discusses in his book, *The Idea of Latin America*, is the point of enunciation of what he terms "Occidentalism." He states that,

> Occidentalism" as O'Gormans's thesis on the "universalism of Western culture" suggests, has two interrelated dimensions: First, it served to locate the geo-historical space of Western culture. But, less obviously, it also fixed the privileged locus of enunciation. It is from the West that the rest of the world is described, conceptualized, and ranked: that is, modernity is the self-description of Europe's role in history rather than an ontological historical process. Without a locus of enunciation self-conceived as Occidental, the Oriental could not have been thought out.[28]

It is this epistemological racism as constructing the world and its standards that the rest of humanity must struggle against within for recognition, and it is to this argu-

---

23. Nelson Maldonado-Torres, "Lewis Gordon: Philosopher of the Human.," 111.
24. See: Nishitani Osamu, (Translated by Trent Maxey), "Anthropos and Humanitas: Two Western Concepts of "Human Being." Naoki Sakai and Jon Solomon (editors), *Translatoin, Biopolitics, Colonial Difference* (Hong Kong: Hong Kong University Press, 2006): 259.
25. Ibid.
26. Ibid: 262.
27. Ibid: 260.
28. See: Walter Mignolo, *The Idea of Latin America*: 35.

ment that I will turn next.

Here, I will look at the work of Nelson Maldonado-Torres, as it relates to the construction of the overrepresentation of Man. According to him, from the beginning of global modernity the *ego conquiro* emerges as the "paradigm of war,"[29] and becomes the central facet of human life. In his book *Against War: Views from the Underside of Modernity*, Maldonado-Torres centrally argues that since 1492 European modernity has become,

> ...inextricably linked with the experience of the warrior and conqueror and the modern colonization, racism, and other forms of social and geopolitical dynamics in the modern world can be understood in terms of the naturalization of the paradigm of war.[30]

It is within this paradigm of existence where war has become naturalized that, according to Maldonado-Torres, ethics as applicable to Western Man are replaced by what he calls the "death ethic of war,"[31] or the "non-ethics of war."[32] As a radical project of "de-colonial love,"[33] Maldonado-Torres uses Emanuel Levinas, Frantz Fanon, and Enrique Dussel as philosophers of the "de-colonial reduction" while making his own theoretical contributions towards a "philosophy of liberation."[34] He chooses to use these three philosophers together because,

> Levinas, Fanon, and Dussel respond critically to the realities of war as they encounter them in the context of Nazism, French imperialism, intolerable Eurocentrism, and the menace of U.S. Americanism and its salvific mission of freedom, all of which are preceded if not tied to each other by a long history of racialization and colonization that goes back to at least 1492.[35]

I think Maldonado-Torres' understanding of the "paradigm of war" has made an important philosophical contribution to our understanding of Man. Most important to my discussion here are the first of two chapters on Frantz Fanon at the center of the book titled, "God and the Other in the Self-Recognition of Imperial Man."[36]

In the anti-black colonial world in which Fanon was writing, the Manichean opposition characterized for him "modern/colonial thinking and power"[37]—a modern/colonial world where the pathological became normal as the colonial and racist context in which he lived in its totality was "a metaphysical transformation of the world."[38] In this transformed world "Imperial Man"

---

29. According to Maldonado-Torres, the "paradigm of war" has been best described by Enrique Dussel who states: "From Heraclitus to Karl von Clausewitz and Henry Kissinger, 'war is the origin of everything,' if by 'everything' one understands the order or system that world dominators control by their power and armies. We are at war—a cold war for those who wage it, a hot war for those who suffer it..." (See Nelson Maldonado-Torres, *Against War*: 3).

30. Ibid: 4.

31. With the term "death ethic of war," Maldonado-Torres is expanding on the work of Steve Martinot. Maldonado-Torres's definition of the term refers to the "constitutive character of coloniality and the naturalization of human difference that is tied to it in the emergence and unfolding of Western modernity." See: Ibid: xii.

32. Maldonado-Torres's term, the "non-ethics of war," refers to "the suspension of what usually goes by ethics not only in war, but in civilization. It is this suspension that allows the production of premature death to become normative, at least for well-selected sectors in society and in the globe." Ibid.

33. Maldonado-Torres borrows this term from Chela Sandoval. See: Chela Sandoval, Methodology of the Oppressed, (Minneapolis: University of Minnesota Press, 2000): 169-170.

34. This is Enrique Dussel's term, and also the title of his multi-volume work of the same title.

35. Nelson Maldonado-Torres, *Against War*: 6.

36. Ibid: 93-121.

37. Ibid: 95.

38. Ibid: 99.

would hold itself up as God, while its colonial subjects would be relegated to the realm of "non-being." It is here that the "non-beings" of colonialism would experience the "colonial death world" which would become,

> the ethical limit of human reality. It is a context in which violence and war are no longer extraordinary, but become instead ordinary features of human existence. This perverse expression of the conversion of the extraordinary into the ordinary represents a "limit" situation, or perhaps even a post-limit situation in the sense that the excess of abnormality goes beyond its climax and begets another reality in which it comes to define the normal.[39]

As the status of "non-being" had become normal, the question then became how did the white colonizers recognize themselves as the 'supreme beings at the center of the universe.' While Fanon did not take up a serious analysis of white consciousness until *The Wretched of the Earth*,[40] to address his argument pertaining to white consciousness Maldonado-Torres begins with a discussion of the "dialectics of lordship and bondage."

Here Maldonado-Torres, taking his lead from Fanon,[41] discusses Hegel's understanding of the "struggle for recognition" which, "takes the form of a dialectic whose terms are those of lordship and bondsman, or master and slave."[42] In this discussion he points out that while the slave must look to the master for recognition, and thus his humanity, "In an Imperial World lordship is the position of a privileged self that does not even turn toward the slave to achieve recognition."[43] The ultimate question then, that also has relevance for us today, is

> If the master/slave dialectic is not overcome by other forms of Spirit but remains a constant explicative factor of human relations defined by the experience of imperialism and colonialism, then we must ask how is it that the master, who in the colonial relation does not look for recognition from the slave, achieves recognition and sustains his position as master?[44]

According To Suha Sabbagh, it was not until *Wretched of the Earth* that Fanon focused on this understanding of white consciousness, but it is through this text that we understand that,

> The West was able to do without the recognition of the 'non-whites' because it has created an image of this native as an inferior entity within the confines of Western discourse. Against the other, Western positional superiority and identity could be established.[45]

It is here through the continuous Manichean production of negative and positive images that the picture of the self and the Other is constructed. According to Maldonado-Torres, this "imperial self-assertion" is constructed through what he calls "the positive."[46] This positive image of the self—or what I call white benevolent innocence[47]—is taken to its height in the imperial world where, "*In empire, God becomes the privileged other who alone can provide authentic recognition to the imperial self.*"[48] So in this

---

39. Ibid: 100.
40. Quoted in Ibid: 107.
41. Fanon discusses Hegel's Master/Slave dialectic in Frantz Fanon, *Black Skin, White Masks*, (New York: Grove Press, 2007): 220-221.
42. Nelson Maldonado-Torres, *Against War*: 103.
43. Ibid: 106.
44. Ibid: 107.
45. Sabbagh, quoted in Ibid: 107.
46. Ibid: 108.
47. See my forthcoming book: Dustin Craun, *White Benevolent Innocence: The Genocidal Mentality of Colonial Modernity*.
48. Ibid: 113.

construction, consciousness of God becomes knowledge of the superior self, and thus the making of God in the image of man, as in the imperial Christian form, which takes on great significance in the production of the modern/colonial self. As Maldonado-Torres understands, in one of his many important contributions to the theory, this form of recognition produces the "egolatry" of Imperial man. He writes,

> A logic of sub-alteration is contained in the process of recognition of Imperial Man. God recognizes Man, Man takes the shape of God, and then others come to be *seen* as the very incarnation of evil. This logic does not respond so much to interests in the conciliation with nature as, more fundamentally, to interests in the subordination of other human beings. Modern imperial man is no pagan. He does not divinize nature, but rather becomes himself God with the sole purpose of enslaving others. Idolatry becomes egolatry, a perverse egolatry that works in the function of the rejection of otherness. At the end, narcissism becomes homicidal, and the command "Thou shall not kill" is transformed into a project of identity based on the principle "I kill, therefore I am.[49]

Despite secularism becoming the center of Western life, according to Maldonado-Torres, Imperial Man through race, the nation-state, and free market capitalism, is able to sustain, "the position of the master as the one and only lord."[50] Despite the shift from a religious center to a mostly secular space, the production of Western/white lordship is still produced through a constant bombardment of Manichean images of the West and the non-West.

---

49. Ibid: 114.
50. Ibid: 119.

III. Striving for *Humanitas* in the Muslim/Arab World

Imperial Man has reared its ugly head consistently at the Muslim/Arab community over the last twelve years, which has resulted in an increasing attempted movement into the world of *Humanitas*. This attempted escape from "the station of *"anthropos"* and becoming a subject who possesses and produces knowledge, i.e. *"humanitas,"*[51] has further augmented this movement that has been going on over the last two-hundred plus years as Muslims have struggled to affirm their humanity in relation to modernity/coloniality. In the early part of the twentieth century the European convert to Islam, Muhammad Asad (Leopold Weiss), already was seeing the cultural destruction brought on by European colonialism in the Muslim world. As he wrote, "For how long will… [Muslims] be able to keep their souls together in the face of the danger that is so insidiously, so relentlessly closing in on them?...A thousand forces – political, social and economic – are hammering at the doors of the Muslim world. Will this world succumb to the pressure of the Western twentieth century and in the process lose not only its own traditional forms but its spiritual roots as well?"[52]

Of course the best example of Muslims/Arabs striving for Western recognition is in the desert-turned-neoliberal-dreamworld of Dubai. This desert fantasy land that boasts of itself that it is making 'supreme lifestyles' for its inhabitants, is obsessed with gigantism, and outdoing the West in every material way possible, in a manner that would frighten Muhammad Asad if he were alive today. In his brilliant essay "Fear and Money in Dubai," Mike Davis writes that the CEO and Emir of Dubai Sheikh Mohammed al-Maktoum has taken his obses-

---

51. Nishitani Osamu, "Anthropos and Humanitas": 269.
52. See: Muhammad Asad, *The Road to Mecca* (St. Louis: Fons Vitae, 2000): 103.

sion with gigantism to such extremes that, "he seems to have imprinted Scott and Venturi's bible of hyper-reality, *Learning From Las Vegas*, in the same way that pious Muslims memorize the *Qur'an*."[53] One of the grossest manifestation of this striving for *Humanitas* is the Burj Dubai, now the tallest building in the world, which when completed will stand 2600 feet tall and will have the world's largest shopping mall, with an area equaling more that 12 million square feet, at its base. This, along with the holy city of Mecca undergoing rapid redevelopment with the biggest (in terms of square feet) and second tallest building in the world, the *Abraj Al Bait* Towers, directly outside of the Grand Mosque, as the most explicit example.

The *Ka'ba* inside the grand mosque, with the *Abraj Al Bait* Towers in the background.
Photo - Dustin Craun, 2013

Despite the fact that Frantz Fanon was writing centrally about the Muslim/Arab world while fighting with the FLN in Algeria, I am always shocked to see how few Muslims know his name today, let alone his work. Of course Fanon is central in understanding the processes of epistemic and cultural destruction brought on by colonialism. As he wrote, "…colonialism is not simply content to impose its rule upon the present and the future of a dominated country. Colonialism is not satisfied merely with holding a people in its grip and emptying the native's brain of all form and content. By a kind of perverse logic, it turns to the past of the oppressed people, and distorts it, disfigures and destroys it."[54]

In his masterful work *Desiring Arabs*, Joseph Massad[55] lays out an important intellectual history at the beginning of the book that shows the ways in which Orientalist discourses were internalized by major Muslim/Arab thinkers since 1798, when Napoleon first invaded Egypt. These discourses existed primarily between the signifying binaries of "decadence/renaissance and tradition/modernity."[56] As the French carried the ideologies of the Enlightenment with them to Egypt, they along with compliant Arab scholars quickly made a call for *Nahda* or a renaissance in the Arab/Muslim

---

53. See: Mike Davis, "Fear and Money in Dubai." Mike Davis (editor), *Evil Paradises: the Dreamworlds of Neoliberalism* (New York: Verso, 2007): 51.

54. Frantz Fanon, *The Wretched of the Earth*, (New York: Grove Press, 1963): 61

55. Massad's work is groundbreaking in the way that Maria Lugones' is, in that he shows how colonialism and Western progressive movements like the Gay International have played a role in shifting sexuality to a more oppressive and different place than it occupied previous to colonization, and Westernization. As he writes, "In adopting this Weltanschauung, Arab intellectuals also internalized the epistemology by which Europeans came to judge civilizations and cultures along the vector of something called "sex," as well as its later derivative, "sexuality," and the overall systematization of culture through the statistical concept of "norms," often corresponding to the "natural" and its "deviant" opposite." See: Joseph A. Massad, *Desiring Arabs*, (Chicago: University of Chicago Press, 2008):6; for his larger arguments around sexuality see pages 99-418.

56. Ibid: 3.

world. Intellectuals like Jamal al-Din Al Afghani, Butrus al-Bustani, and Muhammad Abduh developed deep "epistemological affinity" with Western conceptions of Man or *Humanitas*. As Massad writes,

> These Arab writers would approach the topic at hand by adopting and failing to question these recently invented European notions of "civilization" and "culture" and their commensurate insertion in a social Darwinist idiom of "evolution," "progress," "advancement," "development," "degeneration," and most important, "decadence" and "renaissance."[57]

These discourses that internalize the idea of Islamic civilization as decadent needing a Renaissance, would lead to radical reactions still being felt all over the world today as "modern revivalist Islam," i.e., Wahabism/Salafism, are now very powerful global forces that spread a version of Islam disconnected from its intellectual and spiritual roots, as an almost solely *Fiqh* (Law/Legal) based version of the religion. Massad adds that,

> As Talal Asad explains, 'Abduh, among others, drew on existing Islamic tradition, even when he disagreed with some of it to effect a reform whose ideological lineaments were European. Thus even though the medieval ibn Taymiyyah and the eighteenth-century Muhammad bin 'Abd al-Wahhab's strict and literal interpretation of the Qur'an stripped Sufism of religious legitimacy, the project of modern religious reformers banished (parts of) it in accordance with modernist European ideas while remaining within a certain strand of tradition.[58]

Despite the modernist reformers' arrogance, Sufism is a vital part of Islam, and if we are to make reforms to move away from the oppression of modernity/coloniality, then it must be through a deep engagement with the spiritual as it relates to the destruction brought about by these reformers in alliance with modernity. As Shaykh Abdal-Hakim Murad has written, what is necessary in this context is a

> revival of the spiritual life within Islam. If it is ever to prosper, the 'Islamic revival' must be made to see that it is in crisis, and that its mental resources are proving insufficient to meet contemporary needs. The response to this must be grounded in an act of collective *muhasaba*, of self-examination, in terms that transcend the ideologised neo-Islam of the revivalists, and return to a more classical and indigenously Muslim dialectic.[59]

While the spiritual is central here, and it is where I will turn to in my argument next, it is also central that this spiritual guidance and self-examination lead us to a process of epistemic decolonization; no matter how difficult, and complex that self-examination may be. In this regard, Maldonado-Torres states,

> The mutual reinforcement of epistemological and misanthropic skepticism creates peculiar challenges for people of color. For, while they are aware that modernity promises them full recognition of humanity through the adoption of methodic epistemological skepticism, it often passes unnoticed that the unconditional affirmation of the value of this form of skepticism reinforces the form of skepticism from which they are trying to es-

---

57. Ibid: 5.
58. Ibid: 12.

59. See: Abdul Hakim Murad, "Islamic Spirituality: The Forgotten Revolution."

cape. It is from here that the project of liberation necessitates a process of epistemological decolonization and not one of epistemological assimilation. Epistemological decolonization as a project is not only relevant for people of color. In a way, it is the Europeans' only way out from the hellish circle that they have created. For, while misanthropic skepticism may intend to eliminate skepticism about the value of Man—by making Man more like a God and less than animal-like people—it instead spreads skepticism about the value of humanity as a whole, which in turn foments attitudes of violence and self destruction.[60]

For many of the American Muslim authors I quote in what follows, Islam has been a spiritual and epistemological form of decolonization that has led them to live their lives in alliance and solidarity with Muslims throughout the world.

IV. Turning *Anthropos* on *Humanitas*: Coloniality at the Edge of Islam

If what is called for according to Osamu "is rendering '*humanitas*,' which insists upon its 'universality,' an object of '*anthropologique*' consideration as one version of '*anthropos*,'"[61] then the question becomes what sort of critique do we make when this inversion takes place as we turn to study *Humanitas*? Are we to critique the new *anthropos* by its own standards that it has constructed, or do we dare to construct critiques outside the Western canons of philosophy? To think about these issues it is necessary to turn to Enrique Dussel's idea of Transmodernity.

For Dussel, transmodernity refers to the self-affirmation of cultures that have been occluded by Western modernity…Transmodern thought is postsecular and, therefore, post religious as well…Transmodern thought also recognizes that what is often referred to as religion can be as colonizing as secularism itself… Transmodernity transgresses and transcends. While the first task may be more strictly defined as decolonization, the second indicates the emergence of a transmodern way of thinking. Transmodernity could be thus defined as the complex reality that comes into being through decolonizing processes and transmodern proposals. Transmodernity designates a future beyond the pitfalls of modernity/ coloniality. This is the future that a transmodern way of thinking would aim to promote.[62]

In thinking about transmodern critiques I turn instantly to the thought of the marginalized spiritual and an attempt to move from the *ego-cogito* to experience, or more properly as the Arabic terms it: *dhawq*, a spiritual tasting, as an attempt to free myself from repetitive forms of *taqlid*, or conformism/imitation through tired forms of critique.[63] Thinking through existence from the same epistemology can only make us dizzy, so it is important that we bring in culturally specific epistemologies to critique the new *anthropos*, so as to properly understand what it is, and what it has done from

---

60. Nelson Maldonado-Torres, "Lewis Gordon: Philosopher of the Human": 124.

61. Nishitani Osamu, "Anthropos and Humanitas": 270.

62. See Nelson Maldonado-Torres, "Secularism and Religion in the Modern/Colonial World-System": 383.

63. For further definitions of these terms see: T.J. Winter, "Introduction," *Al-Ghazali On Disciplining the Soul-Kitab Riyadat al-nafs & On Breaking the Two Desires-Kitab Kasr al-shahwatayn-Books XXII and XXIII of The Revival of the Religious Sciences-Ihya 'Ulum al-Din*, (Cambridge, Islamic Texts Society, 1997): LXVI.

multiple perspectives, and in specific locations.

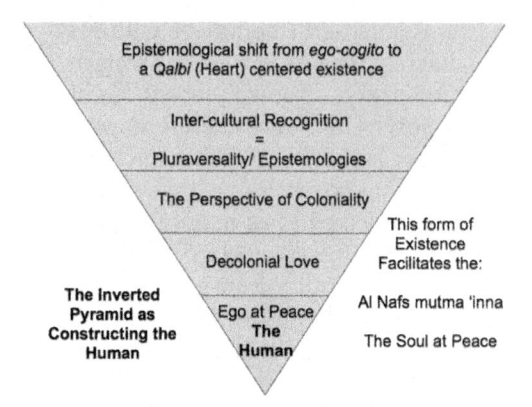

Epistemological shift from ego-cogito to a Qalbi (Heart) centered existence

Inter-cultural Recognition = Pluraversality/ Epistemologies

The Perspective of Coloniality

Decolonial Love

This form of Existence Facilitates the:

The Inverted Pyramid as Constructing the Human

Ego at Peace The Human

Al Nafs mutma 'inna The Soul at Peace

The pyramidal construction of Man from an Islamic perspective shifts our understanding of the seriousness of placing the egolatrous Man above God in constructing reality, while simultaneously allowing us to imagine what would be necessary in creating a transmodern critique in constructing the Human. It is in seeking this spiritual tasting, that I pursue what the great Islamic mystic philosopher of the eleventh century, Abu Hamid al-Ghazali, understood to be the highest level of knowledge. According to al-Ghazali, "The highest type of knowledge...is not that of Reason or that of faith, but that of direct experience. Thus the genuine knowledge of God belongs to this 'experiential' order."[64]

To shift the geo-politics of knowledge, and make what Walter Mignolo terms an "epistemic geo-political move," it is necessary to engage in a form of critique that is deeply engaged in *muhasaba* (self-examination) on three primary levels. These being examination of the self and one's spiritual state, an examination of the dominant structurally intersecting hierarchies that we all interact with (Gender, Race, Class, Religious domination, etc.), and finally an examination of one's local knowledge from where the place of critique is emanating. Foundational to this self/ structural/ societal examination is an understanding of how Western epistemological racism has led towards a global desacralization of knowledge. This to me is the space of critique in-between the pyramidal construction of Man, and the inverted pyramid as constructing the Human. One of the central factors of dehumanization resulting from the colonization of peoples' life worlds that has been grossly under-theorized is this desacralization of knowledge, or what I will call in a forthcoming paper, the coloniality of the sacred. A reality where the sacred or God has been removed from the center of what is considered to be 'valid' or 'scientific' or 'rational' forms of thought. If we are to take seriously epistemologies beyond Western conceptions of knowledge then God and sacred texts must be taken seriously.

In re-centering the sacred in this process of self-examination, many theorists, led by Chicana Feminists, have turned to the idea of "decolonial love." For the UC-Berkeley professor Laura Perez this idea is closely linked to the Mayan "principle of *In'Laketch: tu eres mi otro yo*: you are my other me. Not only are we interwoven, we are one. I am you and you are me. To harm another is thus to literally harm one's own being. This is a basic spiritual law in numerous traditions."[65] One of the most exciting possibilities about the concept of decolonial love is the possibility of looking at what Love means in different faith and spiritual traditions throughout the world, and how this can help lead towards global understanding, and a decolonial move.

I think here of the possible contribution of the marginalized spiritual within Islam, that of Sufism. To make this shift in the geo-politics of knowledge in the context of Islam, what is necessary is the shift away from Descartes and Western modernity's

---

64. See: Majid Fakhry, *A History of Islamic Philosophy* (New York: Columbia University Press, 2004): 256.

65. See: Laura Perez, "Con o Sin Permiso (With or Without Permission): Chicana Badgirls: Las Hociconas," *Chicana Badgirls: Las Hociconas (Exhibition Catalog)* (Albuquerque, New Mexico: 516 Arts, 2009): 5.

centering of human consciousness in the mind, to a re-centering of consciousness in the spiritual heart (*qalb*). This idea is echoed by Subcomandante Marcos and the Zapatistas in their motto to center politics below and to the left (where the heart is), as is understood in Aztec and Mayan cosmology. While the secularism of Western modernity imagines itself as solely rational, and indeed has argued its rationality and casting off of any other type of knowledge as what has made the West supposedly superior to all other knowledge forms, in the Muslim world this separation between the Sacred and reason does not exist. Indeed *Aql* or reason is a central part of classical Islamic theology, and the deduction of its tenets. The difference is that Islam, especially Islamic mysticism, has a firm belief that you cannot simply attain total wisdom or knowledge through reason, but that it must be accompanied with spiritual understanding, the *dhawq* or experiential level of knowledge that Imam Ghazali calls for.

Foundationally, Islam and Christianity have completely different understandings of the concept of original sin. While in Christianity humans are "fallen" to Earth as a result of the sins of Adam and Eve, and thus all of humanity is supposedly born into an original state of sin, in Islamic thought it is said that all of humanity is born into a state of *fitra* (primordial state)[66], "which means that people are born inclined to faith—born with an intuitive awareness of divine purpose and a nature built to receive the prophetic message."[67] According to Shaykh Hamza Yusuf, a prominent Muslim scholar, and White American convert to Islam, what is necessary to nurture this state of *fitra* is to "cultivate this inclination to faith and purity of heart."[68] The difficulty that Muslims face throughout the world in the context of coloniality is a relationship to existence, that from an Islamic perspective is first committing the only unforgivable sin in Islam, that of *shirk* (association), while simultaneously constructing a reality that can only lead people towards an inclination to evil. I will now take up both of these arguments.

The Blackamerican Muslim thinker, Sherman Jackson, best puts these theoretical perspectives into an Islamic context. When looked at in relationship to Rudolf Otto's conception of *mysterium tremendum*, which "refers to that ineffable fear that accompanies the experience of encountering the divine,"[69] it can be seen that as Jackson posits, Man and Whiteness have been made into the all powerful "second creator." Jackson understands the construction of Man, or what he terms, White supremacists to be "second creators" who falsely construct humans as signified objects that create us as something much different than the original state of *fitra* in which God creates us. Accordingly Jackson believes that these "second creators," are committing *shirk* as,

> it is neither graven images nor idols that pose the greatest challenge to God's monopoly on divinity; it is false *mysterium tremendum*, second creators and the sociopolitical reality these produce. As such, it is against these, and not against idols, that modern men and women are likely to find the deepest meaning and resonance in Islam's foundational principle: "There is no god except God (la ilaha illa Allah)." And, on this understanding, the

---

66. This is based on a saying of the Prophet Muhammad, which states that "every child is born in a state of *fitra*." While many Muslims often translate *fitra* here as 'every child is born a Muslim,' Hamza Yusuf writes that the statement here actually means that people are born inclining towards faith in a general term. See Hamza Yusuf, *Purification of the Heart: Signs, Symptoms, and Cures of the Spiritual Diseases of the Heart* (Starlatch Press: 2004): 20-21.

67. Ibid: 21.

68. Ibid.

69. See: Sherman Jackson, *Islam and the Blackamerican: Looking toward the Third Resurrection* (New York: Oxford University Press, USA, 2005): 172-173.

proper response to the problem of human contingency is not to seek to overcome it but to resist and oppose false…"re-creation," *both as subjects and as objects*. In this context, it becomes clear that opposition to white supremacy—or for that matter, any supremacy, including male supremacy or Arab supremacy—is not the exclusive preserve of black nationalism. On the contrary, opposition to white supremacy should be embraced as a manifestation of ultimate allegiance to God and the preservation of God's status as the *only* noncontingent Definer of ultimate value. On this understanding, God, not "the man," becomes the true motivator and ultimate concern of resistance. Indeed, resistance in this context becomes part of the struggle to remain within the penumbra of primordial meanings where God occupies the center of human consciousness. In this light, resisting false *mysterium tremendum* and "second creators" acquires meaning not only for Blackamerican Muslims but for Muslims, period. Whatever color they may be.[70]

It is with this form of resistance in mind that I have written this paper. In attempting to make a decolonial move against these 'second-creators' I have theorized the pyramidal construction of Man, and the inverted pyramid as constructing the Human from an Islamic epistemology centered in the sciences of *Tasawwuf* (Sufism). In Islamic thought the human being as created by God is made up of five parts: the body (*jism*), the mind (*aql*), the spirit (*ruh*), the self (*nafs*), and the heart (*qalb*). The heart as a spiritual organ is central to existence and the human being's relationship with God. As Ibn al-Arabi, who is considered to be one of the greatest mystic-philosophers in the history of Islam, has written,

> The infinite capacity of the heart places it beyond delimitation (*taqyid*) by anything whatsoever. Like Being it is Non-delimited (*mutlaq*), free and absolved from all limitations and constraints. To the extent a person verifies the nature of things by means of [her/his] heart, [she/he] can understand God and the cosmos. But to the extent that [she/he] follows the way of [his/her] reason or rational faculty ('*aql*), [they] will remain in constant constriction and binding. Here the Shaykh points out the root meaning of the term '*aql*, closely connected to the "fetter" ('*iqal*) used to hobble a camel. Reason strives to define and delimit God, but that is impossible. The heart frees God of all constraints and absolves [God] of all limitations. The heart alone is able to perceive God's self disclosures through the faculty of imagination.[71]

The heart therefore is the single most important spiritual aspect of one's life that we can have a constant relationship with as it relates to God and this process of self-purification. It is also the bodily location of our *ruh* which is the "underlying essence of the human individual which survives death."[72] Therefore, if purification of the heart is such a central part of the life of a Muslim, then we must question what type of inclination our existence in the world will lead us towards as it relates to our *nafs* (self). The Quran mentions three levels of *nafs*, these being the *nafs ammara bi'l-su'* (the soul constantly enjoining evil), *Al-nafs al-lawwama* (the 'soul which blames') and after a long inward

---

70. Ibid: 182.

71. See: William C. Chittick, *The Sufi Path of Knowledge: Ibn al-'Arabi's Metaphysics of Imagination* (Albany: State University of New York Press, 1989): 107.

72. Abdul Hakim Murad, "Islamic Spirituality: The Forgotten Revolution."

struggle, the

> *Nafs mutma'inna* (the soul at peace). This is the *nafs* that one strives for in the process of the purifying the heart.[73]

Therefore from an Islamic perspective Man as it is constructed in Modernity facilitates the *nafs ammara bi'l-su'*. This is why to make the decolonial shift to the inverted pyramid as constructing the Human, from an Islamic perspective the self should be at the bottom of existence while God is located as the center of all existence. In Islam this would mean a shift from the *ego-cogito* to *Tawheed* (God Consciousness) where you are conscious of God in every aspect of your life, while your spiritual existence is centered in your *qalb*. This is a shift to a God and therefore a *Qalb* or heart centered existence. To facilitate this it is necessary to make central the spiritual sciences of Islam, which have been marginalized by the orientalist discourses surrounding decadence. Using the term "Islamic Psychology" for Sufism here, Sheykh Murad has written that,

> Islamic psychology is characteristic of the new *ulum* which, although present in latent and implicit form in the Quran, were first systematized in Islamic culture during the early Abbasid period. Given the importance that the Quran attached to obtaining a 'sound heart', we are not surprised to find that the influence of Islamic psychology has been massive and all-pervasive. In the formative first four centuries of Islam, the time when the great works of *tafsir*, *hadith*, grammar, and so forth were laid down, the *ulema* also applied their minds to this problem of *al-qalb al-salim* (the heart at peace). This was first visible when, following the example of the *Tab'in* [the second generation of Muslims], many of the early ascetics, such as sufyan ibn Uyayna, Sufyan al-Thawri, and Abdallah ibn al-Mubarak, had focused their concerns explicitly on the art of purifying the heart. The methods they recommended were frequent fasting, night prayers, and periodic retreats.[74]

Through re-centering *Tasawwuf* Muslims will be better equipped to respond and create alternatives to modernity, as this heart centered existence will facilitate the possibility of developing the *Nafs mutma 'inna* or the soul at peace. From an epistemology centered in Islamic Sufism, then, what is necessary first is to properly understand our consciousness and that it is centered in our heart rather than in our mind. If our hearts are alive, it can be our ultimate center of perception and understanding. Similar to Gloria Anzaldua's understanding of *La Facultad*, which she understands to be a form of "inner knowledge,"[75] is the Islamic concept of *Al Basira* (the spiritual eye of the heart) where one can spiritually sense, if properly developed, and understand reality much more deeply and thoroughly. As al-Ghazali put it in his masterwork of the inner sciences of Islam, *Ihya' ulum al-din*,

> 'Creation' refers to the external, and 'character' to the internal, form. Now, [the human] is composed of a body which perceives with ocular vision [basar] and a spirit [ruh] and a soul [nafs] which perceive with inner sight [basira]. Each of these things has an aspect and a form which is either ugly or beautiful. Furthermore, the soul which perceives with inner sight is of greater worth than the body which sees with ocular vision.[76]

---

73. T.J. Winter, "Introduction": xxviii.

74. Abdul Hakim Murad, "Islamic Spirituality: The Forgotten Revolution."

75. For the concept of *La Facultad*, see Gloria Anzaldua. *Borderlands/ La Frontera: The New Mestiza* (San Francisco: Aunt Lute Books, 1999).

76. Tim Winter (translator), *Al-Ghazali On Disciplining the Soul-Kitab Riyadat al-nafs & On*

In seeing with the eye of our heart we can begin to differentiate between form and meaning, as the outward form of things are not always their internal and spiritual reality. An example is a supermodel who on the outside may look beautiful based on the standards of Western society, but on the inside she may be stricken with anxiety, eating disorders, drug addiction and any number of maladies from being forced to focus only on their external beauty while not considering the internal realities of the heart and soul. Perhaps building on Aime Cesaire's understanding of the Western imperiality as a poison spreading throughout the world, the best example is the West's view of itself, as its most central significations of itself are those of benevolence and innocence. But as the world has seen for far to long, the reality of endless warfare and global genocide is the meaning/ reality behind the form.

Perhaps this is best explained by the early female sufi saint, Rabi'a al-Adawiyya, who stated in verse, "O children of Nothing! Truth can't come in through your eyes/ Nor can speech go out through your mouth to find [God]/ Hearing leads the speaker down the road to anxiety/ And if you follow your hands and feet you will arrive at confusion—/ The real work is in the Heart: Wake up your Heart!/ Because when the Heart is completely awake, Then it needs no Friend."[77] The vision of our hearts has become blinded by the poison of the overrepresentation of white Western Man, and its solely material make-up. If we are to develop the internal tools necessary to break from the chains of modernity, much deeper consideration beyond thought and through the heart as well is necessary by scholars who are experts in both the sciences of decoloniality and the spiritual sciences of Islam. I hope that my small contribution here will be the beginning of many fruitful conversations in this vein. For if we can make ourselves spiritually well, then surely we can develop and incline towards a "decolonial ethics," and "decolonial love," that will help lead us towards a transmodern day, where epistemologies can build from each other, rather than just compete for any opening to speak against the monoculture of the West. As surely the path of love is the one we must walk down, to see each other in the divine light we were born into. As Ibn Arabi most beautifully stated, "I believe in the religion of love/Whatever direction its caravans may take, For love is my religion and my faith."[78]

V. Conclusion: Decolonizing the Heart

If we look at the year 2030 as a benchmark, we see the possibility of the transmodern emerging in terms of demographics as Muslims become more than one quarter of humanity and people of color become the majority population in the United States again for the first time in two hundred plus years.[79] While demographic shifts could produce important political changes, the real question lies in the true heart of the matter, as we think of what an ethical/ theological/ and political decolonial turn would look like. If demographics shift and our epistemological and ontological ways of being stay within the confines of coloniality/ modernity then nothing has really changed. For Muslims this reality is embodied in the verse from the Qur'an that states, "God does not change the condition of a people unless they

---

Breaking the Two Desires-Kitab Kasr al-shahwatayn-Books XXII and XXIII of The Revival of the Religious Sciences-Ihya 'Ulum al-Din (Cambridge, Islamic Texts Society, 1997): 16.

77. See: Charles Upton, *Doorkeeper of the Heart: Versions of Rabi'a* (Putney, Vermont: Threshold Books, 1988): 27.

78. Ibn 'Arabi. *Perfect Harmony: Sufi Poetry of Ibn 'Arabi* (Boston: Shambhala Publications, 2002).

79. See: "The Future of the Global Muslim Population," *Pew Research Religion & Public Life Project*, January 27, 2011, Available at: http://www.pewforum.org/2011/01/27/the-future-of-the-global-muslim-population/ and: Manuel Pastor, Angela Glover Blackwell and Stewart Kwoh, *Uncommon Common Ground: Race and America's Future* (New York, W.W. Norton, 2010).

change what is in themselves."[80] While nearly every form of decolonization has been written about, as this verse attests to, the basis of all decolonial shifts would then begin with the necessary decolonizaton of the heart.

Perhaps then in expanding beyond Dussel, rather than just a theology of liberation, the question I am asking here is what is a spirituality of liberation? For if we are free from the material confines of colonial modernity within the spiritual plane of existence, then it is from that standpoint that all stages of liberation would emanate. To have a spirituality of liberation would invoke the divine assistance (*tawfiq*) that Muslims believe is necessary to undertake the next stages of theological, philosophical, ethical and political layers of struggle. Indeed beyond the political and philosophical realms of decolonization spiritual realities such as prayer have always played a central role within the life of the oppressed amongst Muslims. As two famous sayings of the Prophet Muhammad state so clearly, "Guard yourselves against oppression and so protect your souls from the cry of the oppressed; for surely no barrier exists between the cry of the oppressed and God—even if that cry should come from an atheist," and "Supplication is the true weapon of the believer."[81] Specific supplications for the oppressed have even been collected such as the *Duaa Nasiri* (the prayer of Nasir) which is often recited in groups during great times of conflict and strife in different parts of the Muslim world.[82] From this baseline of a spirituality of liberation which has always been central to Islamic teachings we can then expand to imagine what other decolonial horizons are which have existed and are emerging from throughout the Muslim world.

As the Muslim majority countries continues to go through their slow process of decolonization between the United States global security state and terror war, monarchs, despots, infiltrations, revolutions and counter revolutions much like Latin America experienced in the twentieth century, an in depth study is necessary and project of liberation is necessary on the level which Dussel was able to undertake in his life and times for Muslims throughout the world. Of course the undertaking involved in this project is perhaps even broader than Dussel's as the cultural diversity, political differences and different traditions of struggle from throughout the Muslim world are even more diverse than Latin America, while also being made up of Muslims living in Latin America, and growing Latino/a convert populations in the United States and throughout Latin America.

Our question then as a brief sketch here is, who does the Muslim world look for as its own exemplars of decolonization? These figures range over a period of hundreds of years, from those who resisted enslavement in the America's[83], and colonization in North and West Africa, to Malcolm X's global vision of Islam, what Sohail Daulatzai calls the "Muslim International." This Muslim International is a call to global solidarity within the Muslim world and with peoples throughout the world who face similar forms of oppression. As Daulatzai so clearly states, "Having shaped and been shaped by U.S.-based Black liberation struggles and Third World decolonization in the post-World War II era, the Muslim International is measured by what Aime Cesaire has called "the compass of suffering," connecting geographies of violence and shared territories of struggle against racial terror, global

---

80. Verse 13:11 - M.A.S. Abdel Haleem (translator), *The Qur'an* (New York: Oxford University Press, 2004): 154.

81. Imam Muhammad b. Nasir al-Dar'I; Hamza Yusuf (Translator), *The Prayer of the Oppressed: The Sword of Victory's Lot Over Every Tyranny and Plot* (Danville, CA: Sandala Press, 2010):53. The full text of this prayer is available here: http://sandala.org/wp-content/uploads/2011/04/Dua_Nasiri_Arabic_Translation.pdf

82. This group recitation happens in places such as the emerging hybrid community of Muslims from throughout the world living in the San Francisco Bay Area at Zaytuna College and the Ta'leef Collective.

83. See: Abu Alfa Muhammad Shareef bin Farid, *The Islamic Slave Revolts of Bahia, Brazil* (Pittsburgh, PA: Sankore Institute of Islamic-African Studies International, 1998) and Sylviane A. Diouf, *Servants of Allah: African Muslims Enslaved in the Americas* (New York: New York University Press, 1998).

capital, and war."[84]

For Malcolm X these struggles were indeed "material as well as spiritual," and "political as well as religious," and the interconnectedness of these struggles must be realized in the face of a globalized reality of white supremacy and the facts of coloniality/ modernity. As an example of this, Malcolm X stated that the reality of white supremacy facing African Americans in the United States, "must also be the concern of and the moral responsibility of the entire Muslim World—if you hope to make the principles of the Quran a *Living Reality*."[85] In an era where Islam has been used for political purposes whose means exceed the confines placed on Muslims by religious law (*Sharia*) related to warfare, we are in no way calling to the base form of oppressive resistance used by Al Qaeda and the Taliban reflective of the worst parts of modern warfare which values life no more than the drones, F-16's, and contract armies of the American military. What we are calling for here is an in depth study of those spiritual, theological, philosophical and political thinkers and decolonial examples who came before us from throughout the Muslim International, while also imagining anew what these processes of decolonization look like for us today.

These examples range across leaders and scholars who lived and struggled in vastly different times and places, but for Muslims they start with the Prophets and reach their height with the Prophet Muhammad. Within the era of colonial modernity they range from leaders like Emir Abd el-Kader al-Jaza'iri (1808-1883)[86] who was a religious scholar, a sufi master, and a political and military leader who fought against French colonization in Algeria to Shaykh Amadu Bamba (1853-1927) who fought against the French non-violently and is now venerated as one of the great Sufi saints of West Africa.[87] Further an introductory list could also include: Shaykh Uthman Dan Fodio (1754-1817) and his daughter Nana Asma'u (1793-1864), Imam Shamail Daghestani (1797-1871), Shaykh Omar Mokhtar (1858-1931), Sayyid Muhammad Abd Allah al-Hassan (1856-1920), Shaykh Muhammad Izz ad-Din al-Qassam (1882-1935), Dagistani, Muhammad Iqbal (1877-1938), Said Nursi (1878-1960), Muhammad ibn Adb al-Karim al-Khattabi (1882-1963), Shaykh Ibrahim Niasse (1900-1975), Badshah Khan (1890-1988) and Imam Warith Deen Muhammad (1933-2008).

For each of these thinkers they combined the spiritual, with the theological for political action in vastly different political times, places and eras. From this body of work as well as the long history of relevant texts we could grow a body of work that could take up the mantle started by Dussel in imagining what a theology of liberation, a philosophy of liberation, an ethics of liberation, a politics of liberation, and foundationally a spirituality of liberation could mean for Muslims as we attempt to decolonize our hearts and minds towards a transmodern future.

Just one example of a text from the Muslim International which has been grossly under-studied and could be of great benefit to this undertaking is *Ambiguous Adventure* by Cheikh Hamidou Kane from Senegal. Written in 1962 *Ambiguous Adventure* is seen as a largely autobiographical tale about a young boy Samba Diallo who was raised within a lineage of Sufi Muslim Shaykhs (religious scholars), but instead of following tradition and following his family's long line of classical Islamic education, he is instead the first generation sent to the newly opened French school in French colonized Senegal. The book is a back and forth between tradition and spirituality, and modernity and the disbelief of Westernized life as lived and embodied by Samba Diallo as he moves to France to study for his PhD and then returns to his village in Senegal years later. As Kane reflects throughout the text

---

84. Sohail Daulatzai, *Black Star, Crescent Moon: The Muslim International and Black Freedom beyond America* (Minneapolis, Minnesota University Press, 2013): xxii.

85. Quoted in: Louis A. DeCaro, Jr., *On the Side of My People: A Religious Life of Malcolm X* (New York, New York University Press, 1996): 239.

86. Ahmed Bouyerdene, *Emir Abd el-Kader: Hero and Saint of Islam* (New York: World Wisdom, 2012).

87. See: Cheikh Anta Babou, *Fighting the Greater Jihad: Amadu Bamba and the Founding of the Muridiyya of Senegal, 1853-1913* (Athens, Ohio: Ohio University Press, 2007).

on the role Western epistemology has played in colonizing the heart, mind and spirit he writes of this key moment,

> On the black continent it began to be understood that their true power lay not in the cannons of the first morning, but rather in what followed the cannons... The new school shares at the same time the characteristics of cannon and of magnet. From the cannon it draws its efficacy as an arm of combat. Better than the cannon, it makes conquest permanent. The cannon compels the body, the school bewitches the soul. Where the cannon has made a pit of ashes and of death, in the sticky mold of which men would not have rebounded from the ruins, the new school establishes peace. The morning of rebirth will be a morning of benediction through the appeasing virtue of the new school. From the magnet, the school takes its radiating force. It is bound up with a new order, as a magnetic stone is bound up with a field. The upheaval of the life of man within this new order is similar to the overturn of certain physical laws in a magnetic field. Men are seen to be composing themselves, conquered, along the lines of invisible and imperious forces. Disorder is organized, rebellion is appeased, the mornings of resentment resound with songs of a universal thanksgiving.[88]

---

88. Cheikh Hamdidou Kane, *Ambiguous Adventure*, (Oxford, London: Heinemann Educational Publishers, 1962): 49-50. For an in depth reading of the spiritual aspects of the text see: Rebecca Masterton, "Islamic Mystical Readings of Cheikh Hamidou Kane's *Ambiguous Adventure*," Journal of Islamic Studies (Oxford University Press, 20 (1), 2009): 21-45. Available at: http://jis.oxfordjournals.org/content/20/1/21.short

Works Cited

Abdel Haleem, M.A.S. (translator). *The Qur'an*. New York: Oxford University Press, 2004.

Alcoff, Linda Martin. *Visible Identities: Race, Gender, and the Self (Studies in Feminist Philosophy)*. New York: Oxford University Press, USA, 2005.

al-Dar'I, Imam Muhammad b. Nasir; Yusuf, Hamza (Translator). *The Prayer of the Oppressed: The Sword of Victory's Lot Over Every Tyranny and Plot*. Danville, CA: Sandala Press, 2010. Available at: http://sandala.org/wp-content/uploads/2011/04/Dua_Nasiri_Arabic_Translation.pdf

Anzaldua, Gloria. *Borderlands/ La Frontera: The New Mestiza*. San Francisco: Aunt Lute Books, 1999.

'Arabi, Ibn. *Perfect Harmony: Sufi Poetry of Ibn 'Arabi*. Boston: Shambhala Publications, 2002.

Asad, Muhammad. *The Road to Mecca* (St. Louis: Fons Vitae, 2000).

Babou, Cheikh Anta. *Fighting the Greater Jihad: Amadu Bamba and the Founding of the Muridiyya of Senegal, 1853-1913*. Athens, Ohio: Ohio University Press, 2007.

Bouyerdene, Ahmed. *Emir Abd el-Kader: Hero and Saint of Islam*. New York: World Wisdom, 2012.

Cesaire, Aime. *Discourse on Colonialism*. New York: Monthly Review Press, 2005.

Chittick, William C. *The Sufi Path of Knowledge: Ibn al-'Arabi's Metaphysics of Imagination*. Albany: State University of New York Press, 1989.

Daulatzai, Sohail. *Black Star, Crescent Moon: The Muslim International and Black Freedom beyond America*. Minneapolis, Minnesota University Press, 2013.

Davis, Mike. "Fear and Money in Dubai." In Mike Davis (editor). *Evil Paradises: the Dreamworlds of Neoliberalism*. New York: Verso, 2007.

DeCaro, Jr., Louis A. *On the Side of My People: A Religious Life of Malcolm X*. New York, New York University Press, 1996.

Deloria, Jr., Vine. *The World We Used to Live In: Remembering the Powers of the Medicine Men*. Golden, CO: Fulcrum Publishing, 2006.

Diouf, Sylviane A. *Servants of Allah: African Muslims Enslaved in the Americas*. New York: New York University Press, 1998.

Du Bois, W.E.B. *Darkwater: Voices from Within the Veil*. New York: Schocken, 1999.

Dussel, Enrique. *Philosophy of Liberation*. Translated by Aquilina Martinez and Christine

Morkovsky. Maryknoll, N.Y.: Orbis Books, 1985.

Dussel, Enrique. "Beyond Eurocentrism: The World-System and the Limits of Modernity." In Jameson, Fredric and Miyoshi, Masao (editors). *The Cultures of Globalization*. Durham: Duke University Press, 1998.

Dussel, Enrique. *Ethics of Liberation in the Age of Globalization and Exclusion*. Durham: Duke University Press, 2013.

Fakhry, Majid. *A History of Islamic Philosophy*. New York: Columbia University Press, 2004.

Fanon, Frantz. *Black Skin, White Masks*. New York: Grove Press, 2007.

Fanon, Frantz. *The Wretched of the Earth*. New York: Grove Press, 1963.

Al-Ghazali, Abu Hammid. (Translator: T.J. Winter). *Al-Ghazali On Disciplining the Soul-Kitab Riyadat al-nafs & On Breaking the Two Desires-Kitab Kasr al-shahwatayn-Books XXII and XXIII of The Revival of the Religious Sciences-Ihya 'Ulum al-Din*. Cambridge, Islamic Texts Society, 1997.

Griggs, Richard. "Background on the term "Fourth World."" *Center for World Indigenous Studies*. Available at: http://cwis.org/GML/background/FourthWorld/

Grosfoguel, Ramon; Maldonado-Torres, Nelson; and David Saldivar, Jose (editors). *Latin@s in the World-System: Decolonization Struggles in the Twenty-First Century U.S. Empire*. Boulder: Paradigm Publishers, 2005.

Grosfoguel, Ramon. "World-Systems Analysis in the Context of Transmodernity, Border Thinking, and Global Coloniality." *Review: Fernand Braudel Center*. Vol. XXIX. Number 2, 2006.

Jackson, Sherman. *Islam and the Blackamerican: Looking toward the Third Resurrection*. New York: Oxford University Press, USA, 2005.

Kane, Cheikh Hamdidou. *Ambiguous Adventure*. Oxford, London: Heinemann Educational Publishers, 1962.

Lugones, Maria. "Heterosexualism and the Colonial/ Modern Gender System," *Hypatia*, vol. 22, no. 1, Winter 2007.

Mahmood, Saba. "Secularism, Hermeneutics, and Empire: The Politics of Islamic Reformation." *Public Culture*. Duke University Press, 18:2, 2006.

Maldonado-Torres, Nelson. "On the Coloniality of Being: Contributions to the Development of a Concept." *Cultural Studies*, Vol. 21, Nos. 2-3 March/ May 2007.

Maldonado-Torres, Nelson. *Against War: Views from the Underside of Modernity*. Durham: Duke University Press, 2008a.

Maldonado-Torres, Nelson. "Lewis Gordon: Philosopher of the Human." *The CLR James Journal*. The Caribbean Philosophical Association: Volume 14, Number 1, Spring 2008b.

Maldonado-Torres, Nelson. "Secularism and Religion in the Modern/ Colonial World-System: From Secular Postcoloniality to Postsecular Transmodernity." Mabel Morana, Enrique Dussel, and Carlos A. Jauregui (editors). *Coloniality at Large: Latin America and the Postcolonial Debate*. Durham, NC: Duke University Press, 2008c.

Massad, Joseph A. *Desiring Arabs*. Chicago: University of Chicago Press, 2008.

Masterton, Rebecca. "Islamic Mystical Readings of Cheikh Hamidou Kane's Ambiguous Adventure." *Journal of Islamic Studies*. Oxford University Press: 20 (1), 2009): 21-45. Available at: http://jis.oxfordjournals.org/content/20/1/21.short

Melamed, Jodi. "The Spirit of Neoliberalism: From Racial Liberalism to Neoliberal Multiculturalism." In *Social Text*. 89, Vol. 24, Number 4, Winter 2006, Duke University Press, pp. 1-24.

Mignolo, Walter. *Local Histories/ Global Designs: Coloniality, Subaltern Knowledges, and Border Thinking*. Princeton, N.J.: Princeton University Press, 2000.

Mignolo, Walter. *The Darker Side of the Renaissance: Literacy, Territoriality, and Colonization*. 2nd Ed. Ann Arbor: University of Michigan Press, 2003.

Mignolo, Walter. *The Idea of Latin America*. Malden, MA: Blackwell, 2005.

Mignolo, Walter. "DELINKING: The Rhetoric of Modernity, the Logic of Coloniality and the Grammar of De-coloniality." *Cultural Studies*, Vol. 21, Nos. 2-3 March/ May 2007.

Moosa, Ebrahim. *Ghazali & the Poetics of Imagination*. Chapel Hill, NC: The University of North Carolina Press, 2005.

Morana, Mabel; Dussel, Enrique; and Jauregui, Carlos A (editors). *Coloniality at Large: Latin America and the Postcolonial Debate*. Durham, NC: Duke University Press, 2008.

Murad, Abdal-Hakim. "Islamic Spirituality: The Forgotten Revolution." Masud, UK, no date. Available at: http://www.masud.co.uk/ISLAM/ahm/fgtnrevo.htm

Nasr, Seyyed Hossein. *Knowledge and the Sacred*. New York: SUNY Press, 1989.

Osamu, Nishitani. (Translated by Trent Maxey). "Anthropos and Humanitas: Two Western Concepts of "Human Being." Naoki Sakai and Jon Solomon (editors). *Translatoin, Biopolitics, Colonial Difference*. Hong Kong: Hong Kong University Press, 2006.

Pastor, Manuel; Glover Blackwell, Angela and Kwoh, Stewart. *Uncommon Common Ground: Race and America's Future.* New York, W.W. Norton, 2010.

Perez, Laura. "Con o Sin Permiso (With or Without Permission): Chicana Badgirls: Las Hociconas." *Chicana Badgirls: Las Hociconas (Exhibition Catalog).* Albuquerque, New Mexico: 516 Arts, 2009.

Pew Research Religion & Public Life Project. "The Future of the Global Muslim Population." January 27, 2011. Available at: http://www.pewforum.org/2011/01/27/the-future-of-the-global-muslim-population/

Quijano, Anibal. "Colonialidad y modernidad/racionalidad" in *Los Conquistados. 1492 y la poblacion indigena de las Americas.* Bonilla, Heraclio (editor). Ecuador: Libri Mundi, Tercer Mundo Editores. (1992).

Quijano, Anibal. "Coloniality of Power, Eurocentrism, and Latin America." Translated by Michael Ennis. *Neplanta: Views from the South,* I, no. 3 (2000).

Quijano, Anibal. "Coloniality and Modernity/Rationality." *Cultural Studies* Vol. 21, Nos. 2-3 (March/ May 2007).

Sabbagh, Suha. "Going Against the West from Within: The Emergence of the West as an Other in Frantz Fanon's Work." Ph.D. diss., University of Wisconsin, Madison, 1982.

Sandoval, Chela. *Methodology of the Oppressed.* Minneapolis: University of Minnesota Press, 2000.

Shareef bin Farid, Abu Alfa Muhammad. *The Islamic Slave Revolts of Bahia, Brazil.* Pittsburgh, PA: Sankore Institute of Islamic-African Studies International, 1998.

Upton, Charles. *Doorkeeper of the Heart: Versions of Rabi'a.* Putney, Vermont: Threshold Books, 1988.

Williams Jr, Robert. *The American Indian and Western Legal Thought: The Discourses o Conquest.* Oxford: Oxford University Press, 1992.

Winter, Tim. "Introduction." *Al-Ghazali On Disciplining the Soul-Kitab Riyadat al-nafs & On Breaking the Two Desires-Kitab Kasr al-shahwatayn-Books XXII and XXIII of The Revival of the Religious Sciences-Ihya 'Ulum al-Din.* Cambridge, Islamic Texts Society, 1997.

Winter, Tim (editor). *The Cambridge Companion to Classical Islamic Theology.* Cambridge, UK: Cambridge University Press, 2008.

Wynter, Sylvia. "Unsettling the Coloniality of Being/ Power/ Truth/ Freedom: Towards the Human, After Man, Its Overrepresentation—An Argument," *CR: The New Centennial Review,* 3:3, (Fall 2003): 257-337.

Yusuf, Hamza. *Purification of the Heart: Signs, Symptoms, and Cures of the Spiritual Diseases of the Heart.* Starlatch Press: 2004.

The Voice of a Country of Called 'Forgetfulness': Mahmoud Darwish as Edward Said's "Amateur"

Rehnuma Sazzad

Nottingham Trent University, UK

rehnuma.sazzad@ntu.ac.uk

Abstract: This is a study of two close friends: Edward Said and Mahmoud Darwish—cosmopolitan and humane Palestinians who were fellow compatriots in the fight for the Palestinian cause. Both resigned from the PLO in the wake of the Oslo Accord as a sign of protest to the agreement. However, this was mostly true on Said's part. Darwish said he was a poet; of what use was politics to him? This paper tries to answer this question by exploring the dynamic interplay of poetry and politics in what Said would call Darwish's 'amateurism.' Said's 'amateur' is an intellectual who remains extraordinarily committed to truth and justice through all her/his efforts. An 'amateur's' relentless task is to 'speak truth to power.' In order to perform the task, s/he combines the traits of Gramsci's *'organic intellectual'* and Benda's *'cleric'* in her/himself. Like the *organic intellectual*, s/he persistently challenges hegemonies through advancing progressive ideas and as a Bendaesque moral force, s/he acts against all kinds of subjugations and aggressions. The author argues that an 'amateurish' breaking of barriers took place when Darwish the poet turned into a Palestinian spokesman out of his passion to speak truth to the occupying Israeli power. Consequently, his art and his politics of universal human freedom vis-à-vis Palestine became so inextricably interlinked that he started to fill football stadia with his poetry recitation. Whether he wanted it or not, politics thus became an integral part of Darwish's artistic project.

Palestinian poet Mahmoud Darwish is a landmark figure of the modern world literature. Fittingly, there has been an increasing interest in his great artistry. Understandably, his world recognition on a phenomenal scale advances the Palestinian cause to a great extent. Serene Huleileh writes:

Born on 13 March 1941 in Al Birweh, a quaint village in the Galilee, Mahmoud Darwish went on to live a life that is a poignant example of how far talent and determination, combined with a precarious life, can carry an individual from a simple background into the interna-

---

Rehnuma Sazzad defended her PhD dissertation on Literary and Cultural Studies at Nottingham Trent University in November 2013. Her thesis was based on Edward Said, Mahmoud Darwish, and other foremost Middle Eastern intellectuals. She has written a variety of papers on intellectuals from the region including Said, Darwish, Naguib Mahfouz, Leila Ahmed, Youssef Chahine, Mona Hatoum, and Nawal El Saadawi. She has published pieces on the Bangladeshi-American filmmakers Tareque and Catherine Masud, and the Indian auteur Satyajit Ray. Her research interest is on South Asian history and literary creations, where she aims to foster a deeper cultural dialogue between the Middle Eastern and South Asian regions.

tional halls of fame.[1]

He attended 'International halls of fame' more than once, by winning France's highest medal as Knight of Arts and Belles Lettres, Prince Claus Awards, and the Lannan prize for Cultural Freedom, among many others. My aim here is to project how the poet from 'a simple background' achieved the high accolades by dint of a resistance that Edward Said calls 'amateurism.'

Darwish's modest background reveals a common Palestinian plight. With the birth of Israel, he was ousted from his homeland at the age of six. When the family returned to their erased village, they were declared infiltrators; in official Israeli term, they were 'present-absentees.' As he grew up, he was increasingly in trouble with the authorities for his resistant poetry. Consequently, he left Israel in the 1970s and roamed across various Arab cities. After Israel's 1982 massacre in Beirut, he took refuge in Paris, where his poetic life flourished to the fullest. Naturally, because of being a 'wandering exile,'[2] the Israeli colonialism and American imperialism that uprooted him became key questions in his writings. But as his eminence suggests, his poetic voice achieved greatness by broaching the questions through his idealism of truth, justice, and human emancipation.

This is exactly where Said's idea of 'amateurism' comes in view. Said believes that when intellectuals are confined to their professional knowledge and its perimeters, they are in real danger of being separated from the historico-political world. In order to oppose this withdrawal and the consequent neutrality, Said wants intellectuals to be *'amateurs'* in the French meaning of the term:

> Asked why he used the term amateur rather than 'generalist,' Said replied that he was drawn to the literal meaning of the French word, which means a love of something—'very involved in something without being professional.'[3]

This does not, however, mean that Said nullifies professionalism in a cynical way. Neither does this imply that his 'amateur' has to be a righteous hermit. On the contrary, Said's 'amateur' has a profession to begin with; but s/he is an engaged intellectual, who transcends the boundary of her/his expertise to be involved in a greater politico-cultural struggle. As Said explains above, this happens because of her/his love for and the commitment to a particular cause. S/he is neither 'just a friendly technician' nor 'a full-time Cassandra,' then.[4] Her/his steadfast task is not to produce plain prophecies, but to 'speak truth to power'[5] through her/his writing. Said further explains that the 'amateur' fulfills this role in two ways. First, s/he works as Gramsci's *'organic intellectual'* through the counter-hegemonic writing. Secondly, the twentieth-century French philosopher Benda becomes a role model for her/him. Like Benda's *'cleric'*, s/he always struggles to uphold the universal values of truth, justice and freedom.[6]

I argue here that an 'amateurish' breaking of barriers took place when Darwish the poet turned into a Palestinian spokesman out of his passion to speak truth to the occupying Israeli power. Consequently, his art and his politics of universal human freedom vis-à-vis Palestine became so inextricably interlinked that he started to fill football sta-

---

1. Serene Huleileh, '"I am not mine," Mahmoud Darwish: The Expropriated Poet', Mahmoud Darwish... In the Presence of Absence, http://www.mahmouddarwish.com/ui/english/ShowContent.aspx?ContentId=8 [accessed: 6 April 2010].
2. Edward Said, 'On Mahmoud Darwish', Grand Street 48 (Winter 1994), p.112.
3. Bill Ashcroft and Pal Ahluwalia, *Edward Said* (London: Routledge, 1999), p. 48.
4. Edward Said, *Representations of the Intellectual* (New York: Vintage, 1994), p. 52.
5. Said, *Representations*, p. 63.
6. Said, *Representations*.

dia with his poetry recitation, whether it was in the Arab or the Western worlds. Thus politics is never far from artistic purity, at least as Said's 'worldliness' testifies. Therefore, being a Saidian 'amateur,' Darwish writes combining Gramscian 'organic' intellectualism with Benda's idealistic predisposition. His counter-hegemony resists Israeli-American nullification of his usurped nation. Simultaneiously, like Benda's cleric, he advances the Palestine issue through the universal principles of truth and justice.

As for Darwish's rebellion against Israeli colonialism, it is worth emphasizing here that the core of both Said and Darwish's counter-hegemonic writings against Israel are formed through revolting against the coloniser's non-recognition. In *Orientalism*, Said challenges the constitution of an Oriental's identity shorn off his/her humanity. In the same way, the core of Darwish's poetry is formed by resisting the absence of his conqueror's recognition of his people as humans. 'Write down, I am an Arab!'[7] was his famous poetic outcry against this. The poem 'Identity Card' starting with this statement not only earned him enormous popularity in the 60s but also the title of the 'resistance poet.' Even though Darwish rejected the label and refused to recite this poem later on in life, his poetic oeuvre always remained a resisting project to give voice to the voiceless Palestinians. Starting with the 1960s' fiery poems 'till the more aesthetically polished late poems, his lyrics always defied the degradation of the Palestinian identity as a non-existent one.

Naturally, the reassertion of his nation's denied identity is a predominant theme in Darwish's poetry. Being one of the media of the nation's self-expression, Darwish's poetry brings out the bleak reality of occupation:

> The beloved sun never rose
>   in spite of the day's insistence…
> How long eyes have searched for it
>   & are still waiting…
> & thousands of eyes stare skywards
>   without direction.
> Beyond the eyes they have thrown up
>   walls with high foreheads
> to keep the sun from them…[8]

The poignant description gives us a continuing sunless picture of the occupied territories, where 'thousands of eyes' are 'star(ing) skywards without direction.' Darwish puts his poetry at the forefront of his occupied people's struggle against this dark situation. He calls himself a 'destitute poet as [his people's] caravan leader,' hoping that 'the sun's wounds will guide the caravan' by 'rak(ing) out the rubble of the wall!'[9] The poet is eerily prophetic here, as he symbolises the non-freedom of his people through 'the wall.' Though his poem, 'The Festival & the Sun,' appeared in 1960 in a collection called *Birds without Wings*, it perfectly foreshadowed Israel's so-called 'security wall' in West Bank built in 1994.

Despite the walled-in condition, Darwish's resistance is fuelled by an invincible hope. The hope is boldly expressed in his verses, which turn upside down the usual death and destruction associated with a Palestinian identity in a dominant discourse:

> Twenty songs about sudden death…
> each song: a tribe
> We are in love with causes for falling
> in the streets.
> O noble city of ours bloated with
>   defeat…[10]

Palestinians are dying on the streets without any records. Darwish notes, however, that every 'tribe' has its fair share on the festivity of reasonless death brought upon them by their occupying lords. Despite being ironic about the grave scenario,

---

7. Mahmoud Darwish, *Selected Poems* (Cheadle: Carcanet, translated by Ian Wedde and Fawwaz Tuqan, 1973), p. 25.
8. Darwish, *Selected*, p. 22.
9. Darwish, *Selected*, p. 23.
10. Darwish, *Selected*, p. 73.

he asserts that people still 'longed to survive,' though they were habituated to the 'customary'[11] mourning and repeated funerals for their deceased kinsmen. He further stresses that the instinct to be alive is a strong one, which makes people withstand the humiliation and sufferings of occupation. That is why he chooses to be a determined optimist and describes how the deaths make them value the bravery of their kindred. The persecution of the inhabitants of his 'city' and the deep loss of the survivors become part of its everyday reality. Hence, Darwish's ironic appreciation goes to the bloodshed committed in his 'city,' i.e., homeland symbolised by the 'cross,' because it rescues the 'city' from being non-distinct! Thus its dwellers paradoxically realize how valuable an uninterrupted lifespan is. Once again, this perception preserves the people's fighting spirit:

> I thank you O cross of my city
> I thank you:
> you taught us the colour of carnations & courage.
> O cross O bridge spanning the gulf for us
> from childhood's gaiety
> to old age: now
> we are discovering the city in you ah!
> our beautiful city![12]

Obviously, Darwish's resistance is contained above by allowing death to be defeated by the steely resolve of the people to live and value life and also by the audacity to turn death's regular visit amongst them into an ordinary feature of their life. In fact, such a resolve in the face of the unceasing 'hurricane' of destruction that started off with the Nakba (catastrophe of 1948 that marked the beginning of their dispossession) and continued amidst the 'tears,' 'wound,' and 'bleeding' of the occupied Palestine is Darwish's foremost oppositional strategy against the settler's colonials' insistence on their being a lesser people:

> So be it
> I must feel proud
> of you O wound of my city
> & of you O image of lightning
> in our sad nights.
> Because the street glowers in my face
> you must protect me from the shadow
> & the glances of hate.
> I shall go on serenading happiness
> somewhere beyond the eyelids of frightened eyes.[13]

As a 'caravan leader' of his people, Darwish's support to the cultural resistance against the denied Palestinian existence continues through creating powerful images that are predominantly rooted in their reality, tradition, and life. Against Israeli repression and defeat, they create the vanguard of national pride and self-assurance through the poet's fundamental belief that despite the sufferings inflicted by Israel's settler-colonialism, occupation, and domination, 'the Phoenix, or the Green Bird—as it is called in the Palestinian folk song never ceases to be reborn out of his ashes.'[14] Green, therefore, is an important resisting symbol in his poetry. For example, references to olives are ever-present in the poems. The persona speaking out in 'Identity Card' says that 'to me the most delicious food/is olive oil and thyme.'[15] In the same poem, the Palestinian records:

> My roots
> gripped down before time began
> before the blossoming of ages
> before cypress trees and olive trees…
> before grass sprouted.[16]

---

11. Darwish, *Selected*, p. 74.
12. Darwish, *Selected*, p. 74.
13. Darwish, *Selected*, p. 50.
14. Mahmoud Darwish, 'The Madness of Being a Palestinian', *Journal of Palestine Studies* 15, 1(Autumn 1985), p.138-139.
15. Darwish, *Selected*, p. 25.
16. Darwish, *Selected*, p. 24.

Darwish's very last poem, 'The Dice Player,' brings the green back as usual:

> O land "I love you green," green. An apple
> waving in light and water. Green. Your night
> Green. Your dawn, green. So plant me gently,
> with a mother's kindness, in a fistful of air.
> I am one of your seeds, green...[17]

Discernibly, green does not only stand for the land of olives, basils and thymes, it speaks of an agrarian country on the Mediterranean coast that never ceases to exist in grandeur in its people's minds, despite lacking recognition in the dominant discourse.

As noted before, Darwish's whole oeuvre can be seen as an oppositional project against that discourse. Darwish started off as a forerunner in the dissenting group that was writing in the '60s in Israel in the teeth of Golda Meir's infamous proclamation that 'there are no Palestinians.'[18] From the very beginning, then, his job was to discover the 'image of lightning' in the midst of the 'hurricane' blowing over the country as a result of the longest standing occupation in modern history. Unlike the dominant Israeli discourse, however, his counter-hegemony is an attempt to 'serenade happiness' by upholding the hope of survival for his people, rather than spreading hatred for the occupying force. Therefore, Darwish, like Said, speak of the possibility of resistance under impossible circumstances. 'The Lantern of Wounds' makes it clear:

---

17. Darwish quoted in Mourid Barghouti, "'He is the son of all of you'", *The Guardian* Saturday 16 August 2008, http://www.guardian.co.uk/books/2008/aug/16/poetry [accessed: 3 December 2010].
18. Meir quoted in Gerald Butt, 'Profiles: Golda Meir', BBC News Tuesday April 21 1998, http://news.bbc.co.uk/1/hi/events/israel_at_50/profiles/81288.stm [accessed: 3 December 2010].

> The Sultan grew angry
> & the Sultan occupies all pictures
> & the backs of postcards
> & on his forehead is the tattoo of slaves.
> Then he shouted: 'It is ordered!
> Execute this poem!'
> Execution Square is the anthology of stubborn poems.[19]

Colonial power seems to be absolute as 'The Sultan's' image saturates the prevalent discourse (he 'occupies all pictures' '& the backs of postcards') and enslaves all institutions ('& on his forehead is the tattoo of slaves'). This alludes to the fact that Israel wields overwhelming power over the occupied people. Even so, Darwish explains how ironically the '[e]xecution Square' becomes 'the anthology of stubborn,' i.e., dissenting poems. It is because they are like 'the lightning' that 'cannot be locked in a stalk of maize';[20] they are as true and alive as the forces of nature. Besides, just as 'a stalk of maize' is not an enclosure for something as powerful as 'the lightning,' so is a blockade not a restriction for something as forceful as resistant poetry.

Darwish insists that these are the

> ... songs that have the sun's logic
> & the history of streams
> & the temperament of earthquakes
> that they resemble a tree's roots:
> should they die in one land
> they will blossom in every land![21]

Once again, the images highlight the unstoppable natural force of the voice of resistance. They are no mere figurative language, for Darwish's poetry remained the source of inspiration for Palestinian resistance against Israel's power to curb it mercilessly. Provenly, the vigour of the resistance never dies, because the 'wounds' inflicted

---

19. Darwish, *Selected*, p. 55.
20. Darwish, *Selected*, p. 55.
21. Darwish, *Selected*, p. 55.

by Israel's colonial policies of subjugation, abasement and extirpation paradoxically work as the 'lanterns'[22] assisting the subdued people to walk their way through the endless tunnels of torture. Thus the poet's 'red song' is 'an ember'; even in prison, it creates 'the fire of revolution,' which defies '[t]he Sultan's' sway.[23] Therefore, the poet not only 'ordained' his 'heart' to 'the call of the tempest' of revolution, his verses keep it 'roar(ing)'[24] against the all-powerful authority.

Thus Darwish's 'early fierce poetry registered his resistance to existential and cultural erasure practised by an apartheid colonial state.'[25] In writing against the regular death and destruction, terror and brutality, and painful sufferings of the occupation, his lines speak more directly to the 'masters':

> Don't make a moral of me twice!
>   My masters! O my masters the prophets
>   don't ask the trees about their names
>   don't ask the valleys about their mother…
>   all the hearts of the people
>   are my nationality
>   so take away my passport![26]

Darwish defies his colonial masters who have taken away his political identity. Even from 'the detention room,' he challenges them as they imprison him for his poetry by declaring that he does not require pen and paper for writing, for 'poetry is heartsblood/ salt of bread/ vitreous body of eye.'[27] With the verse that gets written in his mind and body, Darwish defies 'the fetters':

> I shall state this
>   in the detention room
>   in the bath-house
>   in the stable
>   under the whip
>   under handcuffs
>   undergoing the torture of chains:
>
> One million swallows
> On my heart's branches
> Compose the war song.[28]

The design of the first stanza is noticeable. Every line gets a bit away from the starting point of the previous line so as to create the impression that every oppression that the line names is lesser than the previous one, especially as they all fall like cards under the stormy pronouncement the poet makes in the second stanza. In other words, Darwish is saying that the colonial authority can try to undermine his dignity through imprisonment, tortures, and bureaucratic tools like the passport, identity cards, etc., but his 'war song' will always rise above this sort of 'existential erasure.' His words retrieve the lost land and reinscribe it on the cultural map of the world. In 'A Lover from Palestine' the poet says it unambiguously: he 'opened door and window' to their 'stormy night,' i.e., the occupied state asking the night to turn back because 'I have appointments with words & light.'[29] What did the appointed time produce? Obviously, it recreated the land of Palestine whose 'eyes are a thorn in my heart' and 'speech' was 'like the swallows fluttered from my house.'[30]

That is how sheer anger of dispossession does not overshadow the beauty of his poetic imagination. His images are the fulcrum to determine that his verses contain his politics, not the other way round. Therefore, his poetry is not overtly political. Everyday death, destruction and violence of

---

22. Darwish, Selected, p. 55.
23. Darwish, Selected, p. 55.
24. Darwish, Selected, p. 55.
25. Sinan Antoon, 'Farewell Mahmoud Darwish', Al-Ahram Weekly 910 (14 - 20 August 2008), http://weekly.ahram.org.eg/2008/910/fr1.htm [accessed: 16 December 2008].
26. Darwish, Selected, p. 62.
27. Darwish, Selected, p. 70.

---

28. Darwish, Selected, p. 70.
29. Darwish, Selected, p. 64.
30. Darwish, Selected, p. 62.

occupation are alluded to in the poetry. But they are present as a background and not cited as facts. Nor does Darwish let the grim reality of checkpoints, continuous seizures of land, increasing settlements, and so on crush his poetic sensibility. For example, he is never as direct as Noam Chomsky, who plainly states in an interview that Gaza 'is a hell-hole. They don't want it.'[31] Darwish rather speaks poetically:

> The earth is closing on us, pushing us through the last passage, and
> we tear off our limbs to pass through.
> The earth is squeezing us. I wish we were its wheat so we could die and live again. I wish the earth was our mother
> So she'd be kind to us.[32]

The depressing picture of Gaza as 'the last passage' and the sadness of West Bank's ever shrinking territory ('the earth is squeezing us') and the cruel reality of losing land are all evoked without compromising the beauty of the lines. In fact, their suggestive power and beauty are such that they exemplify what Tagore calls, the light that springs from the source of darkness.

Clearly, Darwish's anti-colonialism is signified by his opposition to the darkness of the occupation. At the same time, he situates the Israeli enmity against them in a bigger context of imperialism fed by an Orientalist style East-West divide. Here as well, Darwish shares a viewpoint advanced by Said. Said explains:

> … the roots of European anti-Semitism and Orientalism were really the same… that the Semites, whether Muslim or Jew, were not Christians and not Europeans, and therefore had to be excoriated and confined. What then occurred is that the Zionists took on the view of the Orientalists vis-à-vis the Palestinians; in other words the Palestinians became the subject for the Israeli Orientalist, just as the Muslim and others have been the subject for the colonial or imperial Orientalists.[33]

Indeed, Israel's invasion of Lebanon in 1982 proves the strength of the imperialist hegemony dividing the East from the West. Having been emboldened by the US support, the Western-ally Israel carries out one of the heinous massacres of the eastern (read, 'inferior') Palestinian refugees in Shabra and Shatila camps, among many other atrocities, of course. Beirut killing proves how far the Israeli subjection of the Palestinian 'others' could go. Palestinians' confinement in Beirut refugee camps was not enough; Israel needed to excoriate and uproot them even from their exilic shelter in Lebanon in order to make their absence permanent. Darwish's exquisitely written commemoration of Beirut, *Memory for Forgetfulness*, inevitably acts as a counter narrative to this process of otherization aiming at the erasure of a whole race. More importantly, he surely agrees with Said in showing the deep historical root of the imperial notion of the East-West enmity, as he claims in the memoir that the Palestinian resistance is

> … correcting the ink of a language that (from the siege of Acre in the Middle Ages to the present siege of Beirut whose aim is revenge for all medieval history) has driven the whole area east of the Mediterranean toward a West that has wanted nothing more from slavery than to make enslavement easier?[34]

---

31. Noam Chomsky and Christopher J Lee, 'South Africa, Israel-Palestine, and the Contours of the Contemporary World Order', From Occupied Palestine, http://fromoccupiedpalestine.org/node/1244 [accessed: 14 February 2010].

32. Mahmoud Darwish et al, *Victims of a Map* (London: Al Saqi, translated by Abdullah al-Udhari, 1984), p.13.

33. Edward Said, *Power, Politics and Culture* (London: Bloomsbury, 2005), p. 48.

34. Mahmoud Darwish, *Memory for Forget-*

Arguably, Darwish focuses on the crusades, rather than anti-Semitism, as the source of Western imperialism. History's irony is unmissable in any case. The Jews, who were the 'others' of the Christian West, are now their 'representative' in the East to the extent they adhere to the Zionist colonial agenda, as they are taking revenge on their behalf for their defeat in Acre during the crusades by now punishing Saladin's race.

Darwish's point is that Western imperialism has historically wanted the enslavement of the Levant in one form or another. And that is simply why the American propaganda machine's drumbeating of Israel's virtues overwrites the cruel facts about the invasion. As Said argues, the forceful suppression of a Palestinian experience in Lebanon ensures America's triumphalist exoneration of Israel's crimes in Lebanon.[35] So powerful the exoneration turns out to be that being Palestinian inevitably means facing the cruelty of life through denied rights, needs and opportunities, as the poet records in the memoir. The denial goes so far as to overwrite the Palestinian identity as a tag to the Israeli one. 'The world isn't interested in me,' Darwish tells one of his interviewers. 'It notices me only because it is interested in you.'[36] That is why the poet protested the Tel Aviv protest of the Israeli aggression in Lebanon. Lest it sounds perplexing since the Israelis were announcing their solidarity with the suffering Palestinians, Darwish explains the ground of his protestation:

> I didn't rejoice over the demonstrations in Tel Aviv, which continues to rob us of all our roles. From them the killer and the victim, from them the pain, and the cry; the sword, and the rose; the victory, and the defeat...[37]

Darwish alludes to the victimhood of the holocaust that Israel has been rather abusing since its birth to get Western support for their subjugation of Arab people. The pain of the paradox is understandable. Israel's aggression is so extensive that it overshadows the subjugated people's ability to express their own opposition to their defeat. That is why Darwish writes the counter-hegemonic memoir to give voice to his voiceless people.

Arguably, in a Bendaesque way, truth, justice and humanism remain the source of the Darwishian warfare against the marginalisation and dehumanization of the Palestinians. And what is the truth that the poet upholds? To know the answer to that, we have to listen to Raja Shehadeh, a prominent Palestinian lawyer and writer, who met the poet in Ramallah for an interview during Israel's invasion of the occupied territories in response to the second Intifada (Palestinian mass uprising). Darwish talks to him during a short cessation of the incessant curfews. He describes his new poem, 'A State of Siege,' to Shehadeh as 'a poet's journal that deals with resisting the occupation through searching for beauty in poetics and beauty in nature.'[38] Therefore, beauty, not the horror of the attack, is the truth that inspires him to knit a strong hope in an otherwise bleak war diary. That is why we are told not to expect the poem to be a journalistic report or a detailed record of the invasion. Rather, the beauty emanates from the pieces of feelings, fragments of thoughts, and strings of emotions with which Darwish represents the collective suffering of his people. As with most Darwish poems, the personal is political here:

---

fulness (Berkeley: University of California, translated by Ibrahim Muhawi, 1995), p. 11-2.

35. Edward Said, 'Permission to Narrate', *Journal of Palestine Studies* 13, 3 (Spring 1984).

36. Stuart Klawans, 'Godard's Inferno', *The Nation* 279, 21 (Winter 2004), p. 40.

37. Darwish, *Memory*, p.109-110.

38. Darwish quoted in Raja Shehadeh, 'Mahmoud Darwish – a Poet of Peace in a Time of Conflict', *The Guardian* Friday 7 August 2009, http://www.guardian.co.uk/books/booksblog/2009/aug/07/mahmoud-darwish-poetry-palestine [accessed: 6 November 2009].

> (To a reader :) Don't trust the poem,
>   this daughter of absence,
> she is neither speculation
>   nor intellect,
> she's chasm's sense.[39]

The poet is relaying how it feels to be on the mouth of an abyss, especially when he realizes *why* he and his people are thrown at the chasm. Since the reality of their presence in any shape or form questions the story of their 'absence' dominantly made known by Israel, the siege, invasion and attack are its repeated effort in making this 'absence' true. That is why Darwish ironically says that his poetry must be the 'daughter of absence,' since he never exists 'officially.' This is Darwish's paradoxical way of asserting the plain truth of their existence in opposition to the power's pressure on them to fit into the hegemony it maintains.

Darwish depicts the materialistic effect the hegemony creates in their life through describing the pain of losing the Palestinian land and identity in an intimate way. In *Memory*, Darwish records their forced expulsion and his grandfather's subsequent longing for his land to convey the enormity of the injustice done to them:

> We came from the villages of Galilee. We slept one night by the filthy Rmesh pool, next to pigs and cows. The following morning, we moved north... My grandfather died with his gaze fixed on a land imprisoned behind a fence. A land whose skin they had changed from wheat, sesame, maize, watermelons, and honeydews to tough apples. My grandfather died counting sunsets, seasons, and heartbeats on the fingers of his withered hands. He dropped like a fruit forbidden a branch to lean its age against.[40]

Their ever known land of bountiful 'wheat, sesame, maize, watermelons, and honeydews' turned into a place of 'tough apples,' which was foreign to them. Their life withered away by waiting for a return to the homeland; peace became 'forbidden' in their life. Thus the natural aspirations of a human life were denied, destroyed and disallowed to them, just because another people had a simultaneous claim on their land. Apart from the deep humiliation of the dispossession, the loss of land destroyed a whole way of life. Darwish depicts the uprooting in plain terms:

> I belong there... I was born as everyone
>   is born.
> I have a mother, a house with many
>   windows, brothers, friends, and a
>   prison cell
> with a chilly window! I have a wave
>   snatched by seagulls, a panorama of
>   my own.
> I have a saturated meadow. In the deep
>   horizon of my word, I have a moon,
> A bird's sustenance, and an immortal
>   olive tree.[41]

Having been thrown outside the land, they lose the last remnant of connection to it, which increases the longing for it. Therefore, viewed from exile, even the 'prison cell/with a chilly window' of the usurped homeland does not seem worthy to be lost. The deep attachment to the land that Darwish portrays reflects the scale of injustice related to its loss: 'This land is the skin on my bones, /And my heart/ Flies above its grasses like a bee.'[42] This indomitable love signifies that regaining the homeland is synonymous with achieving justice for Darwish and his people. This is why his verse keeps on asserting their right by defying

---

39. Mahmoud Darwish, *The Butterfly's Burden* (Tarset: Bloodaxe, translated by Fady Joudah, 2007), p. 167.

40. Darwish, *Memory*, p.88.

41. Mahmoud Darwish, *Unfortunately, It Was Paradise* (Berkeley: University of California, translated by Munir Akash et al, 2003), p. 7.

42. Mahmoud Darwish, *The Music of Human Flesh* (London: Heinemann, translated by Denys Johnson-Davies, 1980), p.28.

power's denigration of it: 'I have lived on the land long before swords turned man into prey.'[43]

Thus the poet clings onto the land, which he always felt to be rightfully theirs, despite power's repeated attacks on them to turn this into a lie. The truth is that a group of people simply cannot 'remove' another people from a land just because they want to establish their 'superior' claim on it, or because they 'feel' that it belongs solely to them. And this is what Darwish sets out to explain to the world when he asks,

> Has any other nation ever known so many expulsions, passed through so many exiles, or faced so many massacres without being rewarded with a homeland... I mean its own homeland?[44]

The force of the question can only be disregarded if humanity becomes foreign to itself. Darwish states this clearly in a prose piece written against the Ramallah Siege of 2002: 'From this day on, he who does not become Palestinian in his heart will never understand his true moral identity.'[45]

We have to realize the historical context of such a demanding statement. Darwish represents a dispersed people whose land, identity, wealth, dignity, security, culture, and society and nationhood—everything related to a human existence on earth— evaporated in a nightmare called the Nakba. However, the reality is that there has been no waking up from the nightmare. That is why Darwish writes in his last poem:

> I am fortunate that I am a divinity neighbor...
> It is my misfortune that the cross is the eternal ladder to our tomorrow![46]

The absurdity of the injustice ushered in by the Nakba and its continual aftermaths are brought to light by Darwish through the irony that being a 'divinity neighbor' translates into being a lesser human for him. Indeed, to the Israelis, returning to their Biblical home was not an act of colonization. But for the Palestinians, it makes little difference whether or not religion was on the side of their 'others'; because the Israeli authority did to them exactly what colonizers do to their subjects:

> What difference was it to them whether
> It was Isaac or Ishmael who was God's sacrificial lamb?
>
> Their hell was Hell itself.[47]

Besides, when the 'Hell' breaks loose, the realm of the physical enters the act of resistance. The Arabs use their bodies against the occupier out of sheer desperation of a collective punishment that they never deserve in the first place. This is how crime is begetting crime in the peace-deprived land. However, Darwish insists:

> The martyr clarifies for me: I didn't search beyond the expanse
> for immortal virgins, because I love life on earth, among the pines and figs, but
> I couldn't find a way to it,
> so I looked for it with the last thing I owned:
> blood in the lapis body.[48]

Evidently, Darwish's humanism does not allow him to valorise the martyrs through a religious argument. Rather, his secular consciousness brings a humanistic focus on the situation to explain the paradox

---

43. Darwish, *Unfortunately*, p. 7.
44. Darwish, *Madness*, p. 139.
45. Mahmoud Darwish, 'A War for War's Sake', *Al-Ahram Weekly* 581 (11 - 17 April 2002), http://weekly.ahram.org.eg/2002/581/fr2.htm [accessed: 29 March 2010].
46. Fayeq Oweis, 'The Dice Player by Mahmoud Darwish', Knol (August 2008), http://knol.google.com/k/the-dice-player# [accessed: 20 July 2010].
47. Mahmoud Darwish, *The Adam of Two Edens* (Syracuse, NY: Jusoor and Syracuse University, translated by Husain Haddawi et al, 2000), p.177.
48. Darwish, *Butterfly's*, p. 163.

that those who 'love life' destroy it willingly, since they 'couldn't find a way to it.'

To me, Darwish's universal humanism paves a way forward in lifting both the Israelis and the Palestinians out of their hells in the 'holy' land. Naturally, he renounces meaningless violence on both sides arguing that hostile actions from them simply keep prolonging 'the age of barbarism.' Once again, irony is his weapon:

> The martyr is the daughter of a martyr who is the daughter of a martyr ...
> And nothing happens in this civilized world,
> the age of barbarism is over,
> and the victim is nameless, ordinary
> and the victim... like truth... is relative
> etc., etc.[49]

Endless repetitions of violence triggering off counter-violence irrevocably perpetuate the mutuality of trauma and destroy the desire for peace. Since Israel's military violence starts the process off, it drives away any possibility of human connection between the two groups who are destined to share the same place:

> (To another killer): Had you left the fetus for thirty days, the possibilities would have changed:
> the occupation might end and that suckling
> would not remember the time of siege,[50]

It is no exaggeration, therefore, that Darwish's aesthetics is immersed in his humanism. For instance, the verse below shows how he brings some piece of the sky nearer to his tormented people:

> When the fighter planes disappear, the doves fly
> white, white. Washing the sky's cheek with free wings, reclaiming splendor and sovereignty
> of air and play. Higher and higher
> the doves fly, white, white. I wish the sky
> were real (a man passing between two bombs told me)[51]

When 'the fighter planes' and the 'bombs' become the dominant reality under the sky, Darwish wants his suffering people to look above. After all, like the 'man passing between two bombs,' the rest of the nation wants some respite from the suffering and a scope to get away from the heat and madness. Darwish's poetry materializes that scope through the sky, air, and its free birds above the conflict-ridden world, where peace reigns in abundance. Thus his humane verses give the people an opportunity to inhale the peace from above and lift their spirits up for survival.

The fact is that amidst the trauma, rage, injustice, and violence, something has to soothe the wounded Palestinian hearts. Something has to pave the way for the healing process so that they can start believing in reconciliation. Something has to be the source of strength for them. That is why Darwish's poetry creates a calming effect by knitting the beauty of nature in his verses in order to keep the hope for a better future alive amidst the most impossible situation: 'Alone, we are alone to the dregs, / had it not been for the visits of the rainbow.'[52] However beaten and low the Palestinian life may be and however abandoned they may feel, 'the rainbow' never forgets to visit them to lighten their sorrow. Therefore, Darwish never ceases to

> ... whisper to the shadow: If
> the history of this place were less crowded
> our eulogies to the topography of

---

49. Darwish, *Butterfly's*, p. 167.
50. Darwish, *Butterfly's*, p. 131.
51. Darwish, *Butterfly's*, p. 129.
52. Darwish, *Butterfly's*, p. 133.

poplar trees… would've been more![53]

Clearly, the poet's humanist imagination always emphasizes the greatness of 'the topography of/poplar trees' over history's quarrel about who should live in the vicinity of the trees. Since the quarrel is most shockingly overshadowing the lush beauty 'the topography' offers, Darwish cannot rhapsodise about the quarrel to intensify it in anyway. After all, the history of the land has already been too 'crowded' with claim and counter-claim. And so, emotional outpourings will simply worsen the situation by excavating more and more wounds. Therefore, Darwish employs beauty in a therapeutic way by assigning it the task to heal the unhealable wounds from within.

> I wrote twenty lines about love
> and imagined
> this siege
> has withdrawn twenty meters!…[54]

Evidently, sustaining the inner strength of his people by singing the song of common humanity of both the besieged and the besieger is the ultimate Darwishian way of fighting against the forces of darkness. Should I need to reiterate that such an 'amateurish' way of fighting against the political darkness is a fundamental requirement in every individual, who is worthy to be called an intellectual?

---

53. Darwish, *Butterfly's*, p. 137.
54. Darwish, *Butterfly's*, p. 151.

HUMAN ARCHITECTURE: JOURNAL OF THE SOCIOLOGY OF SELF-KNOWLEDGE
A Publication of OKCIR: The Omar Khayyam Center for Integrative Research in Utopia, Mysticism, and Science (Utopystics)
ISSN: 1540-5699. © COPYRIGHT BY AHEAD PUBLISHING HOUSE (IMPRINT: OKCIR PRESS) AND AUTHORS. ALL RIGHTS RESERVED.

Lisa Suhair Majaj's Geographies of Light: the Lighted Landscape of Hope
(Book Review)

Rehnuma Sazzad

Nottingham Trent University, UK

rehnuma.sazzad@ntu.ac.uk

Abstract: This is a review of the book, *Geographies of Light: the Lighted Landscape of Hope*, a collection of poetry by the Palestinian-American poet Lisa Suhair Majaj, published by Del Sol Press, Washington, D.C, 2009. "Reading Majaj," the reviewer Rehnuma Sazzad states, "we surely realize that whatever differences of skin, colour, or map we may have, we are the neighbours of the stars by dint of inhabiting a tiny planet that has not yet stopped its orbit round its own star." In her view, "The book presents a wonderful landscape, which is filled with the presence of light. The landscape spreads over different continents and establishes the poet's belief and hope in humanity by building up an imaginative geography in which she feels at home."

Lisa Suhair Majaj's Del Sol Press Poetry Prize 2010 winning collection of verses (Del Sol Press, Washington, D.C., 2009, pp. 133) presents a wonderful landscape, which is filled with the presence of light. The landscape spreads over different continents and establishes the poet's belief and hope in humanity by building up an imaginative geography in which she feels at home.

Since the Palestinian-American—born in Iowa, brought up in Amman, educated in Beirut and Michigan, and now living in Cyprus—cannot locate the map she can exclusively claim as her own, she decides to create one for herself through her poetry. How does she draw the lines of this unusual map, though? In my view, Majaj's cartographic skill is the most significant aspect of this collection, for she determines the lines of her imaginative map in a brilliant way. She achieves them by joining the multitude of tiny drops of light emanating from the concrete goodness and warmth of human heart. Majaj excavates her experiences in order to trace the human connection with nature, the fellow human beings, and even the greater

---

Rehnuma Sazzad defended her PhD dissertation on Literary and Cultural Studies at Nottingham Trent University in November 2013. Her thesis was based on Edward Said, Mahmoud Darwish, and other foremost Middle Eastern intellectuals. She has written a variety of papers on intellectuals from the region including Said, Darwish, Naguib Mahfouz, Leila Ahmed, Youssef Chahine, Mona Hatoum, and Nawal El Saadawi. She has published pieces on the Bangladeshi-American filmmakers Tareque and Catherine Masud, and the Indian auteur Satyajit Ray. Her research interest is on South Asian history and literary creations, where she aims to foster a deeper cultural dialogue between the Middle Eastern and South Asian regions.

celestial environment amidst the struggle to live, to come to terms with losses and deep traumas, and of course, the joys of living. Thus, the poet expresses how the light of the human heart becomes visible to her through her life and reality on earth.

Therefore, her poetic mission seems to be to keep knitting the shawl made up of the drops of light that she discovers around her, for one cannot fight against darkness with further darkness. Instead, one needs more and more light-drops to drive it out. Understandably, the drops are not as innumerable as to be readily visible. Therefore, the particles of light that adorn Majaj's landscape delineating her memories, visions, and emotions are hard-earned through her constant search for them. Reading the book, therefore, one is bound to have the feeling that Majaj never ceases to collect the particles to keep forming her ideal map of belonging. As a result, this book of poetry is about keeping focus on the collection, despite the change of places, events and situations that define the poet's life.

I reiterate that her search spans a full gamut of experiences ranging from the pluralistic upbringing, to the sufferings of dislocation, to remembering childhood freedom, to achieving calmness and moving forward. The extract appearing below from the poem, 'Living in History,' beautifully captures her idea of the light being created out of the living history of human existence through all its variations:

> Whatever the skins we live in,
> the names we choose, the gods we claim or disavow,
> may we be like grains of sand on the beach at night:
> a hundred million separate particles
> creating a single expanse on which to lie back
> and study the stars. And may we remember the generosity
> of light: how it travels through unimaginable darkness,
> age after age, to light our small human night. (122)

Her steadfast belief in lighting the 'small human night' is why she declares above that we are not to dwell on our exterior differences. Neither 'the skins we live in' nor 'the gods we claim or disavow' are crucial to her, then. Instead, she wants us to be as rooted to the world as the 'grains of sand on the beach at night' and yet keep looking upwards, just like them, as they fix their gaze at 'the stars,' As hard to reach as it might sound, a silent but powerful strength is embedded in such an ambitious assertion. Majaj aims here to make us realize that the light of the stars visits us by traversing the vast expanses of 'unimaginable darkness.' Similarly, the light of the human soul keeps awake and alive amidst all sorts of deprivations inside the atmosphere of the earth. Majaj makes our communion with the stars possible, then, in order for us to recognize our celestial existence that could be all the more inspiring, if we put things in perspective. Naturally, Majaj's firm answer to all the irreconciliations of her culturally diverse and divided life is a humanistic approach to them to a greater extent. This not only inspires her to write but also gives her a sense of transcendence of all the travails brought about by cultural disintegration.

From this viewpoint, the constitution of the book in seven sections is significant, for each section has a specific temperament as it searches for the humanistic light from a particular angle. For example, the first section deals with the idea of childhood and beginning. It conjures up some warm pictures of the Majaj family, despite its trials to deal with the disorientation of dispossession that seems to be buried underneath the everyday reality, but surfaces from time to time. When this happens, the poet feels that the taste of coffee changes in her mouth, for it

> ... fills with dregs:
> coarse, bitter-sweet, earth-dark,

dense as unclaimed memory. (4)

The sheer fact of the not usually retrieved memory becomes apparent through the image of its 'unclaimed' status. Besides, the memory lying buried deep within is compared to the dregs of some 'dense,' 'coarse,' 'bitter-sweet,' and 'earth-dark' coffee, which makes us realize that we are in the company of a poet of fine sensibility. Simultaneously, we understand that growing up with such burdens of memory was not easy for the child the poet used to be. But the memories of Amman she unfolds tell us that even in her childhood she found a way of dealing with her alienation by connecting her mind with the surroundings:

Banyan trees patient as centuries.
Beirut barely stirring.
The Mediterranean luminous
with the expectation of light. (8)

Evidently, for her, nature bore the first sign of the luminosity lying beyond a war-torn Lebanon that gave her the strength to survive.

I think one of the main attractions of Majaj's poetry is her ability to take the readers to the exact environment of one of the corners of her multiple universes, when she describes it:

Summer held Amman in its
  breathlessness,
Siesta of burning dust, sun melding to
  sky.

Construction chiselled the daze of heat,
shouts of labourers, swirl of stone dust,
weave of weariness, stone-chippers
  tapping
a blood rhythm. (8)

Even if one has never been to Amman, one can experience the heat, daze, burn, and stone-dust of the place. A rhythm arriving out of the melding of the sun and sky also makes us feel the 'breathlessness' of youth under the heat. Moments like this almost makes us forget that we are reading some poetry dealing with the suppressed pain of not finding a sure anchor. And so, we realize why the spirit of the wanderer does not yield: 'My feet grew tired, but I remembered my name.' (15)

The second section continues with the problem of the unsettled origin, but projects it with more longing for light. Nature is proven to be its source, once more. The light of poetic inspiration is found through recreating the images of 'exuberant earth,' 'pine shrubs,' and poppy blossoms, 'fierce tongues beneath transient skies,' (21) which are in effect the fruits of the poet's memory seeds. Memory, therefore, becomes another means to survive:

Uprooted, any stalk or vine
would whither and die. But if the
  taproot
is strong, a transplant can live. (23)

The poet searches for memories to draw strength from them so as to know what aspects of her cultural roots she identifies with. These help her to build a taproot the support of which makes her sail through her frequent transplantations in unknown geographies. As if to reflect her adaptability, her verses in this section both expand into prose poems and shrivel into the shape of an egg!

The third section is about ripening, which the poet brings into sharp focus by the first poem entitled: 'Pomelo Days.' This section is also where we see the sign of a bright poet, since Majaj does not present the ripening as an automated process. On the contrary, she shows her constant reworking of the self as part of her coming of age and beyond it:

I tilt toward the earth, leaning with the
  weather, held
in place by little more than gravity and

the tenacious will
of someone who gathered stones from
   the field, placing them
one atop another, trying to make
   something that would stay.

From how many lives? I build myself up
   as I go. (36)

Majaj's depth of vision is pleasingly visible here. The clambering of cherry trees in her childhood mentioned earlier in the book is now connected with her adult years' struggle to build a stone-structure representing a firm self-identity. It is as if the child in the poet is still collecting 'stones from the field' to build 'something' that will stay in the weather-swept topsy-turvy world, which vehemently draws her to its circumference by a force greater than gravity.

As the life force throws her in the earthly struggle, she keeps working towards her transcendence through the 'Seasons of Fire, Seasons of Light.' This beautiful poem ends the section where these seasons intermingle as the poet changes hemisphere. This is why the fiery autumn of New England reminds her of the lit Lebanon, as she crosses continents, while the gloomy memory of leaving behind the war-torn city lingers around. The memory dictates that during the transition to New England, the war refugees looked upward from the sea and found a canopy of stars keeping them company. Amidst the glint and glare of sumac and maples of North America, therefore, the poet knows that

After the brilliance of autumn,
nothing will be clearer than the
   simplicity of loss. (48)

Nature's company makes the acceptance of loss possible. Loss is not the note, though, on which the beautiful poem ends. The interweaving of New England and Lebanon continues by leading the seeker of light to hope for spring days. In her mind's eye, she sees that the almond trees are blossoming in accord with 'the sea's soft breath,' where the hills have been 'taken by fire' (49), in Lebanon.

In case the readers have the feeling that Majaj's is an affective landscape simply filled up with natural images in order to drive out the losses of non-belonging, I have to point out that the poet's politics of map making runs deeper than that. This is proven when the fourth section throws us into the thick of things. The poet's struggle for a definable political identity is perfectly intelligible here. In 'Guidelines,' she says:

If they ask you where you come from,
say Toledo. Detroit. Mission Viejo.
Fall Springs. Topeka. If they seem
   confused,

help them locate these places on a map,
then inquire casually, Where are you
   from?
Have you been here long? Do you like
   this country? (53)

Majaj seems to have wandered from one point of America to another without being able to decide if she is Arab or American. The use of the caesura emphasizes each of the place of her trajectory and brings out her unsettled condition rhythmically. However, when she is accosted by the question of her point of origin, she has to take time to formulate an answer, which is why the enjambment enhanced by the gap between the verses is brilliant. What answer does she come up with, though? The answer is a startling no answer. Instead, she turns the questions around to reflect that the questioner him/herself is also not indigenous to the land of immigrants. Majaj's success as a poet thus lies in recognizing the perfect moment for irony and utilizing it pointedly.

However, she does not fail to mark the moments residing beyond ironies. We realize that some undecidability hangs permanently on her shoulders, when Majaj depicts an irremovable rift in her identity. In her name poem, she states:

> You call my daily name, *Lisa,*
> the name I've finally declared
> my own, claiming a heritage
> half mine: corn fields silver
> in ripening haze, green music
> of crickets, summer light sloping
> to dusk on the Iowa farm.
>
> The other name fills my mouth,
> A taste faintly metallic,
> Blunt edges around which my tongue
> Moves tentatively: *Suhair,*
> an old fashioned name,
> little star in the night. The second girl,
> small light on a distanced horizon. (63; emphases in original)

The verses, I think, contain the crux of the whole collection and hence, my lengthy citation appears above. Majaj is not an easy combination of Lisa and Suhair. The former contains a dailiness that she associates with the vibrant rural America, one of the sources of her light creating the imaginative geography of her home in the writing. The other source of the light comes from a far distant landscape where a star is keeping vigil. Thus, the poet transforms vigilance, the etymological meaning of Suhair, the Arabic part of her name, into the ground of her constant search for the little dots of light, even when the darkness of night engulfs the surroundings. Another significant point about this part of her name is that it is from a language foreign to her. However, there is a wonderful willingness to keep her ties with a distant language and land alive. In my view, maintaining a complex existence of being both from 'the Iowa farm' and a troubled Arab land by following a beacon of light for the continuous self-transformation towards a better pattern of socio-political existence is the root out of which this beautiful collection of verses branch out.

The beauty of the poems moves us, for its foundation has an idealism the sincerity of which is tangible:

> We might plant together, pluck
> grapes, brew coffee, tell new
> fortunes each day, wash away
> grounds of anger. History could be
> this simple: earth—the final
> claim—cupped like sunlight. (56)

Understandably, these homely, familiar images are the main source of Majaj's earnestness. Nevertheless, the most powerful aspect of the image presented here is the idea of a shared earth. For the poet, the philosophy is quite simple: we are all here to live our ordinary human life through the planting, reaping, brewing, and dreaming of good future under the same sun. Therefore, if our meteorological sharing of the sun is a given, we could transform our history too into an atmosphere reflecting the common aspects of our lived life, rather than the record of conflicts over territoriality and geographical boundaries.

In any case, the fifth section comes as a break from the historico-political musings, since the theme, tone and vision of the poems here are organized around the sweetness of the mother-child bonding. The poet upholds the maternal strength in the poems not only through depicting her affectionate moments with her children but also through highlighting how hard the vocation of motherhood can be. Here we get more glimpses of her sincerity in making her words delineate her experiences in a lifelike way. She describes the deep satisfaction of suckling the child, which is simultaneously arduous and taxing, not least because she nursed 'the baby well into toddlerhood.' (74) Perhaps, the instinct to be as unyielding a shelter for the child as a cold-defying penguin for its chick is what overrides the exhaustion of parenting. Sure enough, Majaj writes:

> I tuck my child beneath my breasts,

ready
to face any danger in his defense, endure icescapes
of hunger, tundras of broken nights—
till my mate returns, scoops up the child,
and sends me staggering to the sea of sleep. (76)

What an insightful picture of men and women's everyday struggle to survive! This is also why we have to believe her that the light she is relentlessly searching for resides inside the humans, for in their ordinariness lies their transcendence!

I think the first poem of the sixth section could not have had a better title, for it truthfully summarises what is discussed in this part: 'Points of Departure.' This is the most overtly and heavily politicized section in the whole book. Yes, it is all about the Palestinian conflict. We see that amid the checkpoints, sentries, cries, memories, documents, and wearies of reaching the debated land, the poet becomes a young girl here, who looks for a border beyond 'the sun's keen blade' (82). Most unsurprisingly, her transcendence does not come from above, for this is the land, where

Sky rims the curve of ocean
opaque as the mountains
mapping the colours of salt. (82)

The unrestrained flow of water has its own mechanism of map making. Since the map is that of salt, there is no quarrel over it. However, the picture is completely different inland. Majaj's prose-poem records how the conflict over the land is plainly killing the zeal for life, as one of the dejected West Bank youth states, 'We are tired, here. We have lost our passion' (83). The poet is deeply affected by the situation. But as we have seen so far, her mission is to rescue whatever little drops of light she can out of the dominant darkness around. This is especially no exception in this part of the collection. Therefore, she does not fail to notice the food varieties, spices, colours of garments, and the fruit platters of West Bank that keep adding to her own map of life.

However, the reality is too overpowering here. Majaj has the perfect image to describe how the conflict is continuously cultivated in the land. She views the surrounding hills as a lasting reservoir of stones that are always 'cropping through the soil of Palestine like a million broken teeth' (83). She can read the hardened but endangered faces of the stone-throwing boys in such an unhinged state. Even so, her instinct is to keep the ray of light alive at least through yearning for peace:

you cry, give us peace!
we cry, give us our lives!

peace grows like any other plant, on the land
it needs earth and water (87)

Once again, Majaj's nature imagery delivers the difficult message in a simple way. 'You' and 'We' have to stop pointing finger at each other. Rather, both the parties must come forward in planting a small tree called 'peace' in the stony soil and give it 'earth and water' for growth.

However, it seems that this idealistic solution will take a lifetime's wait to come about. In the meantime, the reality that governs the lives of 'us' is that of dispossession, 'the pit of exile,' being erased from history, and the numerous razed villages an italicized list of some of which becomes part of the rhythm of a poem, 'For Palestine' (88). In the face of this dissolution of the historic landscape, Majaj's search for light becomes chant-like, as she tries to cover the pain of keeping alive the demolished crevices, windows, steps, 'the houses, the streets, the doorways' in her poetry at the very least:

light pours into the wells
where they threw the bodies

light seeks out the places where sound
was silenced

light streams across stone
light stops at the quarry (92)

This is where Majaj is most Darwish-like, as her words try to put the lost Palestine back into existence and her voice becomes the echo of those silenced forever.

One of the distinct features of Majaj's collection is that the vast injustice meted out to the Palestinians is rendered visible in a story-telling mode. For example, 'These Words' lets us know of a teenage village wife, Rana, who died during labour at a checkpoint, which became an insurmountable barrier between her and the much needed help she sought from doctors at a hospital. Majaj details the incident:

Turned back at the checkpoint
by soldiers indifferent
to fear, or love,

or the fierce labour
of life, she found
only barricades, guns. (98)

Indeed, the pieces of words describe Rana's indescribable pain and sufferings in the face of the merciless barricade and the inhuman apathy. Majaj's negative capability is evident as she wonders how it felt to be the girl who experienced the intolerable waves of pain in the midst of which her baby breathed only to die. In the end, all that remains is a heavy silence of the young mother, her baby, their chronicler, and the readers as well.

In a moment, though, the poet breaks her silence to lash out at the injustice by declaring ironically that if we repeatedly deny that there is anything scandalous in this, the wrongs will be righted. The way Majaj arranges her words in the verse below, the sheer waste of human life is made to glare at us:

Say it fast and over:
this is not a massacre this
is not a massacre this is not
a massacre...
...this is not a
massacre (101)

The last word says it all, however much the world tends to avoid naming the fact. In any case, at the beginning of a befittingly entitled poem, 'Shards,' the poet lists some of the stock phrases with which the world gets away with not encountering the facts on the ground:

A technical failure   terrible accident
  unfortunate
event   regrettable but necessary   we had
to take action   there was no choice
(104; emphasis in original)

We feel the massive cruelty lying behind not only the killings and destructions of the millions of Gazans referred to here but also the nonchalance with which the humanly incomprehensible incidents are turned into mere fragments of harmless news headlines. Thus, Majaj utilizes her words to jolt the world's conscience, and we discover a resistant poet in her.

Understandably, the seventh and the last part of her book is about forming a resistance to injustice that never loses hope for a better future. Therefore, the section opens with a very effective poem, 'No,' by declaring that

Maybe it can't
thwart history: the powerful have
   always known
what they can do, and they do it.
No can't stop an avalanche.
But No could be a retaining wall...
No is steadfast. It knows what it's like
to have nothing in its hands but dignity.
(111)

To me, these lines carry the main strength of the political axis of the collection. When total darkness reigns by stopping even the strength to search for light, Majaj believes a small innocuous word, 'No,' could still support existence by reminding one of one's human dignity. In other words, however dense the darkness is that descends upon the landscapes the poet is connected with, she reaffirms her belief in humanity. This in turn keeps alive her vision of hope. As asphodels, the flowers of Hades and the dead, rise above the earth in search of air, her words want to transcend the immediate reality, which is mostly disheartening, in order to be 'open to the light' (115).

In the end, Majaj's unbudging belief in our essential humanity makes her resistance to injustice so empowering. Her verses make us experience a remarkable uplifting and rejuvenation of spirit. In the ultimate analysis, comparing her lines to the elegance, expanse, and intensity of the Darwishian ones may be left to the judgment of the reader, but who could either forget or disbelieve as sincere a promise as this:

> Low sun flares its crimson light
> across the land. It will rise again
>   tomorrow,
> vigilant and weary as hope. (119)

The success of this prize winning collection should become comprehensible now. The clarity of vision, the sincerity of search, and the power of hope encountered in the book through the verses like the above remind us again and again of our distinct planetary existence. Reading Majaj, we surely realize that whatever differences of skin, colour, or map we may have, we are the neighbours of the stars by dint of inhabiting a tiny planet that has not yet stopped its orbit round its own star.

HUMAN ARCHITECTURE: JOURNAL OF THE SOCIOLOGY OF SELF-KNOWLEDGE
A Publication of OKCIR: The Omar Khayyam Center for Integrative Research in Utopia, Mysticism, and Science (Utopystics)
ISSN: 1540-5699. © COPYRIGHT BY AHEAD PUBLISHING HOUSE (IMPRINT: OKCIR PRESS) AND AUTHORS. ALL RIGHTS RESERVED.

Deep Learning in the Sociological Classroom:
Understanding Craving and Understanding Self

Linda R. Weber

SUNY, Institute of Technology, Utica, NY

flrw@sunyit.edu

Abstract: Deep learning is a dialectical process; the tension between the intellectual understanding and the emotional experience of a subject matter can result in self-insight that has transformative potential. Insight into the self in relationship to the subject matter is the hallmark of this symbolic interactionist understanding of deep learning. Students in two iterations of a senior-level seminar on symbolic interaction abstained from an object of desire for a two-week period; during this time, they blogged about their experiences abstaining, craving, and relapsing. At the end of the two-week period, these blogs were combined to form a qualitative database that was subsequently uploaded into a qualitative data analysis program for phenomenological analysis. The students used this database to write a seminar paper about the overall structure and process of craving that elucidated both the intellectual and the emotional components of learning. This researcher analyzed the students' blogs and papers for signs of deep learning. In general, the integration of the emotional experience with craving and the associated intellectual learning about craving and the transformation of self, signifies that the dialectical process of deep learning about craving can occur in a college classroom.

INTRODUCTION

Does emotion have a place in learning? Intellectual learning takes center stage in the college seminar; students exert effort to learn the material at hand. Yet, those profound emotional experiences that make up our lives are effortlessly integrated into the very fabric of our being. Is there another way of learning whose focus is not solely the intellectual understanding of information as normally encountered in the classroom? The role of emotion in learning about craving is the focus of this study.

This study is neither an assessment of a classroom exercise nor a research project on craving, per se, although some assessment conclusions and understandings about craving can be clearly gleaned. Rather, this study explores the potential of integrating an emotional experience with the intellectu-

Linda R. Weber is an Associate Professor of Sociology at the State University of New York, Institute of Technology, in Utica, New York. Her scholarly work has focused on various applications of symbolic interactionist understandings of trust in relationships. This work on deep learning demonstrates her interest in symbolic interactionism as a pedagogic style as she demonstrates the dialectic of intellectual and emotional learning about craving that leads to the development of a more mature student.

al learning that is already taking place within the sociological classroom as one way of adding depth to the learning experience. The deep learner emerges with an understanding of one's self in relationship to the subject matter, and this understanding may motivate action.

This paper begins with an overview of the theoretical roots of deep learning as experiential learning, continues with the development of craving as an experiential object, follows with the methodological processes at work, and then elaborates on the results of this exercise in relationship to the intellectual, emotional, and self-revelatory process of learning about craving.

Deep Learning as Experiential Learning

> Imagine that there is a fundamental learning experience. It is at once emotional and intellectual, mental and physical, social and personal, totally unique yet freely shared. There is a communal place where this experience becomes positively energized and charged. This is the kind of experience which I call "deep learning." (Bentz 1992:72)

Deep learning is both intellectual and emotional. According to Bentz (1992), intellectual learning, the first element of deep learning, is a rational, cognitive, "philosophical quest for understanding" (p. 72) that focuses on discovering meaning. The traditional educational seminar is organized around this goal. The second element of deep learning is emotion or feeling that emerges from self-revelatory feedback; however, emotional learning is normally considered to be antithetical to intellectual learning. Bentz (1992) proposes that deep learning is the synthesis of the dialectical tension between these two elements, resulting in the production of a more mature social actor. The mature individual is one who has an understanding of one's self in relationship to the intellectual material.

Emotion and self are intimately connected. According to Denzin (1984), emotion is at the core of the self; emotions are "self-feelings" and are both the "self-in-feeling" and those feelings directed toward and about the self. An existing emotion provides insight into the self; for example, when one feels remorse about stealing a vehicle, that remorse reveals a self who values upholding the law. Insight about the self is made possible because emotions are at the core of the self and define its very existence.

Experience evokes emotion. This fundamental proposition is the starting point for the sociological theories of emotion (Denzin 1984). Emotional experiences are powerful because they have transformational potential. Not all experiences are transformational or lead to a change in how one views one's self. Those that are directed toward and about the self can have significant consequences for the self; it is these experiences that I refer to as "emotional experiences." Action is made possible through reflexive (Mead 1934) experience that "transforms the impulses, feelings, and desires of concrete experience into higher-order purposeful action" (Kolb 1984:22) that is based upon foresight of consequences. By viewing oneself as the object toward which the community responds, one finds one's place in the social world; this placement brings with it an understanding of one's self, whether good or bad, that evokes emotions; these revelations are the substance of emotional learning and, thus, have the power to change. Emotional experience is an anti-thesis to the thesis of intellectual understanding. Max Weber's (1968) dictum, "One need not have been Caesar in order to understand Caesar" (p. 5), raises the question of the relationship between experience and understanding (Harrington 2001). First, some argue that one does not have to experience something to understand it intellectually. According to Weber (1968), one can understand another's rational-purposive behavior by understanding its socio-historical context even if one has never participated in such behavior. Second, just because one experiences something does not mean understanding ensues, especially if one is trying to understand another's experience. We cannot actually "feel others' experiences" even while having our own similar experience (Harrington 2001:311); to assume otherwise generates what Harrington (2001) referred to as "naïve empathy view of understanding"(p.311). However, Harrington (2001) argues, and I agree, that there is a "wider legitimate function of feeling and imagination in understanding" (p.313). A more complete understanding emerges from the dialectical tension between our now emotional experience of a phenomenon and our intellectual understanding of the same.

Emotional experiences complement intellectual understanding. Although the exact nature of this relationship between experience and understanding is disputed in the philosophical literature (Ludlow, Nagasawa and Stoljar 2004), it is embodied by the "wow" (Ludlow, Nagasawa and Stoljar 2004) evoked by a new experience. For example, imagine after a lifetime being stereo-blind or unable to see depth, one is able to "see" snow for the first time, even though one is a neurobiologist who technically understands vision:

> One winter day, I was racing from the classroom to the deli for a quick lunch…I stopped short. The snow was falling lazily around me in large, wet flakes. I could see the space between each flake, and all the flakes together produced a beautiful three-dimensional dance. In the past, the snow would have appeared to fall in a flat sheet in one plane slightly in front of me. I would have felt like I was looking in on the snowfall. But now I felt myself within the snowfall, among the snowflakes.… I was overcome with a deep sense of joy…. (Sacks 2006:73)

In the above example, Sue Parry, referred to as "Stereo Sue," has a new relationship with snow now that she is able to directly experience it in three dimensions. Joy emerges from her inclusion within the snowfall as an active participant rather than as an observer. Stereo Sue's immersion in snow is an example of experiential learning that is profoundly emotional and, thus, expands her intellectual understanding of stereovision.

Deep learning is experiential learning of another kind, one which directly acknowledges the importance of emotion. Experiential learning on college campuses has typically taken the form of service learning. Within the service learning context, the student learns while providing a needed service to a community-based organization (Blouin and Perry 2009), for example, tutoring at a local children's center. The form the service takes can be research (Marullo, Moayedi and Cooke 2009) like performing a needs assessment, but frequently, it is the fulfillment of organizational tasks such as program oversight. Observation also provides experiences that promote student learning (Meisel 2008) whether it be visiting a prison or doing a police patrol ride-a-long. A crucial element of all these forms of experiential learning is reactive process brought about by the reflection on an experience (Wurdinger 2005) that is frequently generated by journaling or classroom discussion. While deep learning can take place in these more traditional service learning locations, I believe that deep learning is also possible within the seminar setting if the student has an emotional experience with the subject matter.

The seminar experience can facilitate deep learning if it is properly structured. According to Bentz (1992), the ideal group process that maximizes intellectual learning or truth-seeking is one in which power is leveled (Habermas 1973, Habermas 1979). Emotional learning emerges when one utilizes Satir's (1983) "leveling" or "congruent communication" that involves understanding of one's feelings and, subsequently, non-aggressive communication. When combined with Lang's (1983) "derivatives" or indirect and/or metaphorical statements about the relationship at hand, one can see how the topics of conversation in the group or seminar context can relay meaning, even if indirectly, about the emotional context of the learning that is taking place. Having a comfortable atmosphere in which self-revelatory feedback emerges and is considered in a non-threatening manner creates an environment where deep-learning can find its place in the classroom.

A seminar on symbolic interaction (SI) provides an ideal opportunity for a deep learning experience because deep learning is rooted within this theoretical tradition. First, SI is premised upon the idea that meaning is not inherent within an object but is socially constructed (Blumer 1998/1969). Second, SI is the sociological perspective that places primacy on the self (Cooley 1956, Goffman 1959). Third, the reflexive nature of SI (Mead 1934) is compatible with the reflection at the core of experiential learning that can result in self-transformation. Fourth, the proposition that emotions are rooted in social experience and have self-transformative potential is a well-accepted tenet of SI (Denzin 1984). Finally, SI is compatible with qualitative inquiry (Blumer 1969), an approach that is amenable to addressing the depth of the emotional experiences and consequences of deep learning for self. Methodologically, the symbolic interactionist is forever trying to understand the perspective of the social actor. The SI seminar provides the ideal opportunity for deep learning, but it needs an object upon which to focus.

Craving as an Experiential Object

What is a viable object of a deep learning experience? Understanding alcoholism from the perspective of the social actor as presented in Norman Denzin's work, *The Alcoholic Society* (1993) was the focus of the seminar within which this classroom exercise took place. Denzin's (1993) ideas are insightful and challenging. Although I was convinced that the students had a grasp of his ideas on an intellectual level, I wondered whether the students would better understand the predicament of the alcoholic if they had a "deeper" learning experience. How could one deepen the understanding of alcoholism within a classroom-based exercise?

Craving, an integral part of the alcoholic experience, became the focus of this experiential exercise. Desire, the epitome of symbolic representation in action, is a "wanting" of something that at that moment is out-of-reach; "craving" is a form of desire and is a more concrete concept that applied to the seminar's topic of alcoholism (Denzin 1984, Fitzgerald 2010). I settled upon Drummond's (2001) definition of craving as "the conscious experience of a desire to take a drug" (p. 35). Some propose that craving is the core process of addiction (Elster 1999). However, I did not want the students to think that what they were experiencing was the same craving of addiction, especially to alcohol or drugs, but rather an analogous one (Elster 1999). This constraint was talked about extensively in the seminar; however, the experience generated, while not the same craving as in addiction, was an experience of craving with an object of desire.

My interest was not in physical craving (i.e., that which is due to physical withdrawal symptoms) but in symbolic craving (i.e., craving that is not driven by physiology, but by the symbolic representation of the object of desire, something which occurs long after the physical craving is gone) (Denzin 1984, Isbell 1955). This distinction arises in phenomenological accounts of alcoholism (Elster 1999, Fitzgerald 2010, Jellinek 1960, Lindesmith 1975, Ludlow, Nagasawa and Stoljar 2004, Manderson 1995) that are primarily descriptive in nature and that pay attention to the human experience of addiction. Even though phenomenological accounts of addiction that focus unduly on craving and its relationship to relapse are contradicted by a growing body of empirical literature (Adinoff et al. 2007), I did believe that this approach would provide invaluable insight for the students. But is craving an emotional experience?

Emotion and craving are intertwined. Some scholars argue that emotion is the source of all desire (Irvine 2006); we desire those things that will make us feel good. Euphoria emerges upon the realization of the impending fulfillment of desire; dysphonia emerges upon the continued frustration of desire's fulfillment (Elster 1999). Craving, as a conscious desire (Drummond 2001), has the potential to be a profoundly emotional experience. Likewise, relapse has both an emotional basis and emotional consequences as one's view of oneself as being in-control is threatened (Elster 1999).

In sum, integration of this understanding of both deep learning and craving into a theoretical underpinning of an experiential exercise results in the following:

1) At the beginning, a deep learning exercise needs a purposive action as its focus, like abstaining from an object of desire. According to SI, a driver of purposeful action is one's identity or self, and it is the self that makes its appearance in this approach to deep learning.
2) At the surface, reading the relevant scholarship generates an understanding of craving. A fundamental assumption is that a person identifies with the object of desire, even if the person is not aware of such. One reason for this lack of awareness may be that the person does not have a reflexive relationship with this object.
3) To go deeper, one becomes immersed within the emotional experience of craving. In reflection, an understanding of self emerges within the experience; meaning, one becomes aware of the importance of this object for one's identity. An experience may result in confirmation or rejection of this identity, motivated by pride or self-mortification.
4) As one proceeds, learning becomes deep when the individual is able to integrate one's self experience with the relevant scholarship resulting in a changed self. The statement, "Oh, this is what is meant by ___!" exemplifies an "aha!" moment at the core of deep learning that extends itself to self. Identity changes in this process, even if it is just by the inclusion of a deeper understanding of craving.
5) At the end, the power of deep learning is in its linkage to behavioral change. Behavioral change is not necessary for learning to be deep because changes in identity are necessary but not sufficient for behavioral change as the individual is enmeshed in a social situation wherein change may not be feasible.
6) With this understanding of the theoretical process at work in this classroom exercise, this paper now presents the specific methodology.

Methodological Issues

The immediate methodological dilemma was to create the experience. For two weeks, my students refrained from participating in a behavior that they enjoyed and that was a regular part of their daily lives. My classes undertook this process during two semester-long iterations of ten students each. The objects they chose and the number of students that chose them were as follows: smoking (4), eating chocolate (3), drinking Mountain Dew (1), drinking diet soda (1), eating fast food (1), eating fried food (1), drinking coffee (2), eating bread (1), biting one's nails (2), watching sports (1), using one's IPod (1), using one's cell phone (1), and watching television (1). The twenty students blogged about their experience, using the self-interview described below, for 12 out of the 14 days in the two-week abstention period. For each class, an NVivo database of these blog experiences with craving was utilized by all the students to understand the phenomenon of craving at both an intellectual and emotional level and served as a basis for their seminar papers on craving.

This section on research methods proceeds by explaining the ethical concerns, the limitations of this project, the structure of the seminar, and the qualitative data collection and analytic techniques used to decipher the emotional nature of the craving experience.

Ethical Issues

The IRB chairperson determined that 45 CFR 46 would consider this a classroom exercise at minimum and as research on instructional technique at maximum; the former does not require IRB review, and the latter was considered exempt. An exemption was applied for and received. Human subjects guidelines were nonetheless adhered to in this seminar; the students were informed of the nature of the classroom project at the beginning of the semester, the class was an elective, and students were advised to use the following criteria as they chose their objects of desire: Their objects 1) were legal, 2) did not involve substance abuse, 3) did not create discomfort when blogging or discussing, 4) would not cause harm to themselves or others, and 5) were g-rated. Students chose aliases, and their identities were considered confidential. The students were aware that information from their blogs or papers could be used for conference presentations or for published papers using their aliases. Within this paper, only student aliases are used with some choosing surnames. No students dropped the class as a result of this project, and all students gave the appearance of being comfortable with the objects of desire that they chose.

Limitations of this Project

Each student's experience with craving is limited by the very nature of this learning exercise. First, knowing that one can return to the object of desire at the end of the two week period changes the experience fundamentally. A number of students commented on this constraint, especially Chris, one chocolate abstainer. Second, the objects of desire in this exercise are not illegal as are many objects of desire, especially those from which one is often asked or forced to abstain. Third, unlike many objects of desire, some of the objects chosen by the students do not have a direct effect on physiology. Given these constraints, this exercise tries to parlay each individual experience with craving, no matter how imperfect, into a collective understanding for the class.

Asking the students to experience the phenomenon they were studying is a direct contradiction to phenomenological approaches that require "bracketing" or distancing of one's prior personal experience (Creswell 2007). Personal engagement with craving is what differentiates this deep learning experience from a research experience. As students were subjects of their own research, I asked the students to utilize the first person voice in the discussion portion of their seminar papers. Even though there has long been pressure for students and academics to remove themselves from their writing, this experiential exercise requires them to be a subject of their own writing that demands their presence.

Seminar Structure

This paper is a result of two separate, semester-long experiences with this classroom exercise. The first five weeks of each semester were spent introducing the students to the basic concepts of symbolic interaction, the literature on craving, and the qualitative data manipulation process using QSR NVivo. Data Collection in the form of blogging began midway through the semester and continued for two weeks. For each class separately, I combined all of the students' blogs as one database that the students analyzed for the rest of the semester. The seminar itself was discussion-driven rather than lecture-driven in an attempt to "level" the classroom, and students were frequently asked to lead discussion on the intellectual material for the class. These discussions also included the students' experiences with craving when students were asked to "check in" each time the class met during the abstention process. These experiences were the focus of a relaxed and sometimes humorous discussion about the commonality of their experiences.

The Blogs as Primary Data and the Students' Primary Data Analysis

Data useful in qualitative analysis provides a detailed description of the process being studied (Creswell 2007). The students captured the data by blogging about their experiences. In order to evoke the detail necessary for the students to develop an understanding of craving, a blog "guide" was created that asked the students to address the following, using a story-telling style, in their daily entries: 1) the social and physical situation within which craving emerged, 2) the explanation and description of the specific craving event, 3) the emotions before, during and after craving, 4) the thinking process during and after the craving incident, 5) images or symbolic representations that emerged, and 6) the learning about and the reflection upon one's self (This fifth guideline was added on for the second iteration of this exercise.).

Phenomenological Analysis

To begin, students followed Creswell's (2007) phenomenological analysis and representation process by identifying "significant statements" and identifying one's interpretation of that statement or "meaning." Next, the students grouped these statements into themes that will be discussed in the results section, below. Admittedly, the conceptual element of this kind of data analysis was difficult for the weaker students to achieve, but even these students ended up with some "rough" categories; at the most basic level, the students categorized according to the different foci of the self-interview. Finally, the students were asked to utilize structural and textual phenomenological analysis to assess the context and process of craving, respectively. The central textual or process question addressed in their papers was "What is the experience of craving? Describe it." The central structural or situational question was "What were the conditions (e.g. setting) in which craving occurred?" This distinction between text or process and structure or situation followed Creswell's (2007) simplification of the Stevick-Colaizzi-Keen method of Moustakas (1994).

Students compiled their work in a fifteen-to-twenty page research paper that integrated the scholarly literature on craving and addiction with the students' own structural and textual analysis. These nineteen seminar papers (since one student withdrew mid-semester), with their strengths and weaknesses, formulated most of the data for this paper; in a sense, this paper is an analysis of the students' analyses of craving. I examined these papers and the students' blogs to assess the extent of their learning about craving and their learning about themselves. The results section that follows includes exemplars of these achievements; I tried to be inclusive of all the students' work while being attuned to not focusing solely on the "best" student's work. What follows is not an analysis of craving but an analysis of the students' "deep learning" about craving as indicated by both an intellectual understanding of the material and an emotionally understood and transformed self.

The Results

The central question is whether deep learning about craving occurred in this classroom exercise. Deep learning emerges from the tension created between intellectual learning and emotional experience; deep learning's creation is the more mature social actor, one who has a better understanding of himself or herself and the material at hand. I believe that deep learning is evidenced by the following: 1) intellectual learning about craving, 2) emotionally experiencing craving wherein self emerges and is transformed, and 4) integration of these two elements in a dialectic of learning. Each of these objectives is examined, below. All excerpts from the students' papers are presented mostly as is, with grammatical errors, typos, and misspellings left intact. Clarifying notations by me are set off in brackets and in bold (e.g. [**bold**]).

Deep Learning Thesis: Intellectual Learning about Craving

What did the students intellectually learn about craving? Indicators of intellectual learning include evidence of an understanding of the structure and process of craving and the linking of such to the scholarly literature. The nineteen seminar papers were the primary source of data for this section. The elements of craving identified by the students were as follows: coping strategies, defining the situation, experiencing emotions, responding to the social environment, visualizing objects of desire, feeling physiological symptoms, predisposing traits of the actor, realizing the importance of the object, relapsing, breaking routines, succumbing to social pressures, and resolving stress. This section focuses on two primary elements of craving, identified by the students, that illustrate the overall structure and process of craving: understanding the influence of the social environment and recognizing the importance of visualization of the objects of desire, respectively.

The social structure of craving. The students identified the social situation that evoked craving as one comprised of physical, emotional, and behavioral cues. Thomas evoked Drummond's (2001) understanding of craving to understand the power of cues in relapse. Alice defined a cue as a stimulus that is connected to the behavior as exemplified in the connection that Bella has between the physical presence of coffee and wanting to smoke cigarettes or Jamie has between seeing others use an iPod and his desire to use his own. Cues can also be emotions; Joe illustrated this with Thomas's anger and anxiety that motivate his smoking. Socially, Alice thought that those behaviors that have become habitual are believed to be unconscious by the student. If behavior has become part of a routine, Jamie contended that it is the absence of a constant or part of a routine that serves as a cue. For example, Rainbow Bright always reached for a cigarette when snapping on her seat belt at the beginning of a drive. When trying to stop smoking, she had extreme craving when she entered her car, as did Lucas when trying to abstain from coffee. Whereas some students promoted the idea of the unconscious as a behavioral force, most students believed that it was just inattention to the environment and the ritualized way of responding that gave rise to the actor not knowing what caused his or her behavior. Debbie commented on the problematic of ritual for abstaining and confirms Redish, Jensen, and Johnson's (2008) insights.

The other significant influence in the social environment identified by the students was the social pressure exerted by significant others, namely family and peers. The most important form that social pressure had on craving and subsequent relapse was through the students' desire for social acceptance. According to Rachel, this desire explained both Joe's decision to watch *American Idol* with his new girlfriend's family even though he had vowed to abstain from television and Alex's decision to purchase chocolate at an elementary school fundraiser despite his decision to abstain from chocolate. She connected her observations with those insights on cell phone use by Walsh, White and Young (2009); Rachel touched on the symbolic nature of the cell phone from which she chose to abstain with her statement that "that feeling is a craving for social acceptance" (Rachel's seminar paper). After his own experience with abstaining from TV, Joe recognized that participation or use of the abstained object was a central activity for membership in social groups as seen in McIlwraith's (2008) research on TV addiction.

Notably, the influence of the existing social environment on successful abstention was not a big focus of the students' analyses. Peer and family could be supportive, thereby increasing the probability of success. As an example, Sarah referred to how Alex's wife refrained from buying chocolate for herself. Thomas asserted that these supportive measures could strengthen ties to family and peers, as indicated by Joe's statement: "I also found out how much my friends care, because they helped me through these past 2 weeks" (Joe's Blog). Lucas commented on the importance of his girlfriend's view of him as a motivating force for not drinking coffee. In addition, Bob Frapples initially thought his girlfriend's ripping the cigarette out of his mouth and breaking it in half was a "mood killer" but then thanked her when he realized she was just "trying to help." Debbie connected this positive support as affirmation of Mead's (1934) "me" that propels the "I" to act in a manner consistent with this "me." The lack of support in efforts at change was surprising but may be indicative of the fact that the objects of desire that were forsaken for the two week period were all considered socially acceptable.

Symbolic representations and the process of craving. The students identified the role of symbols as a dominant part of the craving process itself. Images could allow for the satisfaction of a craving, as Jamie asserted using the following example from Alex's blog that illustrated his reflection one evening after the morning's encounter with his forbidden chocolate:

> The muffins were so moist and fresh looking. They had the chocolate chips on top and were sprinkled with some kind of sugar. The shake was cold and heavy like when the window server handed it out to me. (Alex's blog day 1)

Jamie asserted that imagination allowed for vicarious involvement with the object of desire. On his first day, Alex did refrain from the muffins and shake, although he was extremely annoyed at having to do so.

Images of the object that were idealized, wherein the object was "perfect," were often the source of relapse as observed by Sarah. In her seminar paper, she cited Rose's image of a "chilled Mountain Dew freshly opened" (Rose's blog). As Sarah states, "these idealized, images of perfection are a way an individual trying to rationalize giving in to their craving. When something is perfect and special it becomes hard to walk away from knowing that you may not get another chance at it" (Sarah's seminar paper). Alice, who gave up chocolate, linked this insight to research (Rock and Kambouropoulos 2008, Tiggemann and Kemps 2005) that indicated the significance of visual images in generating craving that precipitated relapse. Likewise, Debbie connected Fitzgerald's (2010) work on the power of images.

Images took on a negative quality once the student had been frustrated by failed attempts at abstention. Joe asserted that at their worst moments of craving, these images took on human characteristics, such as

Thomas imagining that the cigarettes at the convenience store were begging him to take them home:

> One image that really stands out in my head was watching a man as I pumped gas smoke outside of the gas station. I could feel my mouth watering and the desire became overwhelming. As I paid for my gas I could see my cigarettes on the shelf, they were begging me to bring them home. It was a very hard for me to walk out without them but I knew that I wouldn't be strong enough to control my urge with the poison at my fingertips. (Thomas's blog)

Negative qualities ascribed to these objects of desire signified the problematic of abstention by emphasizing that they did not have control over their behavior; these items became "poison" for Thomas and "evil chocolate" for Alex. Chris noted that negative visualizations could motivate abstaining by using up visual memory space; he stated that Ann's and Tina's experiences supported this insight by Tiggemann and Kemps (2005).

In this section, the students' connections of their insights into the structure of craving and the symbolic importance of images of the object of desire to the scholarly literature demonstrate the students' intellectual learning about craving. The structure and process of craving include many additional elements, but this section's focus on these two primary elements provides insight into the depth of the intellectual learning at hand. Next, I address evidence of craving as an emotional experience.

Deep Learning Antithesis: Introducing Emotion and Consequences for Self

Does craving represent an emotional experience that can serve as the basis of a deep learning exercise? Two indicators of emotional experience are: 1) the experience of emotion or feelings evoked by the situation; and 2) the experience of the self through reflexivity. Joe's experience with abstaining from TV provided an example of the emotional nature of the experience that generates reflexivity. The general situation was one in which he was meeting his girlfriend's family for the first time on a night they watched *American Idol* together. Excerpts from one day in the life of Joe as found in his blog entry on the tenth day follow:

> **Joe [General Situation]** Today I relapsed! ...After dinner we all were sitting in the living room eating chocolate chip cookie bars that her grandmother had made when I saw her grandfather reach for the remote.
>
> **Joe [Specific Event]** ...It was a family event and if I was to be accepted I needed to participate. So I sat through the whole episode of American Idol watching hopeful's belt their vocal cords out while I cried on the inside.
>
> **Joe [Emotion]** I felt trapped by the situation with no exit strategy. I was flooded with emotions, I was angry at the situation, upset with myself for giving in and depressed for failing the challenge. ...All the while I was happy because it was nice to just relax and watch some entertaining television.
>
> **Joe [Thinking]** My thoughts while watching were at first guilt, yet after a little, I figured the damage had already been done so I enjoyed the program. Afterward I obsessed over possible option of avoiding the relapse situation; I came up with no feasible options.

Joe [Images] My brain was filled with images of my classmates faces as I admit to my defeat. I tried to picture my own face, is it a pained expression, one of joy or sadness. Obviously the images of the performers on the screen fill my thoughts.

The social situation of relapse became apparent when he realized that if he refused to watch television, he might be viewed as an outcast. The reflexive self (Mead 1934) emerged as he saw himself as others might and wondered how this relapse would affect how he and others would view him in the future. Conflicting emotions arose as he struggled with his predicament. Joe "cries inside" at his failure to resist the TV experience; he feels "trapped," "angry," "upset," "depressed," "guilty," and he obsessed over his decision as he reflected on what his classmates might think of him. Joe's experience with craving qualifies as an emotional experience as he was experiencing feelings about the self, as evidenced by his reflection on how others would view him after engagement with craving and relapse. Although Joe's experience is just one example, many other students also had profound emotions as they struggled to abstain from their objects of desire for the two-week period.

Whereas craving itself is emotional, succumbing to one's object of desire is also emotional. The feeling of craving is anxiety-filled; the feeling of relapse releases that anxiety. Ari Davies used the following example by Thomas to illustrate the emotional aspects of relapse:

> I enjoyed the smoke penetrating my lungs while fulfilling my exhausted craving… The craving was overtaking my mind. I couldn't think of anything but what it would feel like to have a few drags…My craving is always so strong when it comes on that I really don't know if I will ever be able to give this up without help of some sort…

The joy of relapse was also identified by Joe, who called it the "rush of relapse," comprised of feelings of "happiness, excitement, and physical pleasure" at the thought of using the object of desire again. Remorse follows the joy of relapse, sometimes immediately. As these negative emotional consequences of relapse gave rise to doubt and threats to self-efficacy (Elster, 1999), they have significant consequences for the self.

Overall, as evidenced in the students' blogs and seminar papers, one can surmise that craving is an emotional experience that is suitable for a deep learning exercise. An emotional experience, as understood within the symbolic interactionist framework, is an experience both of "self-in-feeling," and feeling "by-and-about" the self. Did these experiences with craving transform the self? Emotional experiences that are reflexive have the potential to transform the self; this transformation is one indicator that learning has been deep.

A comparison of Bella's blog entry from the beginning of the experience to an entry at the end of the experience provides evidence of Bella's self-transformation as she attempted to abstain from smoking cigarettes:

> **[Bella: Day 1]:** My emotions were all up and down today first of all the change in nicotine level that was being replaced by other things such as self-doubt, failure and questioning whether I would be able to do this or not….

> **[Bella: Day 10]:** Well the day went well no snags or wants and I am feeling very proud of myself on the days that I do not slip. And I am getting the idea that any goal is attainable if you want it bad enough. Will I go back after this project is done who knows?

Through time, Bella became aware that she was able to see herself as one who could abstain, even if only for brief periods. What had been seen as an insurmountable task had become feasible as Bella became more aware throughout this process of the situational and personal obstacles that influenced relapse.

Another example of self-transformation is provided by Jamie, a student who decided to refrain from using his IPod for two weeks as recounted in the following excerpts from his blog:

[Jamie: Day 2]: The rest of my day did not go so well at all. Everything seemed like it was going wrong. But for some reason, my IPod made it all better. It allowed me to ignore any crap that was going on today. This made me realize how dependent I am on my IPod to make me feel better at any given time I please. … Lastly, I told my friend about my relapse and he told me. "I knew you wouldn't last. You have that thing every time I see you." Seems like this will be way more arduous than I thought.

[Jamie: Day 8]: After this exercise is over, I don't think I can ever look at my IPod the same. It was something that was once hard to let go of, but now it doesn't seem as hard to give up or live without. Before the day started, I was determined to get through the day without using my IPod. Little did I know that I would have no urge to use it; I actually disdained the thought of using it! This mental shift in how I think of my IPod disturbs me a little bit because I wonder what I will think of my IPod when I don't have to do this exercise anymore…

[Jamie: Day 9]: After today was finished, I felt great! I guess just knowing that I can abstain from using my IPod makes me feel like I can abstain from almost anything. I feel like I am officially in control of what I want and what I need. …

Sequential excerpts from Jamie's blog demonstrate learning–in-progress about both himself and his relationship to his IPod. Jamie was a student who came to class with an ear-bud that was "hidden" from view unless you looked closely. He started with an over-confidence about his ability to refrain from his object of desire, as did all students. With his first relapse on the first day, he quickly realized that this was not an easy project. Jamie's blog illustrates the struggles he was undergoing and the consequences for his self-image and self-efficacy. For Jamie, it was clear by the end of the seminar that he had a better understanding of himself in relationship to his iPod.

The power of emotional experience is its ability to generate behavioral change. Both Bella and Jamie felt pride in being able to control their behavior. This pride was common amongst all the students who were successful at abstaining, even if it were only for a short time. Many scholars assert that mastery of one's desires is the key to happiness (Irvine 2006). Mastery, as indicated by a feeling of tranquility or peace that is marked by a reduction in anxiety, allows us to embrace the life that we do live. Control of one's conduct is the hallmark of the socialized being (Mead, 1934), and herein lies emotional experience's importance.

With the evidence of intellectual learning, emotional experience, and self-transformation, this paper now addresses the question of the integration of these three elements in a dialectical process of learning.

Deep Learning: Integrating Intellectual, Emotional, and Self Learning

Does an emotional experience with craving combined with an intellectual understanding of craving result in a deep understanding of craving? Evidence of the dialectic of deep learning is found if the student is able to integrate the intellectual experience with craving and the emotional understanding of self. For this section, I utilize two extended examples of the depth of learning about craving and symbolic interaction that resulted from Bob's emotional experience with craving cigarettes and Lucas's emotional experience with craving coffee. Whereas the blogs reflected the experiential encounters with craving, the seminar papers were where the students were asked to specifically integrate these experiences with other students' experiences and the intellectual material of this seminar; for this reason, the seminar papers were the primary data source for this section.

Bob Frapples, a student who abstained from smoking and who was still successful in being a non-smoker some six months after the end of the classroom exercise, reflected on his experience in his seminar paper. Bob Frapples was raised within a family of avid smokers and had unsuccessfully tried to quit a number of times. He commented on how the object of desire became part of the individual's identity through processes of role embracement and the looking glass self, revealing his intellectual learning about SI and the academic literature as it applies to craving. Bob Frapples went one step further and connected his own experience to the academic insights about craving evoked by abstaining:

> This [abstaining] in essence made them [i.e., the students] undergo a transformation of the self as a result of trying to break ties with an object of desire that they associated themselves with. This can also be seen in *The Alcoholic Society* by Denzin for the alcoholic undergoes a transformation which alters their meanings and language associate with their object of desire. The individuals in the sample [this class] began to disassociate themselves with the object of desire if they found it to be a bad habit. Those who engaged in eating fast food found themselves wishing they ate healthier. Those with addictions to caffeine began to feel better without coffee and thus their view on how much they needed caffeine in their lives changed. Those who smoked began to feel healthier as a result and began to regard smoking as a bad habit. I know I associated smoking with new terms likely "unhealthy" and "disgusting" for during the abstaining period I could feel myself getting healthier and thus distancing myself from my previous sense of self which was known to me and my friends as a smoker (Bob Frapples' seminar paper).

Bob Frapples makes a clear connection between the understanding of self, identity, and behavior and connects that understanding to his own experience. This connection is similar to Tina's understanding of the power of identity revealed in her statement, "because I identified myself as a fast food addict, it is difficult for me to be around my family and friends [when they are eating fast food]" (Tina's seminar paper).

Was Bob's experience an emotional experience? Experiences that give rise to emotions that reflect upon the self are emotional experiences. Insight into the self has transformational potential, and its presence is a necessary condition for deep learning. Bob's abstention from smoking was filled with emotions, mainly anxiety and anger. For example, on day five, Bob went to a drinking party with his friends and "it looked like it was going to be a good night until I saw all the drinkers outside…I felt a large amount of anxiety…I felt completely uncomfortable and I ended up grinding my teeth all night…I know I can think about how much hold nicotine has over me and just how much I am addicted to it. I have been smoking for quite a while now but I never fully understood how much I was" (Bob Frapples' blog). Bob's distinction between "thinking" and "knowing" provides evidence of the force of emotion in learning. Bob Frapples continues to explain the powerful nature of emotional experience that allows him to abstain, even to this day:

> I have in a sense undergone an **Epiphany** through which I no longer associate myself with smoking. Epiphanies are understood as moments of crisis or revelation that disrupt and alter one's fundamental understandings, outlooks and self-images. I can now label smoking as deviant for it is no longer the norm for me. (Bob Frapples' seminar paper)

The dialectical process of deep learning is revealed in Bob's seminar paper. Intellectual learning about craving is integrated with an emotional experience, together generating an understanding of self in relationship to the intellectual and emotional situation at hand, allowing for the individual to participate in self-directed conduct.

Self-knowledge does not demand behavioral change. Even among some of those who gained great insight into his or her self and craving, behavioral change was not long-term; however, even some of the most reluctant participants seemed to experience deep learning. Lucas, who was notoriously unsuccessful in his attempts to abstain from coffee, initially stated at the end of his two-week abstention, "I wish I had learned something insightful during my time abstaining from coffee, but I feel like I focused on it so much that it was just a miserable experience from the first day" (Lucas, blog day 14). Whereas he believes he has no insight initially at the end of his experience, his seminar paper, which he wrote in the last four weeks of class, forced him to engage the intellectual material while reflecting on his and his classmates' abstention experiences; his paper revealed deep insight into craving and himself. For example, as recounted in his blog, Lucas felt guilty and ashamed when he succumbed to his craving for coffee when he believes his girlfriend is sleeping. She, however, is not asleep and catches him. He recounts, "As much as I enjoyed the coffee on the long drive back to ____, I still felt guilty. Some part of me felt the initial, untarnished pride of actually abstaining for so long was lost…I had failed in my own eyes, and in A.'s as well…Of course, I only thought of this after I had finished the coffee" (Lucas, blog day 4). In his seminar paper, he refers to this experience:

> I relate this to George Herbert Mead's concept in symbolic interactionism, the "me" and the "I". The "Me" is the part of the self that is learned through social interaction. The "Me" is how the individual sees him or herself through the eyes of the perceived other. In this case, when I relapsed in front of my significant other, I imagined that her image of me suffered. I internalized how I thought she perceived me then, and because of this my self-image suffered. The "I" is how the individual responds to the attitude of the "other". After we act and internalize society's response, the "I" reacts. I believe the "I" in this case was my impression management that took place after this relapse. I took on the attitude that I would not relapse again, and that I did not in fact need coffee.

Lucas's intellectual understanding of

George Herbert Mead's (1934) dialectical process of self emerges from his engagement with craving and subsequent relapse.

The seminar paper requires him to integrate his intellectual learning with the emotional experience of craving and his understanding of self; for the reluctant participant, this may be forced depth. Either way, Lucas sums up his experience with craving as follows:

> Craving was something I initially considered to be the end result of physical/chemical reactions within the body, and nothing more. Under this research method, craving is in fact the result of pre-existing associations between objects of desire and the desirable meanings we attach to them through sustained social interaction. This is why familiar environments, situations and people can bring on a craving for something like nicotine, long after the physical effects of nicotine withdrawal have worn off. The actual process of craving and addiction is not so much chemically based as it is based in the creation of symbols and socialization. (Lucas' seminar paper)

Lucas's seminar paper revealed some of the deepest insights into craving and his self even though he was only temporarily able to abstain and returned to drinking coffee immediately at the end of the two-week period.

Self-transformations do not have to be followed by behavioral changes in order for learning to be deep. The motivation of the abstainer was one important factor in long-term behavioral change even when self-insight occurred. Some students, like Bob Frapples (e.g., Debbie and coffee, Patricia and nail biting), who seriously wanted to make a life change were able to combine their intellectual learning about craving with self-insight and parlay that into longer-term change. Other students, like Lucas, (e.g., Chris and chocolate), who had little to no motivation to make long-term changes, did not make them; however, these students also evidenced deep insight into craving and self that is indicative of deep learning. In some respects, the reluctant participants gained insight that abstaining from the object of desire was neither an important or desired part of their identities.

Conclusions

Experiential learning of the deep kind is possible within the umbrella of the seminar. Asking the students to be an object of their own inquiry allowed for them to engage with the material in an intimate way. Discussions in the classroom were quite lively as students recounted their experiences with their objects of desire. The objectives of this class were achieved to varying degrees with each of the students. The strongest of the students' works demonstrated the highest level of cognitive understanding into the process of craving, the impact on self of this understanding, and skill at doing thematic analysis. Even the weakest of the students were able to get at a rudimentary understanding of craving although the reflexive understanding of self was definitely not as evident in their transcripts or writings. Adding the experience of craving to the intellectual understanding of craving allowed the students to have an emotional experience that brought them into the learning process.

I think all of the students came away from this experience understanding that desire, experienced as "craving," is a strong social psychological force in behavior. The inclusion of students as their own research subjects allowed for reflexivity, a key component of the kind of consciousness necessary for purposive action (Mead 1934). Vannini (2006) asserts, "if as symbolic interactionists we believe that 'humans will act toward things on the basis of the meanings that the things have for them' (Blumer 1969:2), we should believe that the meanings that an individual has associated with his/her sense of self will significantly shape his or her action, and the meanings associated with action will shape the sense of self" (p. 237). The integration of self with the intellectual material on craving allows for learning to be deep. These experiences that change the self have the potential to change behavior.

Many undergraduates in sociology eventually find employment in the social service sector. Bringing this deeper understanding of craving and his or her relationship to this phenomenon will likely influence their behavior, hopefully in a more tolerant fashion. As one student, who had tried to not text for two weeks, said in her final classroom presentation of her paper, "I will never make light of people and their ongoing struggles to change their behavior again." As many of these students will be working with alcohol and substance abusers in their professional careers, this learning experience will give them a glimmer of an insight into the predicament of these clients. Whereas "one need not be Caesar to understand Caesar" is a dictum of sociology, *verstehen* can be tempered with emotion so that deep learning can find its place in the sociological classroom.

References

Adinoff, B, LM Rilling, MJ Williams, E Schreffler, TS Schepis, T Rosvall and U. Rao. 2007. "Impulsivity, Neural Deficits, and the Addictions: The "Oops" Factor in Relapse." *Journal of Addiction Disorders* 26(Supplement 1):25-39.

Bentz, Valerie Malhotra 1992. "Deep Learning Groups: Combining Emotional and Intellectual Learning." *Clinical Sociology Review* 10:71-89.

Blouin, David D. and Evelyn M. Perry. 2009. "Whom Does Service Learning Really Serve? Community-Based Organizations' Perspectives on Service Learning." *Teaching Sociology* 37(April):120-35.

Blumer, Herbert. 1969. *Symbolic Interactionism: Perspective and Method*. Berkeley: University of California Press.

Blumer, Herbert. 1998/1969. *Symbolic Interactionism: Perspective and Method*. Berkeley: University of California Press.

Cooley, Charles Horton. 1956. *Two Major Works: Social Organization. Human Nature and the Social Order*. Glencoe: Ill., Free Press.

Creswell, John W. 2007. *Qualitative Inquiry and Research Design: Choosing among Five Approaches*. Thousand Oaks, CA: Sage.

Denzin, Norman K. 1984. *On Understanding Emotion*. San Francisco: Jossey-Bass.

Denzin, Norman K. 1993. *The Alcoholic Society: Addiction and Recovery of the Self*: Transaction Publishers.

Drummond, D. Colin. 2001. "Conceptualizing Addiction: Theories of Drug Craving, Ancient and Modern." *Addiction* 96:33-46.

Elster, Jon. 1999. *Strong Feelings: Emotion, Addiction, and Human Behavior*. Cambridge, MA: The MIT Press.

Fitzgerald, John. 2010. "Images of the Desire for Drugs." *Health Sociology Review* 19(2):205-17.

Goffman, Erving. 1959. *The Presentation of Self in Everyday Life*. Oxford England: Doubleday.

Habermas, Jurgen. 1973. *Knowledge and Human Interests*. Boston: Beacon.

Habermas, Jurgen. 1979. *Communication and the Evolution of Society*. Boston: Beacon.

Harrington, Austin. 2001. "Dilthey, Empathy and Verstehen: A Contemporary Reappraisal." *European Journal of Social Theory* 4:311-29.

Irvine, William B. 2006. *On Desire*. New York: Oxford University Press.

Isbell, H. 1955. "Craving for Alchohol." *Quarterly Journal of Studies on Alcohol* 16:38-42.

Jellinek, E.M. 1960. *The Disease Concept of Acoholism*. New Haven, CT: Hillhouse.

Kolb, David A. 1984. *Experiential Learning: Experience as the Source of Learning and Development*. Englewood Cliffs: Prentice-Hall, Inc.

Langs, Robert. 1983. *Unconscious Communication in Everyday Life*. New York: Jason and Aronson.

Lindesmith, Alfred R. 1975. "A Reply to Mcauliffe and Gordon's 'Test of Lindesmith's Theory of Addiction." *American Journal of Sociology* 81(1):147-53.

Ludlow, Peter, Yujin Nagasawa and Daniel Stoljar, eds. 2004. *There's Something About*

Mary: Essays on Phenomenal Consciousness and Frank Jackson's Knowledge Argument (Bradford Books). Cambridge: MIT Press.

Manderson, Desmond. 1995. "Metamorphoses: Clashing Symbols in the Social Construction of Drugs." *Journal of Drug Issues* 25(4):799-816.

Marullo, Sam, Roxanna Moayedi and Deanna Cooke. 2009. "C. Wright Mills's Friendly Critique of Service Learning and an Innovative Response: Cross-Institutional Collaborations for Community-Based Research." *Teaching Sociology* 37(January):61-75.

McIlwraith, Robert D. 2008. "I'm Addiction to Television: The Personality, Imagination, and Tv Watching Patterns of Sefl-Identified Tv Addicts." *Journla of Broadcasting and Electronic Media* 42(3):371-86.

Mead, George Herbert. 1934. *Mind, Self, and Society*. Chicago: University of Chicago Press.

Meisel, Joshua A. 2008. "The Ethics of Observing: Confronting the Harm of Experiential Learning." *Teaching Sociology* 2008(July):196-210.

Moustakas, C. 1994. *Phenomenological Research Methods*. Thousand Oaks, CA: Sage.

Redish, A. David, Steve Jensen, and Adam Johnson. 2008. "A Unified Framework for Addiction: Vulnerabilities in the Decision Process." *Behavioral and Brain Sciences*, 31:415-487.

Rock, Adam J. and Nicolas Kambouropoulos. 2008. "Conceptualizing Craving: Extrapolations from Consciousness Studies." *North American Journal of Psychology* 10(1):127-46.

Sacks, Oliver 2006. "Stereo Sue: Why Two Eyes Are Better Than One.". *The New Yorker* June 19:64-73.

Satir, Virginia. 1983. *Conjoint Family Therapy*. Palo Alto: Science and Behavior Books, Inc.

Tiggemann, M. and E. Kemps. 2005. "The Phenomenology of Food Cravings: The Role of Mental Imagery." *Appetite* 45(3):305-13.

Vannini, Phillip. 2006. "Dead Poets' Society: Teaching, Publish-or-Perish, and Professors' Experiences of Authenticity." *Symbolic Interaction* 29(2):235-57.

Walsh, Shari P., Katherine M. White and Ross McD Young. 2009. "The Phone Connection: A Qualitative Exploration of How Belongingness and Social Identification Relate to Mobile Phone Use Amongst Australian Youth." *Journal of Community & Applied Social Psychology* 19(3):225-40.

Weber, Max. 1968. *Economy and Society*, Vol. I. eds Gunther Roth and Claus Wittich. New York: Bedminster.

Wurdinger, Scott D. 2005. *Using Experiential Learning in the Classroom: Practical Ideas for All Educators*. Latham, MD: Scarecrow-Education.